Praise for *Games, Desi*

"Sharp and Macklin break down the design process in detail from concept to code to completion. What I particularly like about this book is its inclusion of prototyping methods and design patterns that are often overlooked by others. I suspect it will be helpful to designers looking to break new ground outside the AAA space."

—**Brenda Romero,** Game Designer, Romero Games

"There are many books you can read about games. But *Games, Design, and Play* is something new. Colleen Macklin and John Sharp don't just explain what games are—they detail the game design process itself."

—**Eric Zimmerman,** Game Designer & Arts Professor, NYU Game Center

"*Game, Design and Play* is a detailed, thoughtful, and well-researched primer on the multifaceted discipline that is game design."

—**Mare Sheppard,** President, Metanet Software

"I've been studying and teaching game design for over a decade and this is the first time I've read a book that catalogs so many diverse aspects of the game design process. Colleen and John dissect and examine games of all types (not just videogames) and then expertly show you how to put all the pieces together to form your own unique design."

—**Stone Librande,** Lead Designer, Riot Games

"The authors share a wealth of experience, making for a text full of great concepts, thorough process and applied practice. Throughout they provide pertinent examples and use engaging exercises which makes it useful, informative and insightful."

—**Drew Davidson,** Director and Teaching Professor, Entertainment Technology Center, Carnegie Mellon University

"This is a book that fills the much needed space between systems thinking and play theory. Macklin and Sharp balance the process with practicalities, in a way that is as timeless, enjoyable and engaging as the games they discuss."

—**Lindsay Grace,** Associate Professor and Founding Director, American University Game Lab and Studio

"Anyone who seeks to learn or teach about games can use *Games, Design and Play* as an insightful guide to ideas on how games work, methodologies that help us create new experiences, and pleasures found through play. Macklin and Sharp don't seek to restrictively define games or prescribe narrow rules of design. Instead, their text offers a comprehensible yet flexible framework for understanding games and play alongside practical processes for imagining, prototyping, collaborating, and iterating during game development. The approaches described in *Games, Design and Play* are applicable to digital, analog, and hybrid games, and thoroughly illustrated with examples from projects by small teams or individuals. In a time when even large studios find value in fostering small, agile teams, this kind of practical, beginning-to-end handbook to creative development is invaluable."

—Naomi Clark, Assistant Arts Professor, NYU Game Center and Author of
A Game Design Vocabulary

"This is one of the most comprehensive game design books to date. It coalesces academic insights for helpful ways to think about games and play, and guides the reader from scratch to production with thorough advice and best practices drawn from examples of recent, cutting edge independent games. I wish I had a text like this available to me when I was first starting out in my career—it would have made it much easier to come up with a framework for some of the more outlandish ideas I had for games and to communicate them to my teammates."

—Anna Kipnis, Senior Gameplay Programmer, Double Fine Productions

"Colleen Macklin and John Sharp deliver an impressive conceptual and methodological approach to designing and producing games. Perhaps most importantly, *Games, Design and Play* delivers a message to designers that their games will go out into the world and be part of society and culture. The approach is both rich and approachable for undergraduate, graduate and aspiring game developers alike."

—Casey O'Donnell, Associate Professor, Michigan State University and Author of
Developer's Dilemma

"If for some reason you've decided on a career in game development, you could do a lot worse than Macklin and Sharp's book. While most texts on game design float in a vague sea of buzzwords and nostalgia, *Games, Design and Play* is rooted in example after example of real work being done by real game artists. Books on game-making tend to fixate on the technical "how to," GD&P dabbles in the far more essential 'why to.'"

—anna anthropy, Play Designer, Sorry Not Sorry Games

Games, Design and Play

A Detailed Approach to Iterative Game Design

Colleen Macklin

John Sharp

♠♦Addison-Wesley

Boston • Columbus • Indianapolis • New York • San Francisco • Amsterdam
Cape Town • Dubai • London • Madrid • Milan • Munich • Paris
Montreal • Toronto • Delhi • Mexico City • São Paulo • Sydney
Hong Kong • Seoul • Singapore • Taipei • Tokyo

For information about buying this title in bulk quantities, or for special sales opportunities (which may include electronic versions; custom cover designs; and content particular to your business, training goals, marketing focus, or branding interests), please contact our corporate sales department at corpsales@pearsoned.com or (800) 382-3419.

For government sales inquiries, please contact governmentsales@pearsoned.com.

For questions about sales outside the U.S., please contact intlcs@pearson.com.

Visit us on the Web: informit.com/aw

Library of Congress Control Number: 2016938039

Copyright © 2016 Pearson Education, Inc.

ISBN-13: 978-0-134-39207-3
ISBN-10: 0-134-39207-8

Text printed in the United States on recycled paper.

19 2021

Editor-in-Chief
Mark Taub

Senior Acquisitions Editor
Laura Lewin

Senior Development Editor
Chris Zahn

Managing Editor
John Fuller

Project Editors
Becky Winter,
Tracey Croom

Copy Editor
Gill Editorial Services

Indexer
John S. Lewis Indexing Services

Proofreader
Deborah Williams

Technical Reviewers
Naomi Clark
Chris Dodson
Merritt Kopas

Editorial Assistant
Olivia Basegio

Cover Designer
Chuti Prasertsith

Book Designer
Bumpy Design

Compositor
Danielle Foster

NC 04.15.2021 1347

Contents at a Glance

Contents

Preface

Games, Design and Play is a book that goes from a foundation in game design concepts to the roll-your-sleeves-up work of actually designing a game. With examples drawn from independently produced games, it's also a window into the process and thinking of actual game designers working to further what games can do and express. It's an exciting time in videogames—and this book is your key to getting involved!

We're Colleen Macklin and John Sharp, two game designers and educators. This book is a distillation of all we have learned from designing games, from the lessons of other game designers, and from the games we've played and studied. *Games, Design and Play* also draws on our experiences in other creative fields—DJing, VJing, graphic design, interaction design, photography, even teaching. We've developed and honed an approach to understanding games, play, and game design over our combined 35 years of design and teaching experience, and we have worked hard to capture it here.

Another Book on Game Design?

You might ask, "How is this book different from some of the other game design books out there?" Indeed, there already are some very good books, and we've been inspired by many of them. Our play-oriented approach is very much in line with Tracy Fullerton's *Game Design Workshop*,[1] and we have learned much from Katie Salen and Eric Zimmerman's seminal game design book, *Rules of Play*.[2] anna anthropy and Naomi Clark's *A Game Design Vocabulary*[3] influenced our approach to examples, not to mention the influence their work as game designers and critics has on us.

Even with all these great resources, we still found a gap. The primary thing that *Games, Design and Play* does differently is in the details—literally. Many game design books are fairly high level, considering games and game design primarily from an abstract point of view. Or they describe an overall game design methodology but don't get into the details of game design and the play experiences game designers create. Still other game design books approach videogames from a computer-science perspective, using games as a frame for learning game programming but skipping over the details of the design and playtesting process.

Games, Design and Play differs in that it connects the conceptual and design considerations of games with the process of actually designing a videogame from start to finish, from idea to

---

1   Tracy Fullerton, *Game Design Workshop*. 3rd edition, 2014.

2   Katie Salen and Eric Zimmerman, *Rules of Play*, 2003.

3   anna anthropy and Naomi Clark, *A Game Design Vocabulary: Exploring the Foundational Principles Behind Good Game Design*, 2014.

prototype to playtest and finally, a fully realized design. To put it another way, *Games, Design and Play* is a practitioner's guide to designing games. It looks closely at games, identifies how games work, and shows you how to design one from idea to fully realized game.

Game Design, Game Development, and Game Production

While *Games, Design and Play* is a book that takes you through the details of game design, there are certain things we left out—namely, game development. This is a game design book, not a game development book. What's the difference? **Game design** is the practice of conceiving of and creating the way a game works, including the core actions, themes, and most importantly, the game's play experience. Game design requires an understanding of different kinds of games, how they work, and the processes game designers use to create them.

Game development, on the other hand, encompasses the creation of the game, including game design, programming, art production, writing, sound design, level design, producing, testing, marketing, business development, and more. These activities might correspond to roles on larger game development teams, or in an independently made game, they might be undertaken by one person or a small team. In this light, we will not be addressing programming, modeling, animating, music scores, or any other aspect of videogame development except as they relate to game design. There are already some very good books that show you how to program games, including Jeremy Gibson Bond's *Introduction to Game Design, Prototyping, and Development*.[4] We also will show some bits of the art production process, but not how to use art and animation production tools like Photoshop and Maya. There are some great resources out there for that, too, including The Gnomon Workshop's video tutorials[5] and books such as *Drawing Basics and Video Game Art*[6] by Chris Solarski and Paul Wells' *Understanding Animation*.[7] For sound design and production, we would highly recommend Michael Sweet's *Writing Interactive Music for Video Games: A Composer's Guide*.[8]

An important distinction to also make here is the difference between design and production. *Games, Design and Play* is a detailed set of principles and processes for understanding and designing games, but it only scratches the surface of the production processes that happen once a game's design is complete. The relationship between architecture and construction is a useful comparison. Architects design buildings, but they do not build them. The building

---

4   Jeremy Bond Gibson, *Introduction to Game Design, Prototyping and Development*, 2014.

5   The Gnomon Workshop, www.thegnomonworkshop.com/.

6   Chris Solarski, *Drawing Basics and Video Game Art*, 2012.

7   Paul Wells, *Understanding Animation*, 1998.

8   Michael Sweet, *Writing Interactive Music for Video Games: A Composer's Guide*, 2014.

process is handled by engineers and construction crews. Construction can't happen, or at least can't happen smoothly, until the building is designed. The same goes for games—they need to be designed before they can be produced. **Game production** is then the process of producing the game indicated by the game's design. As you work through the book and the iterative game design methodology in Part III, "Practice," you will encounter some of the important aspects of production, but we don't go into anywhere near as much detail as we do on conceptualizing, prototyping, playtesting, and evaluating a game's design. As we mentioned earlier, there are many good resources and tutorials out there for code, art production, and sound, and often, in the production of your game, you will find solutions to specific production problems by simply searching for them online.

Games By and For Everyone

Another important thing about this book: most of our examples come from independently produced games made by small teams or individuals with goals ranging from the commercial to the artistic. We focus on indie games for a number of reasons. For one, these are often the most interesting and diverse games. The scale of these games is also more realistic for individuals and small teams. Changes in distribution and marketing over the past decade have made it possible for individuals and small teams to create and release games. On a personal level, we're both involved in the independent games community and have been for nearly a decade, so indie games are what we know and love. Perhaps most important, these are the kinds of games we make and play. The games we have made fit that category and include everything from cardgames and sports to iPhone word puzzle games and experimental arcade games.

Videogames are often organized into genres—platformers, shooters, sports simulations, massively multiplayer online (MMOs), role-playing games (RPGs), and so on. While we all enjoy particular genres, it isn't how we like to begin the design of our games. Genres can limit thinking, leading us to think in terms of what play experiences we want to borrow or improve instead of the play experiences we want to provide our players. Instead of focusing on the kinds of play, genre tends to focus thinking on other games in the same genre. We become hide-bound to the conventions, which keeps us from thinking more inventively about play. This is why there are so many indie platformers, stealth games, and mobile physics puzzle games: we allow ourselves to get caught in genre traps. In this book, we prefer to think about the kinds of play, not games circumscribed by genre.

This doesn't mean that what you learn from this book can't be applied in large-scale game industry context. However, this aspect of game development is often beholden to licensed content, sequels, and genres that have become increasingly predictable. *Games, Design and Play* hopes to show another path for gamemaking and provides a process that is play focused, not product oriented. This may seem like a subtle distinction, but it's the key to creating game experiences that focus on the act of play, unburdened from what a game normally is or is expected to be. Does this mean that we think all AAA games are bad? Definitely not.

Some break the mold, and many are a lot of fun to play. But we also think that as videogames continue to grow and mature as a medium, it's important to keep experimenting, trying new things, and pushing the boundaries.

You Are What You Play

This book is written from the perspective that games are an exciting art form with a wide array of styles, forms, and messages. We're interested in games by and for everyone, not tied to a particular platform or console—games that are digital, nondigital, and everything in-between. One reason for focusing on all forms of games is that from a design standpoint, there's much to learn and apply between different kinds of games. Physical sports can inspire videogames, and so can cardgames, boardgames, and playground games like hide and seek and tag. And it's a two-way street: videogames can inspire nondigital game designs, too. The more kinds of games we play, the more we learn and can apply to our own ideas.

One of the first things you will notice about this book is the emphasis on play and play experiences. In fact, throughout the book we use *gameplay* and *play experience* interchangeably. We do this to challenge our mind-set about games. Instead of focusing on the idea that we are designing games, we prefer to think about designing opportunities for play. By *play*, we mean the thinking and actions that emerge when we engage with games. Or, we mean the ways in which we engage with each other through the rules of the game—devising creative strategies and solutions to the problems games create for us, or enjoying the intersections of player participation and the game's images, sounds, and story. So in this book, we prioritize play as the primary experience our games provide. We also think this is a really good way to break out of expected genres and styles of games. By focusing on designing play instead of designing a game, we can choose many different approaches to take us there. We believe that thinking like this helps us create better and more interesting play experiences for our players. We'll explore and expand on this throughout the book.

How This Book Works

We wanted to write a game design book that guides you through the entire process of designing a videogame. When we teach an introductory game design class—whether to our college students or young people through the various curricula we've designed—we see how challenging it is to learn all of the important concepts of games, from rules to goals to feedback systems. Designing videogames adds a whole new set of challenges, from coming up with an initial concept to creating the rules and goals of the game to communicate your ideas, to testing and refining your design until it's solid. But these concepts and skills are all the nuts and bolts we need to design play experiences. So, we've set out to include all of the parts we think you'll need to design a game from start to finish.

Games, Design and Play is divided into three parts: Part I, "Concepts," Part II, "Process," and Part III, "Practice." Part I takes you through the definitions and principles of a play-based approach to game design. By the end of Part I, you will have the terminology and conceptual framework for understanding games and play from a game designer's point of view. The chapters in Part I include the following:

- Chapter 1, "Games, Design and Play," explores the component parts of games and considers how game designers use them to create play experiences.
- Chapter 2, "Basic Game Design Tools," looks more deeply at the foundational principles of game design.
- Chapter 3, "The Kinds of Play," examines the kinds of play games provide.
- Chapter 4, "The Player Experience," considers how players learn and come to understand a videogame and what it is asking of them.

Part II, "Process," steps outside the concepts of game design and looks at some of the core processes and techniques through which the iterative game design process unfolds. These chapters introduce important methods and documents that will make the game design process smoother and more enjoyable. The chapters in Part II include the following:

- Chapter 5, "The Iterative Game Design Process," provides a quick overview of the game design process.
- Chapter 6, "Design Values," introduces an important tool for guiding a game's design through the iterative process, including three case studies showing how design values can guide a game's design.
- Chapter 7, "Game Design Documentation," looks at the three main documentation tools of game design: the design document, schematics, and tracking spreadsheets.
- Chapter 8, "Collaboration and Teamwork," covers the often-overlooked but important considerations of collaborative projects, including team agreements, and considerations for resolving team conflicts.

Part III, "Practice," then puts game design into action. The chapters move through the iterative game design process of conceptualizing, prototyping, playtesting, and evaluating the design of games as play machines. The chapters in Part III include the following:

- Chapter 9, "Conceptualizing Your Game," details techniques for exploring and establishing ideas for a game's design, including a number of brainstorming methods and considerations for capturing the designer's motivations for creating a game.
- Chapter 10, "Prototyping Your Game," moves into the intentions and approaches to giving form to game design ideas through prototypes.
- Chapter 11, "Playtesting Your Game," considers the role of playtesting and lays out a series of approaches to playtesting prototypes of a game's design.

- Chapter 12, "Evaluating Your Game," establishes the importance of reflection on the results of playtests and provides a methodology for making the most of playtesting feedback to improve a game's design.

- Chapter 13, "Moving from Design to Production," outlines a means of determining when a game's design is complete and looks at a series of case studies that approach iterative game design in different ways.

Like our teaching, this book takes the old adage, "learn the rules before you break them," to heart. By focusing on a broad understanding of what games, play, and design can be, those familiar with basic iterative processes will likely see familiar patterns. We believe the best way to expand a discipline is by first mastering its foundational principles. So we use the best practices we've learned as designers and educators to show a tried-and-true path through the design of play experiences. And as you master them, you'll likely want to tweak the process in small and large ways. This is to be expected—we look forward to hearing how you have refined and revised the principles, processes, and practices presented here.

The Beginning of Something

If this is your first time designing a game, we welcome you to what we think is one of the most exciting creative practices around. Game design is challenging, but it's all worth it when you see your game being played and enjoyed by people. If you've made games already, we hope this book offers inspiration and some new ways to do things. And for teachers, we hope that it is a useful addition to your classroom. It's been playtested in ours and we're happy with the results. We hope you are, too. So let's begin.

John Sharp and Colleen Macklin
Brooklyn, New York
Spring 2016

Acknowledgments

Game design is more often than not a collaborative effort. This book was no different. Certainly, the two of us worked together on planning, writing, editing, and so on, but there were many others involved, too. Thanks are due to our external reviewers Naomi Clark, Chris Dodson, and Merritt Kopas, whose feedback on in-progress drafts was essential in strengthening the book. Jonathan Beilin worked with us on many of the details, while Shuangshuang Huo's photography is found throughout the book.

We must also thank our students at Parsons School of Design at The New School who play-tested the book with us over the past couple of years. And before that, we thank our students over the past decade of teaching game design—John's students at the Savannah College of Art and Design-Atlanta, and both of our students at Parsons.

Without the amazing games coming out of the many facets of indie games, we wouldn't have the material to write this book. A particular shout-out to those who spent time talking with us about their approach to game design—we really appreciate it. Our friend and business partner Eric Zimmerman has shaped our thinking about games in big and small ways; his generosity is deeply appreciated.

Last but certainly not least, John would like to thank Nancy for keeping the joy fully stocked. And Colleen thanks Renee for being an enthusiastic collaborator in the game of life.

About the Authors

Colleen Macklin is a game designer, interactive artist, and educator. Much of her work focuses on social change and learning and the potential of play for both.

John Sharp is a game designer, graphic designer, art historian, educator, and curator. He makes games, teaches game and interaction design, and researches and writes about games, design, art, and play.

Together, they are associate professors in the School of Art, Media, and Technology at Parsons School of Design at The New School where they codirect PETLab (Prototyping, Education, and Technology Lab), a research group focused on games and game design as forms of social discourse. Along with Eric Zimmerman, Colleen and John are members of the game design collective Local No. 12, which makes games out of culture.

PART I

CONCEPTS

CHAPTER 1

GAMES, DESIGN AND PLAY

The first step in learning any medium is

understanding its basic elements. In this chapter,

we begin taking games apart to see how they work.

We identify the six basic elements of play design:

actions, goals, rules, objects, playspace, and players.

When we talk about playing games, we often talk about them in the same way we do movies, books, and music—as a form of mass media. This isn't a surprise—since the rise of the Magnavox Odyssey, *Pong,* and the Atari VCS in the 1970s, games have often been treated as simply another kind of entertainment media. And videogames *are* the same in many ways—we learn about, purchase, and experience games in quite similar ways to movies, music, even books. But just because games are packaged, marketed, and sold like the products of other mediums doesn't mean they are conceived of, designed, and produced the same way.

Let's look past the marketing and distribution to the actual experience videogames provide—play. But what does that mean, to play a videogame? Is it like playing a movie? When you play a movie, you are watching a series of prerecorded images and sounds. You may interpret a movie differently when you watch it multiple times, or you may notice different shots, characters, settings, or plot elements, but the movie itself doesn't change. But when we play a game, we aren't just watching, reading, and listening (though we do these things while playing). With games, players have to interact, to be involved, for the game to happen.

This sounds more like playing music—as in performing it, not listening to it. Musicians play music by following the notes the composer wrote.[1] In games, players do something similar—they follow the rules written by the game's designer. So playing music and playing games are a little more alike. When playing music, you are following a score. In the same way a musician will interpret a score and make it their own, players interpret and act inside a game's rules. There is one big difference between music and games, though—games change based on player input in ways that music does not. In most cases, a music score is static, but a game will change based on what the player does. And as a result, gameplay experiences can be different almost every time, sometimes in big ways, sometimes in ways that are barely perceptible.

When we talk about playing games, we are talking about players taking an active role that has an impact on the substance and quality of the play experience. In fact, you might say that a game doesn't take form until it is played. Take the game hopscotch (see Figure 1.1). By itself, it is at most some lines on the ground and a rock or marker of some sort. But add a set of rules and a couple of players, and it turns into a mechanism for generating play. The drawn lines and the rock are explained in the rules, outlining how players jump and throw the rock to see if they can hop through the environment defined by the lines.

This is how games work. The game itself is a process that produces play when interacted with. Though we often think of games as being like movies, comics, and music—art and entertainment media—they are also like pocket knives, printing presses, and car engines. By this we mean that games are put into motion by players in the same way these devices are; a pocket knife won't do much but sit there until someone picks it up and uses the little scissors to trim a thread.

---

1   anna anthropy draws a similar analogy in Chapter 3 of her book, *Rise of the Videogame Zinesters: How Freaks, Normals, Amateurs, Artists, Dreamers, Drop-outs, Queers, Housewives, and People Like You Are Taking Back an Art Form,* using theater and the performance of a script.

Figure 1.1   A hopscotch board.

Thinking of games as machines is a **systems dynamics** approach to game design—considering how the elements in a game come together to create different dynamics. To get a better understanding of this, consider a familiar machine—a car. A car as a system has objects (steering wheel, turn signal, gas pedal) and dynamics (steer, signal, accelerate) that connect and interact to make the car work. The relationships between these elements—their dynamics, the inputs, and the different outputs they create—come together to create the experience that is driving. A car can be operated in many ways. It may have different types of inputs, such as the driver—a race car driver, a student driver, a London taxi driver. Other inputs come from the environmental conditions, the quality of the road, or other cars and pedestrians. (Let's hope not as a collision!) Depending on these inputs, the car may be operated differently and result in different types of outputs. A fast and wild ride on a racetrack, an awkward parallel parking job, a slow trip in rush hour traffic. And that's just one type of system. There are many, from cars to computers to coffeemakers, each with its purposes, styles, and outputs.

Instead of focusing on the stuff in the world, systems dynamics suggests we should look at the actions and the interactions between the stuff. Systems are made up of objects, which have relationships to one another, all of which are driven by a function or a goal.[2] A game is a kind of system. It takes inputs and generates different kinds of outputs. The elements of the game interact and produce different dynamics. In the case of hopscotch, the game's design crafts relationships between the drawn lines, the rock players throw, and the rules that enable play. This structure is created by the game's designer (or designers in many cases, but we will get to

---

2   For more on systems dynamics, check out Donella Meadows' excellent *Thinking in Systems: A Primer.*

that in Chapter 8, "Collaboration and Teamwork"). Without the game design, the rock and lines are just that—a rock and some lines. They are given meaning and purpose through the act of crafting the rules and the configuration of the rock and the lines—in other words, the act of game design. It's the players that ultimately make the game come to life, just as the interactions between things in the world create the situations and events we live with. When viewing things through the lens of systems, attention gets paid to not just the things, but the dynamic relationships between them and what happens when they interact. And it is the players that determine the purpose of their play experience. Players might play hopscotch in order to move through the game the most quickly, or to play with a flair that prioritizes style over speed. Or maybe they are playing simply as a way to pass the time.

This is one of the ways we can think about games: games are systems that dynamically generate play. Fast play, funny play, silly play, serious play, expressive play, reflective play, competitive play, cooperative play—you name a kind of physical, intellectual, and emotional response, and there are games that produce it through play. This is true of all sorts of games, no matter what they are—cardgames, boardgames, text adventures, mobile games, sports, 3D games, and on and on.

While games are systems from the vantage point of systems thinking, they are also works created to express, convey, and provide experiences. Games are just as much about expression and experience as any other medium. This suggests another way to approach games—as a form of expression closer to poetry, literature, and art than to pocket knives and steam engines. Games have style—visual, aural, written, experiential—and they create emotional responses and experiences for players to reflect upon. We want to understand games as things that generate experiences and different dynamics—in a word, play. Hopscotch is illustrative: the system is composed of a few simple rules, chalk and a rock produce exceptional experiences—jumping, laughing, focused concentration, opportunities for performance, competition, fellowship, and any number of other outcomes we wouldn't expect from such basic materials.

This is the real power of game design—creating play experiences that can entertain, express, connect, cause reflection, and many other kinds of thought and emotion. Part of what makes game design so much fun, but also makes it so challenging, is that the game designer designs something—a game—that produces something else—play. That play, in turn, generates physical, intellectual, and emotional responses. These responses can only be seen when the parts of the machine are assembled and the play begins. And so in this book, we hope to explore how game design is the design of play by keeping in mind how games generate play and how play in turn creates experience and meaning.

The Basic Elements of Play Design

To begin understanding how games work as designed systems for generating play, we need to identify the basic elements from which games are made. The problem is, the parts differ from game to game in pretty drastic ways. Even more perplexing, many of the parts are hidden from us or take an intangible form. For example, a car engine (at least a classic car engine) can be taken apart and understood by looking at the parts and how they operate in relation to one another. On the other hand, a transistor radio is a bit more difficult to decipher by just looking at its component parts. However, when we play with a transistor radio, we get a pretty good sense of what it does, at least at a higher level. When we turn the tuning knob, we find radio stations at different frequencies. Move the antenna, and we pick them up more or less clearly. We can adjust the volume. And when we move to a different city, we receive different stations. Looking at the insides of the radio might not tell us much about what this machine does, but fiddling around with it helps us understand how it works and might even reveal other things related to it, such as the properties of radio waves.

Some games are easy to take apart and see what's there (car engines), and some are more mysterious (radios). However, despite the many differences in games, we can identify the six basic elements in games: actions, goals, rules, objects, playspaces, and players. Rather than get too far into the invisible realm of games, let's look at a game with most of its elements visible for us to see: football, or as we call it in the United States, soccer (see Figure 1.2).

The best place to start is with **actions**, as this is the most obvious designed aspect of a game. Actions are the things players get to do while playing a game. The main actions in soccer are

Figure 1.2 A soccer game.

kicking the ball and running on the field (see Figure 1.2). These two core actions combine in interesting ways as the teams try to get the ball in the other team's goal. Around them emerge other actions, like dribbling the ball or passing it from player to player.

What lets players know what actions they can perform? The **rules** define what players are able to do—moving the ball with their feet, trying to get the ball inside the net, playing within a limited period of time, and so on. A game's rules are equally concerned with what players *cannot* do. With soccer, the most important limitation is banning the use of hands by all players but the goalkeepers. In this respect, the rules governing actions in games are about both permitting and limiting. Rules are the invisible structure that holds a game together. We can't see the rules of soccer without checking a rules book, yet they are always present, defining the play experience.

In games, rules are a source of player creativity, choice, and expression. This might seem paradoxical because in most cases we think of rules as limiting what we can do. However, the restrictions rules place upon players are also what make games fun. Rules give us opportunities to try new things, develop strategies, and find enjoyment within a play experience. Think of a fantastic moment in a soccer game you've watched or played—an amazing bicycle kick, or a well-timed tackle to stop an attempt to score, a kick that gracefully arcs into the net. These are only possible because of the rules of the game.

That brings us to next basic element of games: **goals**. A game's goal defines what players try to achieve while playing. The actions and rules of a game make more sense when we know the game's goal. If soccer didn't have the stated goal of score the most goals in the allotted period of time, what would the players do? Just kick the ball back and forth? More than likely, the players would make up their own goals to give structure to their play. This is what separates games from toys.[3] By itself, outside the rules of the game, a soccer ball is a toy. We can do whatever we want with it—throw it, kick it, draw a face on it even. But inside a game, the ball and everything else take on special meaning. Sometimes this meaning is to win, as in competitive soccer, but sometimes it is simply to spend time with friends and family during a backyard soccer game. In other cases, the goal is much more self-directed, like trying to make a character in *The Sims* rich and famous or building a replica of the Taj Mahal inside *Minecraft*. In other cases, the goal is simply the experience of the game, like in Mattie Brice's *Mainichi*, a game created to provide a window into daily life.

Without the ball, soccer players would just be running around, and without the two nets, they wouldn't have a location for attempting to kick the ball or to keep the ball out of. This brings us to the fourth basic element of games: **objects**. Objects are the things players interact with during play. There are two types of objects in soccer—the ball and the two nets at either end of the field. In some games, resources are also objects in the game—such as Monopoly money or the amount of health a videogame character has. To put these objects into use and to help

---

3   The difference between games and toys (among other things) is thoughtfully described in Greg Costikyan's 1994 essay "I Have No Words & I Must Design" from the British role-playing journal *Interactive Fantasy*.

create physical and conceptual relationships between them, there needs to be a **playspace**. In the case of soccer, this is the field, the defined area within which the game takes place and the objects are located. Together, the objects and the playspace constitute the main physical, tangible elements of a game. Objects are defined by a game's rules and are necessary for the game to happen.

The last basic element of games is the **players**. They are part of the game's design, too, right? Without players, the ball and nets just sit there on the field, and the rules are just words on a page. Players put the game that is soccer into motion through their pursuit of the goals using actions and objects within the playspace, all governed by the game's rules. Players are the most important part of any game, as they are the operator that makes the game go.

We now have a working list of the "moving parts" of games and play experiences: actions, goals, rules, objects, playspace, and players. Together, these constitute the basic elements of game design.

From Six Elements, Limitless Play Experiences

Crafting the basic elements of the actions, goals, rules, objects, and playspace and how they come together to create play—that's the role of the game designer. You make decisions about what kind of play experience you want players to have, and you then design a game that will give players that kind of experience.

Of course, not all games combine these elements in the same way. Take the goals of a game. In soccer, the goal is to be the team with the most points when time runs out. This drives the entire experience, at least in competitive matches, putting everything else about the game in service of this goal. But in a game like Exquisite Corpse (see Figure 1.3), the goal is to have an experience rather than to compete. Exquisite Corpse begins with a folded sheet of paper. The first player draws on one of the surfaces, making sure her drawing slightly overlaps the adjacent panels. The paper is then refolded so the next player has one of the mostly blank panels. Play continues until all panels are drawn upon. The paper is then unfolded, and the players see the image they collaboratively created. In the case of Exquisite Corpse, there is a goal that shapes the play experience but in a less heavy-handed way. There's no score in Exquisite Corpse and no points to count. The goal is to create a drawing together. So a goal can be the driving reason to play, as in soccer, or simply a catalyst for a playful experience, like in Exquisite Corpse.

Playspaces can take many forms as well, depending on the intended play experience. The fields of sports, the materials of boardgames, the fantastic environments of 3D videogames, the graph paper of tabletop role-playing games—these are just a few of the kinds of playspaces our games can use. The playspace of a game should be designed to encourage and support the kind of play experience you want your players to have. If you want a playspace that is mostly in

Figure 1.3   An Exquisite Corpse drawing.

the player's imagination, you might consider a simple, abstract map for tracking players' collective discoveries. If you want to provide players with a rich story world of your own design, you might consider a more detailed 3D game.

The actions performed while playing a game can vary wildly, too, from game to game. The most typical action of videogames is shooting. But really, if we look more closely, the actions are much more granular and interconnected: walking, running, and crawling; looking and hearing; aiming and shooting. Games like The Chinese Room's *Dear Esther* (see Figure 1.4) show that these actions can be reconfigured to allow all sorts of other kinds of play experiences. In *Dear Esther*, the player interacts with the game through the standard first-person perspective. They look and move through a designed space not unlike a full-scale movie set. Though the player aims their view, they are never doing so to shoot. By removing this one action, the designers of *Dear Esther* create a play experience focused on the exploration of a storyworld that feels radically different, even though it lacks only one standard action.

Game designers determine the specifics of these core elements of a game, but they have little control over what the player does with them while playing the game. That is why the **iterative game design process**—involving conceptualizing, prototyping, testing, and evaluating—is so important. We will get into this more in Parts II and III of this book, but by approaching game design as the design of play and focusing on what happens when a game is put into motion, game designers can methodically shape and refine the play experience of their games.

This is easier said than done. Game design produces second-order play experiences for players. By this, we mean that game developers create the game, but the player is the one who decides how, when, and why to play it. **Second-order design** is a concept loosely borrowed from mathematics and propositional logic. An equation is a proposition, and the insertion of variables is first-order

Figure 1.4   A screenshot from The Chinese Room's *Dear Esther.*

logic. Second-order logic is what emerges when the variables begin to interact. In the context of game design, those variables are the players and how they engage with a game. When do they play? Why do they play? What do they do while playing? What do they feel while playing? Unexpected outcomes emerge when a player plays within the dynamic system of a game.

Katie Salen and Eric Zimmerman refer to this as the **space of possibility** of a game[4]—the potential experiences a game designer creates through their combination of objects, playspace, players, rules, actions, and goals. A game's space of possibility can be focused and specific about what the player will do and experience, and it can be broad and open-ended. anna anthropy's *Queers in Love at the End of the World* is a text-based game in which the player spends the last ten seconds before the world ends with her partner. anna has defined the scenario as well as the options of what the player can do within these precious seconds. There is limited time and a limited number of actions to choose from. *Queers in Love…* has a defined space of possibility because anna had a very specific kind of experience she wanted to share with players. She was more interested in creating a focused play experience that led to reflection than in creating a play experience that offered an open-ended space of possibility for player actions.

On the other hand, there is *Minecraft,* the open-ended sandbox in which players collect materials so they can create things like buildings, vehicles, and tools. This has led to an endless set of unexpected outcomes—scale models of the *Starship Enterprise,* functioning rollercoasters, and replicas of entire cities. The space of possibility in *Minecraft* is quite broad, allowing players to

---

4   Katie Salen and Eric Zimmerman, *Rules of Play.*

develop their own goals. Even in this seemingly endless possibility, there are limits, however. Players tend to create buildings and vehicles but not sports or forms of life, for example.

In the case of anna anthropy's text-based game *Queers in Love at the End of the World*, the possibility space is narrow because anna has a particular expression to convey to players. In Mojang's *Minecraft*, the space of possibility is so broad as to seem endless. This, ultimately, is what approaching game design as play design is about—understanding that games create spaces of possibility defined by player experience as much as by game design. The more focused the designer wants the experience to be, the smaller the space. The more the designer wants the players to develop their own experience, the more open the space of possibility will be.

A game's space of possibility is something we as players never really see in complete form. Instead, it is a quasi-theoretical understanding of the many play experiences players can have inside a game. The thing is, our understanding of a game's space of possibility is always changing. Take basketball as an example. Until 1980, no one ever realized that it was possible for a player to jump under the backboard in the space between the rim and the baseline.[5] But when Dr. J leapt from one side of the basket to the other in that underneath space, suddenly a whole new set of possibilities was added to the game.

What lets a player understand a game's space of possibility is **game state**. Game state refers to a particular moment in the game—where the players and objects are in the playspace, the current score, the progress toward completing the game's goal, and so on. Every time a game is played, it is going to have a different sequence of states, as players will move through their play experiences in different ways. This brings us back around to the second-order nature of games. A game's design is the creation of a space of possibility that changes from moment to moment based on player input. In real-time games in particular, the game state is in constant flux as play is ongoing. In turn-based games, the state changes less frequently but is still in motion and changing based on player engagement. This is what makes games such a powerful medium—we as game designers create spaces of possibility from the basic elements of games. And players, in turn, bring our games to life through their play.

Getting from Here to There

Designing a game that creates a particular kind of play experience is much easier said than done. This requires us to approach games as designers rather than as players. Making the change from player to designer is not so different from transitioning from being a sausage-eater to a sausage-maker—seeing the messy behind-the-scenes work involved in the process can be unsettling. The next three chapters of Part I, "Concepts," look more closely at games

---

5   Dr. J's scoop shot is forever immortalized on YouTube (https://www.youtube.com/watch?v=NjdEP7I2fRA) and in Dave Hickey's classic essay, "The Heresy of Zone Defense," published in his book *Air Guitar*.

from a designer's point of view. Together, these chapters create a play-focused approach to game design. For those new to game design, the chapters in Part I form an understanding of what game designers see and think about when playing and making games. And for those already thinking about games as a designer, these chapters provide our outlook on games as a broad medium suitable for entertainment and expression alike.

Chapter 2, "Basic Game Design Tools," focuses on the basic tools and principles for shaping play experiences. We look at tools like constraint, abstraction, decision-making, and theme to help us see how game designers create a range of play experiences.

Chapter 3, "The Kinds of Play," explores the types of play experiences we can create for our players. This encourages designers to think about games as play experiences rather than as media products. Competitive, cooperative, chance-based, whimsical, performative, expressive, and simulation-based play are all looked at in detail. We look at a variety of games in the process to help us understand the incredible range of play experiences we can provide our players.

Chapter 4, "The Player Experience," examines the ways players perceive games, how they make sense of the information encountered while playing, how they decide what actions to take, and how they understand their role in the game. In other words, this is what we ask of players during play experiences.

Summary

When game designers think of games as frameworks for play experiences, they recognize that games are generative. There are many kinds of games, but they all share the same basic elements: actions, rules, goals, objects, playspace, and players. These parts interact to generate play. As a designer, the challenge of creating play experiences is that they represent a second-order design problem: we are designing the play experience indirectly through the game. But there are ways to accomplish this, and the upcoming chapters will show you how.

The basic elements of games:

- *Actions:* The activities players carry out in pursuit of the game's goals
- *Goals:* The outcome players try to achieve through their play, whether they be measurable or purely experiential
- *Rules:* The instructions for how the game works
- *Objects:* The things players use to achieve the game's goals
- *Playspace:* The space, defined by the rules, on which the game is played
- *Players:* The operators of the game

Additional important concepts:

- *Second-order design:* Designing games is a second-order design activity because we create the play experience indirectly through a combination of rules, actions, and goals. The game only takes form when activated by the player.

- *Space of possibility:* Because games are interactive, they provide for players a variety of possible actions and interpretations. While a designer can't predetermine all the possible actions and experiences players will have, they can limit or open up the space of possibility through the game's combination of actions, rules, goals, playspace, and objects.

- *Game state:* The "snapshot" of the current status of game elements, player progress through a game, and toward the game's (or player's) goals. Game state is constantly in flux based on player engagement with the game.

Exercises

1. Identify the basic elements in a game of your choice (actions, goals, rules, objects, play-space, players).

2. As a thought experiment, swap one element between two games: a single rule, one action, the goal, or the playspace. For example, what if you applied the playspace of chess to basketball? Imagine how the play experience would change based on this swap.

3. Pick a simple game you played as a child. Try to map out its space of possibility, taking into account the goals, actions, objects, rules, and playspace as the parameters inside of which you played the game. The map might be a visual flowchart or a drawing trying to show the space of possibility on a single screen or a moment in the game.

4. Pick a real-time game and a turn-based game. Observe people playing each. Make a log of all the game states for each game. After you have created the game state logs, review them to see how they show the game's space of possibility and how the basic elements interact.

CHAPTER 2

BASIC GAME DESIGN TOOLS

One of the first things we do when learning a new field is to become familiar with the tools of the trade. In this chapter we look at the core tools of game design: constraint; direct and indirect interaction; goals; challenge; the interplay of skill, strategy, chance and uncertainty; decision-making and feedback; abstraction; theme; storytelling and context.

Now that we've identified the basic elements game designers work with in the creation of games, the next step is considering the tools used to shape and combine these elements into experiences for players. When you think about tools, you probably think of game engines, animation tools, programming languages, sound design, or 3D modeling software. These are tools used as part of game design and development, but they aren't what we are talking about here. Game design tools aren't like the wrenches or screwdrivers you might think of for working on machines. Instead, the basic tools of game design are more like the foundational principles of visual art—symmetry, contrast and hierarchy, for example. This sort of tool helps designers understand the parameters of game design in the same way that color, line, form, and composition establish the basic parameters of visual art.

There are ten basic tools for designing games: constraint; direct and indirect interaction; goals; challenge; the interplay of skill, strategy, chance, and uncertainty; decision-making and feedback; abstraction; theme; storytelling; and context of play.

Constraint

Part of what makes games fun are the unusual ways they let us interact with the world. If, in soccer, all players really wanted to do was put the ball in the other team's net, wouldn't it be easier just to carry it there or maybe throw it? Soccer players could certainly do that, but would it be much fun? By constraining the way players can put the ball in the net using anything *but* their hands, the goal suddenly becomes much more interesting. This is **constraint**—putting limits on player actions and interactions with the objects, other players, and the playspace with the intention of creating a play experience.

When carefully designed, constraint provides more satisfying play experiences. An important concept here is what Bernard Suits calls the **lusory attitude**[1]—players are willing to accept, and even invite, less efficient or logical means of engaging with a game in exchange for the potential of the play experience. Constraint is one of the main ways to shape a game's actions to generate challenge, creative strategies, and engagement for players.

A great example of constraint in a videogame is Messhof's *Flywrench* (see Figure 2.1). It is a platformer with a twist—instead of running and jumping through a horizontal landscape, the player flies a small ship through a twisting and turning series of corridors and other environments. The ship's natural state is falling. But if it falls into a wall, the player dies. To keep aloft, the player has to flap. This is the first constraint in the game—navigating the ship to avoid bumping into walls and other obstacles.

On top of this, the environment the player navigates is filled with barriers and obstacles of different colors. To pass through them, the ship must be the same color as the barrier or obstacle.

---

1   Bernhard Suits, *The Grasshopper: Games, Life and Utopia*, 1978.

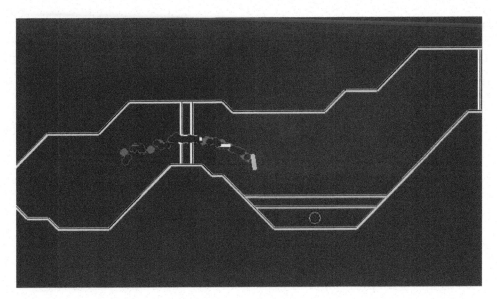

Figure 2.1 A screenshot from *Flywrench.*

Each state of the ship changes the ship's color—dropping is white, flapping is red, and spinning is green. So not only does the player have to navigate the environment without touching the walls, they also have to time the changing state of the ship to allow it to pass through the barriers while keeping the ship moving in the right direction. This is the second constraint—color-matching. Together, these two design decisions create a layered set of constraints that establish the core challenge of the game. (We'll get more into challenge later in this chapter.)

Flywrench's constraints are so finely tuned that the player needs to fail over and over again to develop the skills to time their movements with micro-twitch accuracy. *Flywrench* creates a fast and exciting play experience by challenging players with tightly calibrated constraints on movement and timing.

Another helpful example of constraint is Young Horses' *Octodad* (see Figure 2.2). Instead of having a typical humanoid player character with a rigid skeletal system, *Octodad* asks the player to maneuver and control a boneless, floppy, handless octopus as he carries out mundane tasks. This constraint—moving around a space and interacting with objects with a floppy octopus body—creates a playfully frustrating experience for players as they mop the floor or clean the refrigerator. This is very close to Suit's example of the lusory attitude—golf. Why use expensive sticks to knock a ball in a hole if you could carry it there more easily with your hands? Or, in *Octodad*, why use a floppy suit-wearing octopus when you could use a traditional person? In both cases, it is because of the experience the games provide.

Figure 2.2   A screenshot from *Octodad*.

Yet one more approach to constraint is found in Shawn Allen's *Treachery in Beatdown City* (see Figure 2.3). The game is a mix of turn-based combat and 1990s scrolling beat-em ups. Players have to juggle resource collection, move selection, and hand-to-hand combat in a way that pulls their attention in multiple directions. The role of time in making all these decisions is one way in which Shawn works with constraint—players needing to make choices around the

Figure 2.3   A screenshot from *Treachery in Beatdown City*.

timing of their actions. Another way constraint comes into play is the interaction of two play types (a concept we'll look at more closely in Chapter 3, "The Kinds of Play"). By interleaving two styles of play—turn-based combat and a real-time beat-em up fighting game—the player is confronted with actions and goals that run against expectation.

In many ways, constraint is the "secret sauce" of game design. Much of the satisfaction we derive from playing games comes from well-designed constraints. This often involves coming up with unexpectedly satisfying limitations that turn everyday objects, activities, and spaces into something new and exciting. In the case of *Flywrench*, it is a constraint of precise movement and timing, and in *Octodad*, it is a constraint of unorthodox and awkward control. With *Treachery in Beatdown City*, it is constraint of time and of unexpected play types.

Direct and Indirect Actions

When talking about constraint and goals, we're more often than not thinking about the actions players perform during play. An important pair of tools game designers use to shape play experiences are direct and indirect actions. **Direct actions** are those in which the player has immediate interaction with objects and the playspace, while **indirect actions** are those that occur without direct contact by the player or the primary objects they use while playing. Pinball serves as a great example here (see Figure 2.4). Players directly interact with the ball through the use of flippers. At the same time, players indirectly interact with the bumpers, ramps, holes, and other features by hitting the ball with the flippers. If a player hits the ball at a bumper, it is going to bounce off in predictable but not completely knowable ways due to the mechanical push triggered by the ball's

Figure 2.4   A game of pinball.

impact. The player might directly act on the ball by hitting it at a precise time with the paddle, but ultimately this leads to a variety of indirect actions as the physics of the ball and other objects in the pinball game interact. So hitting the ball with a flipper might lead to the ball passing under a spinner at the entrance to a ramp, which will add to a score multiplier, which increases the value of the trip around the ramp. All of these related events and chain reactions emerge from a single hit of the ball with a flipper. This is one of the ways in which players can set into motion effects both anticipated and unexpected within a game.

These stacked interactions of objects speak to the importance of designing the implications of how different objects interact with one another within the playspace. Designers have to think about the characteristics of the objects and what these properties may cause to happen within the game's space of possibility. Done well, the relationship between direct and indirect actions can create a dynamic sense of engagement with a game. Secret Crush's *SUNBURN!* (see Figure 2.5) is a great example of this kind of dynamic system. In the game, the player controls the captain of a spaceship that just exploded deep in outer space. All the ship's crew has made a pact to die together, so the captain must jump from planet to planet to gather the crew together and then plunge them all into the sun. To do this, the captain must interact with the planets and their gravitational pulls and the stretchy bungee cord that connects the captain to the crew members. The properties of the planets, the sun, the rope, and the crew members interact in ways that are mostly out of the control of the player. Because of this, the player must observe how their direct actions lead to indirect interactions between the other objects to make sure they are able to successfully complete each level.

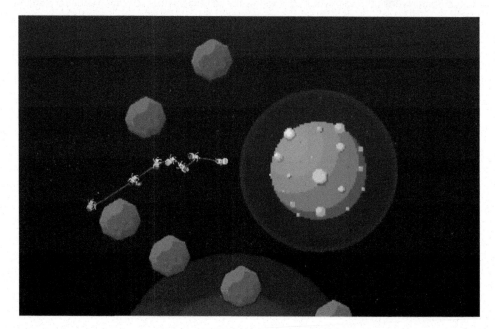

Figure 2.5 A screenshot from *SUNBURN!*.

A different way to think about direct and indirect action comes from Ed Key and David Kanaga's *Proteus* (see Figure 2.6). Like pinball and *SUNBURN!*, similar cascading actions occur in the game, but less in pursuit of player goals and more in the spirit of experiencing a world that seems alive. In *Proteus*, the player explores a pixelated island in first-person view. There are no clear goals or threats, so the player is left to explore and find out what happens. As they move, their presence affects other creatures and phenomena in the world. When the player approaches what looks like some little frogs, the creatures hop away, generating a set of tones. When the player sits still, elements in the environment change, and in special locations, they experience new sounds and images. All of these events are indirectly triggered by their presence; the player's only direct actions are movement or non-movement and where the player looks. Ultimately, the player's movements "play" the island, like a musician plays a score, triggering visual and audio events to bring the island to life, setting off cascading effects in the world.

Figure 2.6   A screenshot from *Proteus*.

The concepts of direct and indirect actions are the tools game designers use to create unexpected outcomes in games. A balance between the two can provide players with a sense of individual agency through direct action and through indirect action, creating a dynamic, interactive system to play within. The more direct actions a player has access to, the more fine-tuned the player's control can be of their experience. With more indirect actions, there is less control but a greater sense of discovery with how the world works.

Goals

As we discussed in Chapter 1, "Games, Design and Play," the goal of a game gives shape and purpose to what the players are trying to achieve while playing. Sometimes the goals are quantifiable, and therefore strong, while in other cases, they are experiential and loose. Without a goal, players won't know to what end they are following the rules. Soccer is an example of a quantifiable, and therefore strong, goal—one that guides and gives purpose to the play experience. On the other end of the spectrum is Jane Friedhoff's *Slam City Oracles* (see Figure 2.7). Players take on the role of one of two young girls in a world filled with snack food, fantastic buildings, pinwheels, and other quirky objects. The goal? Bounce around the environment with a friend, and in the process knock things around—riot grrrls in a perfectly playful world. The player can bounce higher and higher or just stick around one area and slam to their heart's content. While there is a score, it is intentionally complex with absurdly high numbers that provide humor more than a measure of player performance. For a player of *Slam City Oracles*, the outcome isn't the focus; it's the process of getting there and the different things that happen along the way.

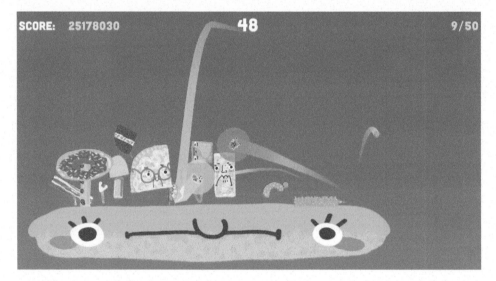

Figure 2.7 A screenshot from *Slam City Oracles*.

A middle ground between Soccer and *Slam City Oracles* is Liam Burke's Dog Eat Dog (see Figure 2.8), a paper-and-pencil role-playing game. Instead of a clearly stated quantifiable goal that drives the play experience, Dog Eat Dog explores ideas around colonization and what happens to cultures when they are confronted with external cultural forces. And instead of loose experiential goals, Dog Eat Dog provides structure and quantifiable outcomes, but those outcomes are not the focus of the play, and to call them goals might be stretching the definition. Instead, they are outcomes that provide a way of ending the story, giving players a sense of how their performance in the game led to the fate of the characters and the island.

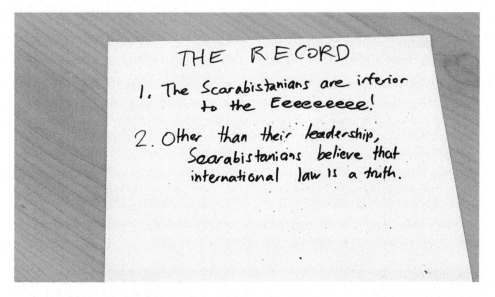

Figure 2.8   A game of Dog Eat Dog.

Play begins with players naming and creating a set of traits for their fictional Pacific islands nation and then doing the same for the colonizing nation. Players are given one rule to start:

> The natives are inferior to the occupation people.

Players then add to this a list of rules that are followed in the engagement between the two cultures. As an asymmetrical game, one player takes on the role of the occupying nation, while all others play the role of natives to the country. Players take turns setting up scenes in which two or more of the characters engage in a situation. If in the course of the scene a disagreement occurs about what is happening or how things resolve within a given situation, then the rules come into play to help resolve them. At the end of scenes, judgment is passed on whether everyone followed the rules, with coins taken and received to account for everyone's behavior. The Natives then add one new rule to the list, and the next scene begins. Play continues until one side runs out of tokens. At that point, players recount the epilogue, which tells the story of how the occupied nation fared. If the Occupation ended the game without tokens, then the epilogue should recount how and why the occupying nation gave the power back to the Natives. If one of the Natives ended without tokens, then the Natives should talk about how the occupation impacted them. After all the epilogues are stated, the players still holding tokens decide the final fate of the islands.

As a group, players tell a story together. At the same time, each player manages their tokens so that they can define how the end of story is told. The purpose of the game's experience is the unfolding story, from beginning to the end. In the case of Dog Eat Dog, there is a quantifiable goal articulated by the tokens, one that delineates the end state of the game, but it is not the focus or purpose of the play experience. The experience is the real drive, and the goal is simply a catalyst to allow that experience to unfold.

Games can also have layered goals. Take Tale of Tales' *Sunset* (see Figure 2.9). Players take on the role of Angela Burnes, a housekeeper for a wealthy man living in a fictional country in the middle of a civil war. The game consists of a series of days, each with a different list of house-keeping tasks for Angela to complete. Each subtask—wash the windows, unpack a few boxes, wash dishes—is necessary to complete as part of the larger goal of a day's work. The overarch-ing goal is to complete Angela's assignment at the house, which is done by completing the smaller goals within a given day. In the case of *Sunset*, there are three layers of goals: complete an assigned task, finish a day's task list, and complete the game. But these more structured goals build to the experience of the game's story. And so in this way, *Sunset's* structured goals build toward a looser experiential goal—learn about Angela's life.

Hang frames in a cosy arrangement.

Figure 2.9 A screenshot from *Sunset.*

Goals are a really useful tool for game designers. They are one of the only ways we can guide players' experiences in engaging with the actions, objects, and playspaces we design. A game's goal frames the play experience, suggesting to players how they might engage the game. The goals shape the space of possibility for players. A game's goals also shape how players perceive the available actions and objects within the playspace. Do they approach them as a means to an end or simply as an experience unto themselves?

Challenge

One of the things that designers use to craft a player's experience of trying to reach their goal is **challenge**. All games provide some level of challenge, even if the players provide it themselves. Challenge is often described in relation to the psychologist Mihaly Csikszentmihalyi's idea of the **flow state**.[2] For Csikszentmihalyi, flow is described as a state of high focus and enjoyment. Perhaps most famous is his chart of the flow state, showing the "flow channel" between anxiety and boredom, rising with skill and challenge (see Figure 2.10).

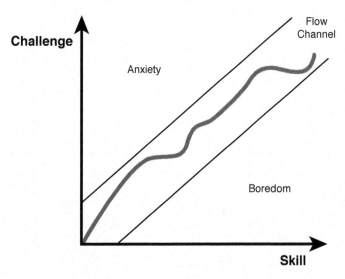

Figure 2.10 A representation of the flow state.

Many game designers use the concept of flow state to describe an ideal difficulty for level design, increasing the challenge to fit evolving player skill by just the right amount to avoid spiking into the anxiety zone or plummeting toward boredom.

Certainly, flow can be a useful concept for game designers, but here's a word of caution about the idea of flow. It can be tempting to correlate a state of flow with good game design, but just as many movies might provide us with an escape from ordinary life or a happy ending, not all movies need to be that way. Sometimes great films are made about ordinary life; or their endings aren't happy. For games, flow is a response to challenge meeting the player's skill level, and it creates a kind of play that can be highly satisfying. But equally satisfying are games that don't challenge players' skill. Instead, the game might confront the player with a challenging narrative or an experience that the player can enjoy regardless of skill. So, flow can be experienced in games, but it's not the only kind of experience players can have in games, and it's not better

---

2   Mihaly Csikszentmihalyi, *Creativity: Flow and the Psychology of Discovery and Invention,* New York: Harper Perennial. 1996.

than other kinds of experiences. The flow state is simply something the game designer might try to develop for or might not. It really depends on the values the designer wants to explore with their game. We'll get more to this idea of design values in Chapter 6, "Design Values."

An alternate concept to flow that emerges from challenge is **absorption**. Players can become deeply engaged in their play experience, but not in a way that is about a single state of being like flow suggests. A good example of absorption comes from the folkgame ninja (see Figure 2.11). Players gather in a circle an arm's length apart. The game begins when all players freeze in a "ninja" pose. Players then take turns trying to hit the hand of an adjacent player in one smooth movement ending in a new ninja pose. The player who is attacked can move only the hand aimed at by the attacker. The game tends to pull players deep into the game, taking on the silly premise of ninja-posing without self-conscious worries. In other words, the players become absorbed in the game and give themselves over to it in the spirit of Bernard Suits' lusory attitude discussed in earlier in this chapter.

Figure 2.11 A game of ninja. Photo by Scott Chamberlin / Elliot Trinidad. Used with permission of the IndieCade International Festival of Independent Games.

The point of this digression into flow and absorption is to simply say that challenge can generate these—and other—kinds of experiences with games, but that challenge, as a tool, can be used in varying degrees and for a variety of purposes. One purpose, which we will touch on later, is to encourage player skill development. As players encounter new and increasing challenges in a game, they must get better at overcoming them. This entails developing one's skill at the actions in the game. Another kind of challenge can be to achieve the goal of the game. In soccer, it can be to score the most points by the end of the time, for instance. Another kind of challenge might be found in the content of the game; the game might provide players with content that challenges their notions of gender, for instance.

Lea Schönfelder and Peter Lu's *Perfect Woman* (see Figure 2.12) is a good example of all three kinds of challenge (skill, goal, and content). *Perfect Woman* is a game using computer vision (the Kinect) that provides the player with the (almost impossible) goals of trying to attain exceptional personal, professional, and familial success defined by the "lean in" lives expected of many 21st century women. To do so, the player is asked to strike increasingly difficult poses with their own body to match the body of their in-game character, and ultimately, to attain their life goals. Instead of difficulty being determined solely by player skill moving through each level, it is also based on the choices players make during the game during different life stages. For example, if the player chooses to be a street kid in the beginning of the game, it will be very difficult for her to attain the correct pose for a rich woman later in life. But if they chose princess, it will be easier. As Lea Schönfelder describes it:

> "…it is almost impossible for the player to always live their 'perfect life.' It may be okay for a while, but eventually your life history will catch up to you and you will have a real conflict with all the different aspects of your life that 'need to be perfect,' such as work, family, friends, individuality, health, to name a few."[3]

Figure 2.12 *Perfect Woman.*

---

3   *Gamasutra*, "Road to the IGF: Lea Schönfelder and Peter Lu's Perfect Woman" by Christian Nutt, 2013.

The goal of the game—to balance all the way to a long life—entails balancing one's physical skill in the game as well as one's life choices. Challenge in *Perfect Woman* operates on multiple levels and serves to embody (pun intended) the difficulties of attaining life balance.

Think of challenge as a knob that you can turn up or down, like heat to a pot on a stove, to influence the intensity of a player's experience, help them develop their skills at the game, provide meaningful effort toward the game's goal, and to give them access to concepts that can be difficult to express in any other medium.

Skill, Strategy, Chance, and Uncertainty

Emerging from challenge is a quartet of concepts that have a deep connection to one another: skill, strategy, chance, and uncertainty. **Skill** is the degree to which a player has mastered an action within a game, while **strategy** is the ability of the player to determine the best ways to perform the actions of the game in order to achieve their goals. The more **chance**, the harder it is for a player to develop strategies, regardless of their skill. This is because no matter how much one practices, there is **uncertainty** that can lead to unpredictable events in a game.[4] The less chance, the more room there is for them to develop strategies. In game design terms, how much of the play experience is driven by the quality of player actions and the decisions that the player makes relative to the things that happen outside the player's control?

Take darts as an example (see Figure 2.13). The game requires a high degree of skill in throwing the darts at the board. Players make decisions about how to aim, and they develop strategies.

Figure 2.13 A game of darts and a game of roulette.

---

4   Greg Costikyan's book, *Uncertainty in Games*, provides a deep dive into ideas around chance and uncertainty.

The game contains no chance at all. There is, however, uncertainty around where the opponents will throw their darts, which impacts the player's strategies, causing on-the-fly changes to a player's pursuit of winning.

At the other end of the spectrum, there is roulette (see Figure 2.13, right). There is very little skill involved. The player simply picks a color, a number, or a grouping of numbers and then hopes they guessed correctly. So while there are decisions to make, they are made without much to go on—the result is purely based on chance, and completely uncertain. There isn't meaningful information to take in and process to guide decisions beyond the basic probabilities of hitting a certain color, number type, grouping, or individual number. This isn't to say there isn't fun in chance-based play, but it is of a different nature than in skill-based games.

Sometimes, uncertainty comes through the interaction of a player's direct actions and the interplay of objects within the playspace indirectly caused by the player. The Japanese arcade game pachinko (see Figure 2.14) is a perfect example—players shoot balls into a vertical maze of pins and gates with the goal of getting the ball to a payout at the bottom of the maze. The arrangement of the pins and gates makes it difficult to predict how the ball will travel through the maze. Players can learn the responsiveness of the pins and gates as a means of developing strategies for getting the ball through the maze, but there is always a degree of uncertainty in what will happen.

Figure 2.14   A pachinko machine. Fashionslide

Basketball (see Figure 2.15) is a good example of a game that relies on skill and strategy, has no chance, but has plenty of uncertainty. The game is one that rewards height and speed, and of course dribbling, passing, and shooting skills, but it also awards smart decision-making and team play. On offense, players move the ball around from player to player to get the best opportunity to shoot a high-percentage shot. On defense, the goal is to keep the other team from having opportunities to shoot or at least make easy baskets. Players can predict many things—how the ball will bounce off the rim after a missed shot, where teammates will go on the floor to be ready to catch a pass, and what the opposing team will do when the player with the ball shoots.

Figure 2.15 A game of basketball.

Though there is no chance in basketball in the strict sense (we don't roll a die in the game or randomly generate the game's elements), there is plenty of uncertainty. At what angle will the ball come off the rim? Will a teammate be waiting in the corner for a pass? Will the other team run to the goal to rebound the ball? Everything the opponents do requires analysis and reaction and thinking about what is the best way to achieve the goal of scoring more points. Basketball is a sport where players develop skill and manage uncertainty by reacting quickly to the constantly changing state of the game.

Poker, on the other hand, mixes chance and skill in a way that requires players to develop strategies around the heavy dose of randomness inherent in the game. Let's use Texas hold 'em as an example. As in most card games, the deck is shuffled before play begins, and no one gets to look at the order of the cards. To begin play, everyone is dealt two cards face down. Players then make bets on their hands. This is a tricky time to bet in the game, as there is so much chance and uncertainty. What is in the other players' hands? What's still in the deck? Players have seen only 2 of the 52 cards. That means they have no idea which cards are in the other players' hands. This requires players to have a good sense of probabilities around poker hands. After the first round of betting, the dealer plays out 3 cards face-up in the middle of the table. These are considered shared and can be factored into all players' hands. Even by the end of the game, players only know the identity of 7 of the 52 cards in the deck. That's only about 15% of the deck, leaving a lot of uncertainty and chance in play. So players are left to rely on their knowledge of the probabilities of the different poker hands like four of a kind, full house, two of a kind, and so on. Just as important is their ability to guess what their opponents are up to. Will the other players remember two aces have already passed through in the previous hand? Is one opponent bluffing about having a great hand? Did the other player who folded early do so as a longer-term strategy?

The interaction of player skill and strategy are impacted by the ways the game's designer uses chance and allows for uncertainty, whether within the space of possibility of the game or through the actions of other players or through players' pursuit of goals. Finding the balance of these is one of the greater challenges in game design.

Decision-Making and Feedback

There are two related game design tools to consider when thinking about how players understand a game's state: the **decision-making** and **feedback** that propel a player through their play experience. Let's use bicycles as an example here. For a bike to go forward, the rider has to pedal it. But while doing the pedaling, the rider is making hundreds of decisions every second—how fast should they go? Which direction should they head? Are there cars, pedestrians, or other cyclists to keep an eye on? While operating a bicycle, the rider has to make lots of decisions.

Games also require that players constantly evaluate what is happening while continuing to carry out their actions in the game. This is what Katie Salen and Eric Zimmerman refer to as the "action-outcome unit."[5] All play experiences are made of a sequence of actions—pedal the bike—that have outcomes—the bike moves forward—that lead to the next action—turn the handle bars—that lead to the next outcome—the bike turns left. Ultimately, this is what gameplay is made up of: dozens, even hundreds or thousands, of small decisions that each creates a change in the game's state. From these, play experiences emerge, shaped along the way by the goals and subgoals, however loose or strong they might be.

---

5   Katie Salen and Eric Zimmerman, *Rules of Play*, 2003, pg. 62.

Let's look at a game of chess (see Figure 2.16). Chess is a turn-based game. One player takes a turn, then the other, and so on. This allows more time for decision-making and thus for interpreting the game's state. For instance, one player moves her knight a few squares in front of the other's king. Check! The second player is in trouble now, so he has to do something or the first player will win. Her actions have had an effect on how close she is to winning and how close he is to losing. So he has to react accordingly to the effects of her move. Maybe he decides to move his bishop to take her knight, which eases up the pressure on his king.

Figure 2.16   A game of chess.

Because each player has time to contemplate their actions, the game gains the "thinking person's pastime" reputation it has. In order to understand the game's state, to assess the available options, and to then make a decision about what action to take with a play piece, the player needs to be able to "read" the game. And in turn, the opponent needs to be able to understand the impact the player's move had on the game's state.

Turn-based play encourages deliberate decision-making. But what happens if we make chess a real-time game? Bennett Foddy's *Speed Chess* (see Figure 2.17) does just that—and makes it a 16-player game to boot. In *Speed Chess*, eight players per side use NES-style controllers to move their play pieces across the board as quickly as possible. No need to wait your turn, as it's a mad dash for the king in 30 seconds or less. Because every play piece is moving at the same time, the game becomes something completely different from chess. *Speed Chess* is more like a chaotic sport, where coordination between teammates is attempted, but because of the sheer speed of the game, players are not always successful. That's ok, though, because the next game is just a few seconds away. *Speed Chess* is a real-time game, where all the movements of players happen simultaneously and the state of the game board is constantly changing. That's the point of the game, really—things are happening so fast no one can really understand the game state as a whole or the more granular actions and their outcomes and impacts on the game state.

Figure 2.17 *Speed Chess.* Photo by Bennett Foddy.

A well-designed game provides feedback on player actions. When a player does something—move the left stick on a controller, for example—the object moves to the left. But there are other forms of feedback in the game, too, that are essential to the player knowing what is going on. Meshoff's *Nidhogg* (see Figure 2.18) provides a good example of this. In *Nidhogg*, two players square off in a sword fight in which they try to defeat their opponent by stabbing them fencing-style, or punching them, or even throwing their sword at them. The goal of the game is to make it to the other side of the game world. The first one there wins. Players can parry, run, jump, and crawl to beat their opponent. The game is constantly taking player input and giving feedback to confirm the action and to show the consequences of that action. When the player moves the character side to side, they walk, which provides feedback on the player's actions—the movements of a controller stick. Or when the player thrusts their sword by pushing the X button, the little character dutifully responds. The game also provides feedback on player progress by showing which player is in the lead by transitioning to screens that are closer to their goal and showing the direction they should run in with an arrow graphic at the top of the screen. Finally, when a player reaches their goal, they are given feedback on the outcome of the game by being ceremoniously eaten by a gigantic serpent and declared the winner.

Figure 2.18 A screenshot from *Nidhogg*.

Even games with looser goals and more experiential play experiences are composed of these decision-then-feedback loops. Porpentine's *Howling Dogs* (see Figure 2.19) is a great example. It is a text-based game in which players make choices about their movement through the game's environment. This being a text-based game, the actions—choosing a text branch within a body of text—will lead to an outcome—the loading of the corresponding text. Clicking on a highlighted link results in new text. The players choose between "hydration unit" and "food dispenser" and are then told about the results of that choice and given one or more choices to continue from there. These decisions aren't building toward a measurable or competitive

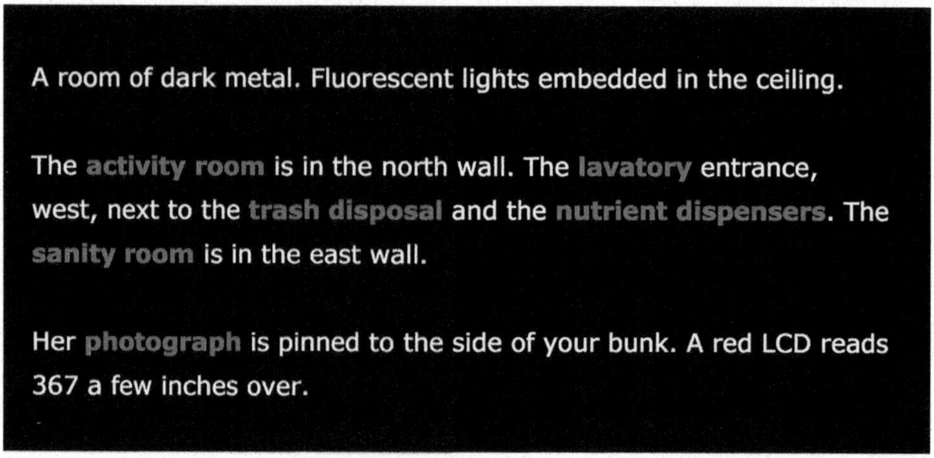

A room of dark metal. Fluorescent lights embedded in the ceiling.

The activity room is in the north wall. The lavatory entrance, west, next to the trash disposal and the nutrient dispensers. The sanity room is in the east wall.

Her photograph is pinned to the side of your bunk. A red LCD reads 367 a few inches over.

Figure 2.19 A screenshot from *Howling Dogs*.

outcome, but instead informing the course the story will take. And so while choices about how the player moves through Porpentine's game don't generate a score, they do have poetic as well as story-changing impact on the play experience.

Games are made out of a continuous cycle of small decision-feedback loops, each providing players with information on the game state. Ultimately, that is what game design is all about: creating play experiences fueled by player consideration and interaction. In chess, the turn-based structure allows deeper player contemplation, while the frantic real-time nature of *Speed Chess* prioritizes instinctual responses. And in games like *Howling Dogs*, the choices prioritize experience rather than player control. The more clearly a game designer crafts the ability of players to understand the game state and the impact of their actions on it, the more chance players have to feel empowered in their play.

Abstraction

Let's look at **abstraction**, another important game design tool. The most common way to think about abstraction in games is found with the abstract strategy game Go (see Figure 2.20). The board is a grid, the pieces simple black-and-white stones. In this case, abstraction refers to the fact that the game doesn't represent anything in particular. Compare this to the boardgame The Game of Life (see Figure 2.20), in which everything is representational—the little cars and passengers, the road and bridges, the buildings, and the money. Go embodies a kind of abstraction for games, but there are two other forms of abstraction game designers use to craft play experiences: abstraction of real-world activities, and abstraction of systems.

Figure 2.20   The boardgames Go and The Game of Life. The Game of Life photo by Fabian Bromann, used under Creative Commons Attribution 2.0 Generic license.

A classic example of abstracting real-world activities is the relationship between tennis and Atari's *Pong* (see Figure 2.21). In tennis, players can move to any spot on their side of the net; they can hit the ball to any spot on the opponent's side of the court they are able; they can hit the ball high or low, soft or hard, with or without spin; and so on. But in *Pong*, tennis has been simplified in a number of ways: players travel in a straight line along the baseline; the ball can only travel along a single plane; there is limited opportunity to control the direction the ball travels when hit.

Figure 2.21   Tennis and *Pong*. Tennis photo by Madchester, File: London 2012 Federer-Isner Quarterfinal Warm Up.jpg, Used under CC 3.0 SA Unported. *Pong* photo by Rob Boudon, used under Creative Commons Attribution 2.0 Generic license.

In other words, *Pong* is an abstraction of tennis. It takes a real-world game and reimagines it as a videogame. The process of abstraction involves reducing the real-world game down to an essential form that is appropriate for the new medium (and for the technology at hand). The tennis court is flattened, play only happens along a flat plane, the player and racket are replaced by a paddle that can only move along a single line, and force of swinging is removed altogether. As a result, a new play experience is created.

A different approach to abstraction is found in Matt Leacock's Pandemic (see Figure 2.22). Players work together to protect the world from a set of four deadly diseases. This is done on a gameboard with a simplified map of the world, player tokens and identity cards, color-coded cubes representing the diseases, a deck of cards representing a selected list of international cities, and a set of cards representing disease outbreaks. Players are assigned roles like Dispatcher, Medic, and Scientist, each with unique abilities. Together, the players work to cure the four diseases by moving around the gameboard, healing cities and treating virus outbreaks.

Pandemic uses abstraction differently than *Pong*. Instead of using abstraction to create a playful structure around something we already do in the real world, Pandemic models a real-world

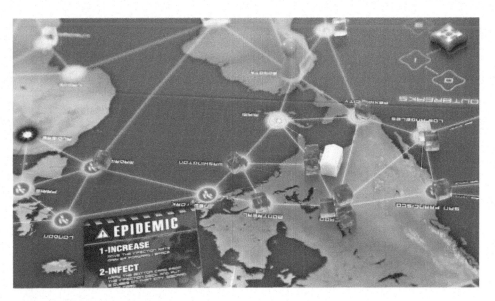

Figure 2.22   The boardgame Pandemic.

phenomenon—the spread of viruses—into a game system. This is all done by abstracting real-world systems and actions. Instead of traveling by car, plane, or boat, players simply move their pieces from city to city following the rules of the game. Another example is the way Pandemic abstracts epidemiology. The diseases spread by placing cubes on the cities, and they are cured by removing the viruses. This is a modeling of how viruses spread and are cured, but within the structures of a game, it also is how play and fun are produced.

We have three different ways we can use abstraction as a design tool: as a nonrepresentational approach to the design of game elements (Go), as a means of reimagining everyday activities to suit the medium (*Pong*), and as a way of simplifying real-world systems into game form (Pandemic). Abstraction gets rid of extraneous details and lets game designers focus on what's fun about the interaction of the game goals, the actions players can take to reach those goals, and the objects and playspaces.

Theme

The next basic game design tool is **theme**. A game's theme is the logical framework for how the game represents itself. Designers use it to shape the player experience and help them understand the game more quickly and intuitively.

Take chess as an example again. Chess doesn't have a story, at least not an implicit one. In fact, when we talk about chess, many people call it an abstract strategy game. (The *abstract* in *abstract strategy game* refers to the game not having representational qualities, similar to Go.)

But chess does represent something through the appearance and movements of its pieces and its board—namely, a war of territorial acquisition. The king is the ruler, with his powerful queen by his side. His advisors, the bishops, are nearby, while his military, the knights, are just to the side of the bishops. And on the outside of the knights are the rooks who form the outer protective guard. In front of them are the pawns, or the foot soldiers. And on the opposite side of the board is an identically organized opposing force.

Players very much engage in strategic warfare when playing chess, with the goal of taking down the opponent's king, conquering and controlling his territory. And the actions for each object in the game—the six kinds of play pieces—move in a way that relates to their role. The king is weak and slow and must be protected; the queen is powerful and fast; the two rooks begin along the edges and move in straight lines that define edges; the pawns are plentiful but slow. So even an abstract strategy game like chess has a theme that impacts the way we think about the game and its play. Theme is essentially a conceptual handle for players to be able to grasp how the world might work. And as they play, theme provides a way to interpret the decisions and their outcomes on the game's space of possibility.

A different approach to theme comes from the two-player cooperative game *Way* (see Figure 2.23). *Way* has a more explicit theme—two players in very different environments, dressed

Figure 2.23   A screenshot from *Way*.

in the clothes of two different cultures, trying to find ways to communicate with one another without a shared spoken or written language. All the actions players perform to achieve the goals are designed to support the idea of having to establish a language through which the player can communicate. Players are able to indicate emotional states and use gestures to suggest speed, direction and anything else the players are able to convey through a simple gesture system. The game's goal—move through the puzzle-based platform levels—supports the theme of communication quite well. It is impossible for a player new to the game to solve most levels without assistance from the other player. *Way* illustrates how theme can be handled through a mix of design and visual representation to help us reflect on communication and cooperation. *Way* then is "about" something, which provides the thematic framing for the entire design of the game, and in turn, the play experience.

Kentucky Route Zero by Cardboard Computer (see Figure 2.24) represents yet another use of theme in games. It has a very strong theme in terms of its mood, its art style, and its interaction model. The player is an observer on a storyworld centering on a truck driver named Conway who travels along the eponymous Kentucky Route Zero. The game draws on old graphic text adventures and point-and-click adventure games combined with a clean, minimal illustration style and cinematic animations. While the interactivity and the story of *Kentucky Route Zero* are not as tightly coupled to theme as they are in *Way*, they do work well together to create an atmospheric play experience. Everything about the sensory elements of the game supports the moody, magical story inside the game. *Kentucky Route Zero* explores an aesthetic theme that envelopes the player in a space of possibility more focused on atmosphere and narrative.

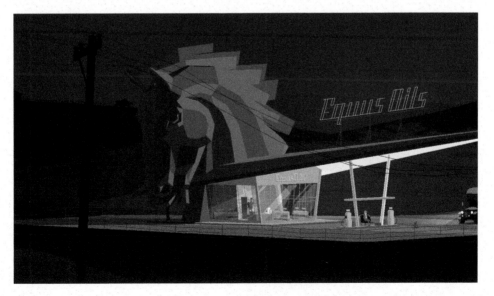

Figure 2.24 A screenshot from *Kentucky Route Zero*.

What we see with theme is that a game's goals, actions, sensory style, story, and world can be combined in all sorts of ways depending on what kind of play experience you want to provide. Sometimes, as with chess, the designer wants a light theme coupled with strong game design and a near-abstract presentation layer that helps the player understand their role and provide context for interpreting their decisions and outcomes. Sometimes the designer wants a conceptual theme tightly integrated with the game's goals and actions and light but supportive visuals and sound, as demonstrated with *Way*. And sometimes the designer wants theme to provide a particular kind of tone that is expressive, as in *Kentucky Route Zero*.

Storytelling

This brings us to the next game design tool: **storytelling**. Often, a game's theme is embedded in its story, as happens with film, comics, literature, and more. Many games are constructed around **storyworlds** within which players inhabit characters and carry out actions via their avatars. Decisions made by the characters lead to the unfolding of the story. Of course, we can tell stories through sports—recounting the tale of the winning goal just seconds before the match ends—or in boardgames—recounting the story of how the players came to almost, but not quite, eliminate the four viruses in Pandemic. But in many videogames, the story is a larger part of the experience. The layered impact of our actions and the advancing of the story often go hand-in-hand. The less directly we control our role in a game, the more story cues help us make sense of what happens and how well we are advancing the story.

In the game *Braid* (see Figure 2.25), players control the main character, Tim, who has lost his princess. To help Tim find her, the player navigates Tim through a puzzle platformer game.

Figure 2.25 Three forms of storytelling in *Braid*: (clockwise from top left): the menu, the level introduction texts, and the gameplay itself.

Instead of controlling anything and everything about Tim, the player can only make Tim move along platforms, up and down ladders, and they can make Tim jump. That is it. Through these limited forms of action, the player interacts with the storyworld and unfolds Tim's journey to find his princess. Tim also has some control of one other aspect of the game—time. The player can rewind time, and in the process, undo the things the player has made Tim do. This opens up a whole new vantage point on the game and the storyworld of *Braid*. Each time-related interaction with the world provides a place to consider different ideas relating to our actions and how they impact the world around us.

Braid becomes a game that uses story as another element in the production of play. The story in *Braid* unfolds through several conduits: the written story elements read at the beginning of each level, through the actions carried out by the player to move through each level, and through the meta-narrative formed through the game menu, represented by a cut-away view of Tim's house. Together, these elements produce the story of *Braid*.

In the case of The Fullbright Company's *Gone Home* (see Figure 2.26), the storytelling involves similar elements of exposition, player action, and contextual information. But in *Gone Home*, the whole point of the game is the player interacting with the environment to experience the story. *Gone Home* lacks many of the elements we might expect from a 3D game—no shooting, no enemies to vanquish, and no "winning" or score. Instead, players move through the space to piece together the story of Katie's sister Sam, and more generally, Katie and Sam's parents. The goal of *Gone Home* then is experiencing the story. To do this, The Fullbright Company made moving and looking the primary actions of the game. The player looks at the house, they look at the objects in the house, and through these and key audio snippets, they piece together the story.

Figure 2.26   A screenshot from *Gone Home*. Screenshot courtesy of The Fullbright Company.

Liam Burke's Dog Eat Dog illustrates another way storytelling can emerge from a play experience. The game provides a structure and context, while the players generate the story themselves through their decisions and interactions with one another. As a result, the stories players generate through the tabletop role-playing game generally share broad thematic elements, but they differ substantially in terms of the details.

Sometimes, a game's story is the full play experience. Dietrich Squinkifer's *Conversations We Have in My Head* (see Figure 2.27) is a story-driven game about one character's memories of their relationship with a second character. The two are on a walk in which the first character, Quarky, reminisces on this childhood relationship. At points in Quarky's monologue, the player can select responses from the second character. These insert slight branches in Quarky's thoughts, but they stay on track in thinking back on the childhood. If the player doesn't make a choice, the story continues to unfold. The story *is* the game in *Conversations We Have in My Head*.

Figure 2.27   A screenshot from *Conversations We Have in My Head*.

In these examples, we see story emerging through an interplay of text, player action, and the game's challenge and goals (*Braid*); story emerging through the navigation of playspace and interaction with objects (*Gone Home*); story emerging through the game's structure (Dog Eat Dog); and story being the primary activity and content of a game (*Conversations We Have in My Head*).

Context of Play

The last basic tool of game design is the **context** within which a game is played. Taking into account where the game is played and by whom has a real impact on the experience. Will players be playing on their phone or tablet? In a public space? Alone or with friends and family? Of course, game designers can't always predict this, but taking it into account can make a big difference for the player. Imagine trying to play a mobile phone game that has hour-long play sessions, and you will soon see why most mobile games have shorter sessions developed around the concept of playing during a commute, in between meetings, or at a coffee shop waiting for a friend to arrive.

Speaking of mobile games, take the iPhone app, *Tiny Games*, by Hide and Seek (see Figure 2.28). *Tiny Games* includes just that: a slew of tiny physical games meant to be played in short sessions in a variety of contexts. The first thing the player sees when opening the app is a question: "Where are you?" The player can select Home, Walk, Road, Bar, In Line, or Work. Selecting "Home" and "two players" might get you the game "Knife Fork Spoon," based on the folkgame Rock, Paper, Scissors, to be played while waiting for a piece of bread to pop out of the toaster. Each round, the winner keeps the utensil the other player played. By the end of the game (when the toast is done), players have the utensils remaining for their meal. This game is designed to be played with a friend in a kitchen, and as with all of the *Tiny Games*, is meant for a specific context.

Figure 2.28 A screenshot from *Tiny Games*.

Another example of designing for context is Jenga Classic, Jenga Giant, and Drunk Jenga, all based on Leslie Scott's classic game Jenga. In Jenga, players remove one block at a time from a tower constructed of 54 blocks, placing the block on top of the structure. Over time, the structure becomes more and more unstable, leading to the exciting climax of the blocks tumbling down. Interesting aside: Jenga is one of the few games that ends with a loser (the person who made the tower topple) rather than a winner.

Because of its popularity and the simple nature of the game's materials (54 wooden blocks), it has been remade and redesigned by players for different contexts. Jenga Giant is a version of the game with much larger blocks, which makes the toppling much more of a spectacle. It's popular in bars and backyards, whereas classic Jenga is more often played on household tabletops. This is design for context—making a version of the game that's fun in a different context; the larger blocks of Jenga Giant provide players and spectators with a large, easy-to-see sculptural game. The development of the larger version of Jenga then leads to the DIY modification called Drunk Jenga or Drinking Jenga, depending on your circle of friends. In this game, each block has an instruction written on it in marker like: "ladies drink," "tell a secret," or, in more racy variants, "remove an article of clothing."

Tiny Games is a set of games that are designed to fit a variety of contexts, considering where the game is played, when it is played, and how many players there are as the primary setting for the game to unfold. The Jenga variants described here are the same game, with slightly different forms and somewhat different features all developed to fit different contexts (home, bar, outdoors). Context provides the setting for a game but can also change the nature of the gameplay, leading to new variations and forms.

Summary

Game design uses a series of basic tools that are not so different from the basic principles of visual art. These basic tools are used to combine the six elements (actions, goals, rules, objects, playspace, and players) in ways that can generate endless possibilities for player experience.

The 10 basic tools of game design are constraint; direct and indirect actions; goals; challenge; skill, strategy, chance, and uncertainty; decision-making and feedback; abstraction; theme; storytelling; and the context of play. Each can be used alone, in combination, or to design new games.

- *Constraint:* The limitations we put on players through the design of the actions, objects, and playspace of a game.
- *Direct and indirect actions:* Direct actions are the kinds of actions that allow players to have immediate interaction with objects and the playspace. Indirect actions are those that occur without direct contact by the player or the primary objects they use to perform actions.

- *Goals:* A game's goals give shape and purpose to play experiences by giving players objectives.

- *Challenge:* The ways in which a game resists players. Sometimes challenge comes from the difficulty of achieving a game's goals, and sometimes it comes from the concepts embodied in the game.

- *Skill, strategy, chance, and uncertainty:* Skill is the mastery of a game's actions, whereas strategy is a player's ability to determine a path to achieving the game's (or their own) goals. Chance is the use of randomization in a game, whereas uncertainty is the unpredictable nature of what will happen as a game is played.

- *Decision-making and feedback:* Based on the game state and players' pursuit of the game's or their own goals, players make decisions about what their next action should be. To understand the game state, the player interprets the feedback the game provides on their last actions and the changes brought about in the game state by that action.

- *Abstraction:* The modeling of complex phenomenon into game form.

- *Theme:* The logical framework for how a game is represented.

- *Storytelling:* A series of tools for shaping player experience that borrow from traditional narrative structures.

- *Context of Play:* The consideration of when, where, with whom, and other aspects of when players play a game.

Exercises

1. Think about your favorite game and what would make it easy to achieve the game's goals, and then think about how the game designer used constraint to make the goal fun to pursue.

2. Choose a game with direct action—perhaps a sport where the ball is directly handled by players—and make that interaction indirect. Now try making indirect action direct. What does it change about the nature of the game?

3. Take a purely strategic game like chess and add an element of chance to it. How does this change the play experience?

4. Watch a game that allows for strategic play. Keep a log of the game state to help you examine the role of uncertainty in the play experience.

5. Find examples of games using abstraction to model the real world. How close is the game system to the real-world system? Where does it depart from the real-world system?

6. Pick a game you like, and consider how it uses theme and storytelling. How do the theme and story relate to how players engage with the game?

7. Pick a game you play at home. Reimagine the play experience if it were played in a public park.

CHAPTER 3

THE KINDS OF PLAY

This chapter is a catalog of many of the different kinds of play experiences game designers create using the basic game design tools. These kinds of play include: competitive and cooperative play, play based on skill, experience or chance, whimsical play, role-playing, performative and expressive play, and simulation-based play.

Videogames are usually thought of in terms of genre—first person shooter, puzzle platformer, survival, horror, and so on. This provides one way to make it easy for players to understand what a game is and for developers to operate within the conventions of expected play experiences. But this also has a couple of side effects—it treats games like categorized commodities rather than lived experiences, and it limits the potential of what game designers can try to create for players. Instead of thinking about genre, we prefer to think about the kinds of play our games provide players. This allows us to imagine what the experience will be without set boundaries, beyond marketing niches.

Thinking broadly about the kinds of play lets us focus on the sort of play experience we want to give our players. Lots of fast decisions they don't have to think much about? A smaller number of decisions that require strategy and analysis? Or very simple interactions that emphasize the visual, aural, and emotional experience? Lots of story? No story at all? Cut-throat competition? Or cooperation instead? A game that emphasizes designer expression? Or one that puts player performance at the forefront? These are just a handful of the things that make up play experiences.

This chapter breaks down some of the primary kinds of player tastes, looking beyond genres like first person shooters or puzzle games or platformers to focus on the more essential play types. We categorize the kinds of play as competitive and cooperative play; play based on skill, experience, or chance; whimsical play; role-playing; performative and expressive play; and simulation-based play.

One important note before we begin. Like tastes in food, the kinds of play are not mutually exclusive. Where a dish might call for garlic, onions, oregano, and thyme, so a game's design may require a mix of competition, player expression, and whimsy. Keep this in mind as you review this chapter. We delineate the kinds of play to bring clarity and focus to how they work, but ultimately, how they are blended is up to you.

Competitive Play

In a competitive game, some players will win and some will lose. This creates a context of competition in which players or teams of players try to come out ahead of their opponent, whomever or whatever that might be. For example, in soccer, the winner is the team that gets the most points by the end of the game's time limit. This is certainly the case with sports and most multiplayer games.

Messhoff's *Nidhogg* (see Figure 3.1) is a **local multiplayer game**—a videogame played by two or more players gathered in the same space in front of a shared screen. In *Nidhogg*, all the actions players perform are in service of pitting one player's skills against the other's—running, jumping and ducking, and thrusting or throwing a sword. The goal: to make it to the far end of the world before her opponent does. To gain an advantage, the player must attack her opponent to get past him, if only by a split-second advantage. There's a laser-like focus to *Nidhogg*. Everything about the game's design encourages you to compete against your opponent. There isn't much else you can do within the game's space of possibility.

Figure 3.1   A screenshot from *Nidhogg*.

One of the things we find often in competitive games is **yomi**. Yomi is the Japanese concept for knowing the mind of your opponent. It's usually applied to one-on-one competition, but it can also be found in sports, where one team analyzes the other team's past play to predict future actions, all in service of gaining strategic advantage. In a game like *Nidhogg*, this means trying to predict what the opponent is going to do so that the player can make a move that takes advantage of the weaknesses in her opponent's strategic tendencies. Yomi often comes in layers. In a game of *Nidhogg*, the player may think that her opponent is going to parry with his sword. But he guesses that's what she thinks he'll do, so he thinks he'll jump instead. But she knows he knows she thinks he'll parry, so she gets ready for him to do something else. This example illustrates how recursive yomi can be, where strategies and counter-strategies are all devised by trying to get inside an opponent's head.

This is where competition in some games gets really fascinating—designed spaces where players can think about not only their own decisions, but those of their opponents, too. Yomi is when the interplay of a player's skill and strategies come up against the uncertainty of another player's skill and strategy. What drives this is the pursuit of the game's goals by both players. So yomi is most seen in games with explicit goals in which one player or team wins and the other loses.

Competition isn't always head to head. In videogames, players often compete with one another in single-player games. Take Semi Secret Software's *Canabalt* (see Figure 3.2), a single player "endless runner" in which the player controls a little runner heading across a side-scrolling environment. The player has one action they can take: jump. This allows them to propel the player character over obstacles on the rooftops, avoid objects that fall from the sky, and jump from building to building. The longer the player lasts, the faster the game gets, until the player character hits its maximum speed. The only way to slow down is to run into obstacles on the rooftops.

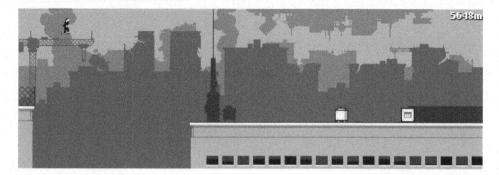

Figure 3.2 A screenshot from *Canabalt*.

In *Canabalt*, the score measures the distance the player ran before getting crushed by a falling object or falling off a roof. At the end of a game, the score is posted to the scoreboard, and the player has the opportunity to share their score via Twitter. This creates a form of competition in which one player sees another's score and compares it to their own. Sometimes *Canabalt* tournaments are run, in which the game is projected on a big screen, and players take turns playing, with the winner being the player with the longest run. This creates a different kind of **asynchronous competition** in which players are playing in one another's presence with a group of spectators.

Another basic form of competition comes in players competing against the game itself—the challenge of reaching a game's goals, in other words. A great example is Captain Game's *Desert Golfing* (see Figure 3.3). The name is quite descriptive. Using an *Angry Birds*-style gesture, the

Figure 3.3 A screenshot from *Desert Golfing*.

player aims and "hits" a golf ball toward a hole in the desert. Players are competing against the game in two key ways—navigating the ball around the terrain, and mastering the aim-and-shoot action. This kind of player-versus-game competition is another way to think about challenge. A game like *Desert Golfing* provides the player with pleasure through the pursuit of mastery by providing resistance and challenge. Players pit themselves against the game, doing their best to overcome the obstacles the game places in their path.

In looking at *Nidhogg, Canabalt,* and *Desert Golfing,* we see three approaches to designing competition—**head-to-head competition**, which adds layers of complexity to the decisions players make; **asynchronous competition,** in which players compete, but in ways measured by their performance rather than by the outcome of head-to-head play; and **competition against the machine**, which emphasizes the challenge of mastering actions to pursue the game's goal.

Within competitive games that pit players against one another directly, there are two additional ideas to consider—symmetrical and asymmetrical competition. Die Gute Fabrik's *Johann Sebastian Joust* (see Figure 3.4) is an example of **symmetrical competition**. Players have the same abilities—to move around the playspace, to hold their PlayStation Move Motion controllers aloft, and to use their bodies to jostle their opponent's controller to knock one another out of play. We call this *symmetrical competition* because the players have shared actions with which they compete with one another in pursuit of a common goal. In the case of *JS Joust*, this is to be the last player with his controller still active. This kind of play is found in most competitive games, as it is the most common approach to designing competitive play.

Figure 3.4   Johann Sebastian Joust. Photo by Brent Knepper.

Asymmetrical competition is found in games in which players have different actions, objects, or goals. A great example is Chris Hecker's *Spy Party* (see Figure 3.5). The game pits one player, the sniper, against another player, the spy. The spy plays one of a dozen or so characters attending a party, with all the other characters operating as **nonplayer characters** (characters controlled by the computer). The spy moves around the room, "talks" with other guests, and performs a series of missions in the hopes of remaining undetected. The sniper's goal is to figure out which character the spy controls as he maneuvers around a crowded party. The sniper can look at the room and zoom in to get a closer look, and if she thinks she has figured out who the spy is, she has one bullet with which to shoot him. If the spy remains undetected at the end of the allotted time, he wins. If the sniper shoots the spy before time ends, she wins. If the sniper shoots the wrong person, then the spy wins. The game sets up a wonderful "cat and mouse" asymmetry that, while still in prerelease, has already spawned a fan WIKI and innumerable "Let's Play" videos.

Figure 3.5   Screenshots of the sniper view (top) and the spy view (bottom).

Cooperative Play

Though it is by far the most prevalent form of play, competition isn't the only way to interact with other players. Sometimes, people feel like cooperating. These are play experiences in which players work together to achieve the game's goals. One of the things about cooperative play is that when it goes well, it is one of the best kinds of fun you can have. You and your collaborators are in sync, making things happen that none of you could do on your own. Like a well-executed pass in a soccer match leading to a goal, you are in sync with someone else, working to meet a shared goal.

One of our favorite cooperative games is Valve's *Portal 2* (see Figure 3.6). There is a single-player campaign, but in our opinion, the more enjoyable play experience is the two-player cooperative campaign. The players inhabit ATLAS and P-body, two robots inside Aperture Laboratories' test center. Working together, they solve the spatial puzzles of the game. In some cases, the two have to time their actions, while in other situations one player has to create portals for the other. Throughout, the level design and puzzle design create a collaborative, cooperative play experience.

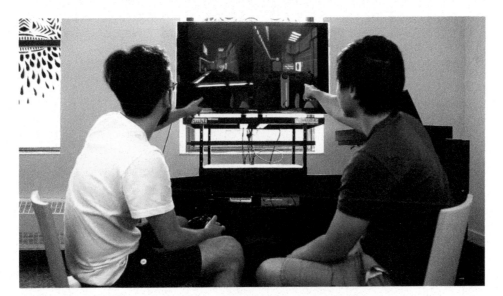

Figure 3.6 Our friends Brian and Robert conferring during a game of *Portal 2*.

Portal 2 is also a great example of **symmetrical cooperative play**. This refers to games in which the cooperating players get to use the same actions and have the same basic attributes. With *Portal 2*, both player characters look different, but they shoot portals, run, and jump in the same way. Neither has a built-in "role" in the collaboration. This leaves space for the players to develop and put into action strategies that may end up with one player doing one thing and another doing something else. The important point here is that this is left to the players to decide, not the designers.

An example of **asymmetrical cooperative play** is Matt Leacock's board game Pandemic. In Pandemic, players work together to protect the world from a set of four deadly diseases. If the players don't work together, the game will easily defeat them. Together, the players work to cure each disease by moving around the gameboard, healing cities and treating virus outbreaks. Players are assigned roles like Dispatcher, Medic, and Scientist that each have their own special abilities. These different roles assumed by the players create the asymmetry. The Medic can clear up diseases more quickly, while the Dispatcher can facilitate the movement of other players around the board. This creates asymmetrical cooperation in which the players work to figure out how to best utilize the differences in the characters to achieve the game's goal.

Coco & Co.'s videogame *Way* (see Figure 3.7) is another great example of cooperative play, drawing on the symmetrical cooperation model in an interesting way. *Way* is a two-player puzzle platformer where players take turns solving puzzles over the Internet. The active player doesn't know exactly how to solve the puzzle because they can't see everything in the playspace, while the inactive player can see the full puzzle space. *Way* quickly becomes about learning to communicate through nonverbal cues to solve the puzzles so that the players can share

Figure 3.7 A screenshot from *Way*.

information with one another. The active player will move in a particular direction, or perform a particular task, and the inactive player will try to convey whether or not the active player is getting closer to or further from the solution using body language. *Way* is an example of a third kind of cooperative play: **symbiotic cooperation**. By this, we mean the players are reliant on one another to play the game. Without the assistance of the other player, it is close to impossible to make your way through the game with all of its invisible platforms.

What we see with cooperative play is the design challenge of creating a truly collaborative experience for players, one in which it is impossible to meet the game's goals alone, requiring players to work with each other to find success. Whether it be symmetrical, asymmetrical or symbiotic, cooperative play is an important kind of play.

Skill-Based Play

With both competitive and cooperative play, players are asked to develop skill to perform the game's actions in pursuit of its goals. Soccer asks us to have skills in order to run, start, stop, and change directions, but also to become deft in manipulating the ball with our feet, our knees, the tops of our head, and even our chests. This is one core kind of play: **skill-based play**. We can further break skill down into active skill and mental skill.

Team Meat's *Super Meat Boy* is a great example of a game that requires **active skills**. The game falls decidedly in the "masocore" category of games that require a good deal of skill around precise movement and timing. The player controls Meat Boy, who has the goal of getting from point A to point B, where Bandage Girl awaits. To do this, the player must move Meat Boy around through side-to-side movement and jumping. Like many platformers, *Super Meat Boy* requires nuanced twitch response and timing. Unlike the other SMB, *Super Mario Bros.*, *Super Meat Boy* requires players to make use of speed and pin-point accurate timing to climb walls. To play the game, you need to develop skills to gauge distances and time jumps and wall climbs. And, like many incredibly challenging games, developing those skills involves failing over and over again and learning from hundreds, sometimes thousands, of failures.

For **mental skill**, a great example is Thekla Inc.'s *The Witness* (see Figure 3.8). The player explores an empty island filled with a series of path-tracing puzzles that unlock buildings, turn on machines, and generally bring the island to life. While the player does have to move around the world and trace the puzzles, the challenges they confront are mostly mental. For example, in some of the puzzles, they must remember the path of an adjacent puzzle and then trace its mirror image on an otherwise invisible puzzle space. The execution of this is easy enough, but the mental challenge of remembering and inverting the sequence is where the skill lies.

Figure 3.8 A screenshot from *The Witness*.

Still other games combine these qualities to create play experiences that draw upon both active and mental skill. *Portal* comes to mind here. The game's designer, Kim Swift, wanted to put pressure on the player's ability to enact the solution to the puzzle. To do this, Kim added time pressure. The player has to make precisely timed portals that allow them to shoot the portal, jump through, duck, and then shoot another portal, all while avoiding the high-energy pellets. To know when, the player must think through the spatial puzzle, execute well-timed portal shots, and then move through them to avoid being hit by the pellet. So the game requires both excellent hand-eye coordination and timing, but also the additional mental skill of sorting out a solution to the puzzle.

What connects these three examples—*Super Meat Boy*, *The Witness*, and *Portal*—is the design of challenges that put pressure on different kinds and combinations of skill. The more accurate or developed the skill requirements, the more time it will require of players to get to the point they have acquired the requisite skill mastery. This might limit the number of players who will be willing to commit to playing and mastering these skills, but it also makes the rewards of achieving victories great.

Experience-Based Play

What if you want to provide players with an experience that isn't built out of overcoming skill-based challenge but instead focuses on other aspects of the play experience? A good example of this is The Chinese Room's *Dear Esther* (see Figure 3.9). The player explores an island on which they find a series of letters a man wrote to his deceased wife. By moving through the island, exploring the contents of buildings and reading the letters, the player unfolds the story of the man and his wife. So long as the player understands the basic mechanisms for navigating a 3D first-person game (not something we can easily take for granted, as we will discuss in Chapter 4, "The Player Experience"), they will be able to experience the story the developers created. The core of the experience is exploration, enjoying the design of the spaces, and of course, unfolding the story between the man and wife.

Figure 3.9 A screenshot from *Dear Esther*.

In text-based games like Christine Love's *Analogue: A Hate Story* (see Figure 3.10), players experience a story through a combination of text, image, and interaction prompts. The player takes the role of someone in the future who has stumbled upon a broken computer system. Sometimes players are asked to type inputs into a command-line prompt, while in other situations they simply make choices from a list of options. Yes, there are decisions to be made, but because the game isn't competitive or skill based, the player is left to focus on the text and the images and to consider the meaning of the story.

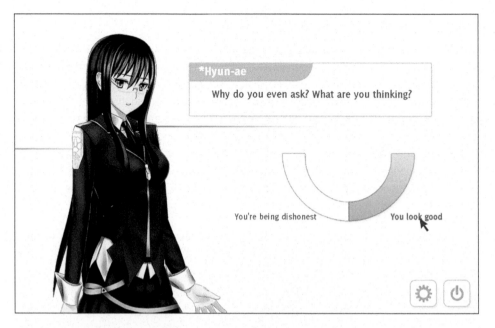

Figure 3.10   A screenshot from *Analogue: A Hate Story*.

Even within games that are competitive on the surface, players can find other forms of experience. The folkgame ninja is a great example. Players stand in a circle and take turns making
one move that ends in a "ninja" pose. The basic goal is to hit the hands of one of the adjacent
players, while avoiding having your own hands hit. Though this sets up a competitive premise
and does involve physical and strategic skill, most games of ninja are played with emphasis on
acting like a ninja, being part of the experience as a group, but not really on winning or losing.
As ninja suggests, many games can be played for experience instead of competition or skill
development, as long as the game's designer has left room within the space of possibility.

In these three examples, we can see three approaches to experiential play—that of navigating a
3D space to experience a story (*Dear Esther*), that of a combination of text and image to piece a
story together (*Analogue: A Hate Story*), and that of physical activity that emphasizes communal
engagement over winning (ninja).

Games of Chance and Uncertainty

The games we've looked at so far in this chapter have focused on play styles in which the
structure and outcome of the experience are in the hands of the player or the game's designer.
But what happens when you bring chance into the mix? This is, of course, the basis of many
cardgames like poker or blackjack. But we can find this sort of mix in other games, too.

A game that mixes chance and skill in interesting ways is Sirvo LLC's *Threes* (see Figure 3.11), a mobile puzzle game in which players drag tiles around to combine them into multiples of threes. A 1 tile and a 2 tile create a 3 tile, which combined with another 3 makes a 6, two of which create a 12, 24, 48, and so on. Every move the player makes concludes with a randomly selected tile loading onto the grid, so the player never knows exactly what is coming down the pipe. When the grid is filled with tiles and there are no more possible moves, the game is over.

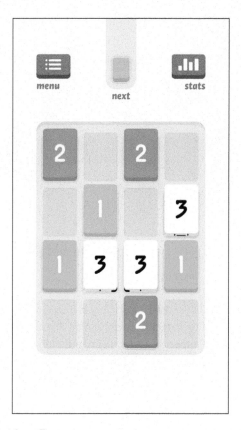

Figure 3.11 A screenshot from *Threes*.

Players have to develop strategies to combine as many tiles as possible with each move. So *Threes* is a game involving the strategic management of uncertainty—the player doesn't know exactly what kind of tile they will get, so part of their strategy is about managing their moves to anticipate a variety of outcomes. The game does provide players with some information, however. There is an indicator letting the player know what color tile will drop next. This comes in handy in thinking through the placement of tiles, particularly when the board is nearly filled. In this light, *Threes* is a game that encourages players to develop skills to navigate uncertain events in the game, plan their next actions, and develop longer-term strategies around obtaining the game's goal.

Android: Netrunner (see Figure 3.12), Lukas Litzsinger's reboot of Richard Garfield's Netrunner, is an asymmetrical card game in which one player, the Runner, attacks the other player, the Corporation, to steal Agenda points from the Corporation. The Corporation, in turn, tries to defend itself while secretly scoring Agenda points before the Runner can steal them.

Figure 3.12   A game of Android: Netrunner.

The game mixes strategy, skill, chance, and uncertainty in interesting ways. Before the game starts, the two players construct their deck of cards for play. The players then separately shuffle their decks so that the cards will appear in a random order during the course of play. If the players have constructed their decks well, they will have strategies for playing Agendas (if they are the Corporation), or in the case of Runners, stealing Agendas. Players have to weigh the probabilities of a particular card appearing in the flow of the game. As a result, if there is a card that the player really wants to use, they have to put in three of that card (the maximum allowed). In a deck of 45 cards, that means 1/15 of the player's deck is that particular card, giving them a fair chance in the flow of a game that they will draw that particular card in time to put it to use.

But just getting one particular type of card to come up isn't enough to succeed. Players have to think through strategies involving the possible interplay of several different kinds of cards and think through the probabilities of them emerging in ways that allow them to be played together. So players have to develop strategies that take advantage of the actions chosen for that deck, such as developing "engines"—or chains of cards—that help pursue or protect Agendas, remembering what cards are in their deck, which have already been played, and which are likely to come up soon. They must then balance these strategies against the chance of the shuffled deck by managing their own uncertainty of the strategies of their opponent. Android: Netrunner requires that players intuit the strategies their opponent will put into play, trying to make sense of the available information and guess what lurks in their deck, or in the case of the Corporations, their unrezzed cards (the still face-down cards the Corporation has put into play).

The proportion in which you use strategy, skill, chance, and uncertainty is one of your considerations as a designer. It's like cooking and the choice you have between sweet, salty, sour, and spicy, or how and in what proportions you combine all four. Like many aspects of game design, chance is like a tasty spice. The right amount makes food taste great, too much can be overbearing, and not enough can make things bland. And our tastes change as we move through life. To young children, Candy Land (see Figure 3.13) seems like the best game ever. (Play it with a four-year-old some time; you'll see.) But at some point, the complete lack of choice and the total reliance on chance gets old. There is no player decision-making in the game. Players just spin the spinner (or draw cards, if you are playing an older version) and then move accordingly. For children, the illustrations and the imaginative play of the Candy Land world is more than enough to make the game fun, but for many others, that just isn't enough.

Figure 3.13   A game of Candy Land.

Purely chance-based games remove decision-making from the player experience. *Threes* suggests smart ways to use strategy and chance to enhance the variety of decision-making for players. Android: Netrunner employs strategy, chance, and skill built over multiple games (and losses) to create a unique play experience. Android: Netrunner is a great example of a game that requires mental skill within a chance-based context. And Candy Land reminds us that chance has to be carefully managed to keep players engaged.

Whimsical Play

And now for something completely different. While most games designed around the interplay of strategy, chance, and uncertainty tend to be pretty serious, there are other play styles that are funny and whimsical. This sort of play feels like a ride at an amusement park (see Figure 3.14) or kids rolling down a hill. Whimsical play emphasizes silly actions, unexpected results, and creating a sense of euphoria by generating dizziness and a play experience that you need to feel to understand. Three videogames that embody this sort of experience are Kaho Abe's *Hit Me*, Bennett Foddy's *QWOP*, and Keita Takahashi's *Tenya Wanya Teens*.

Figure 3.14   A ride at Coney Island.

Hit Me (see Figure 3.15) is a videogame (actually, more of a combination digital/physical game) in which two players don safety hats outfitted with big red buttons and then proceed to try to push one another's button. Literally. The two players simultaneously strain to reach the other's button on their helmet and keep their own helmet out of reach. Thanks to the circle within which the game takes place, the two players are forced to stay close together, which increases the chaotically silly energy of the game. That the game is played with a group of spectators is important, as this further adds to the silliness—people laugh, gasp, and cheer as the players try to hit one another's buttons. *Hit Me* becomes a caricature of cartoon-like combat. Should a player hit their opponent's button, style points are earned by having the best picture taken. (The buttons also house cameras pointed at the opponent.) The judge and spectators reward style points for the best pictures. This changes the dynamics of the game. It becomes as much about the picture-taking as about the physical interactions. Everything from the design of the hats to the actions and goal of taking creative photographs of the other player as you hit their button creates a whimsical experience framed by the silly behaviors players enact in pursuit of their goals.

Figure 3.15   A game of *Hit Me*.

Another game with lots of whimsy is Bennett Foddy's *QWOP* (see Figure 3.16). The game seems straightforward: players try to propel a runner along a track using the Q, W, O, and P keys on a QWERTY keyboard. Things get challenging, and funny, based on the way the keys are mapped to the runner's skeletal system. Instead of making the act of walking trivial like most video-games do, the Q and W map to the runner's thighs, while the O and the P to the runner's calves. This sets up a very challenging goal—keep the player upright and moving forward. The upper body is completely at the whim of the positioning of the legs, often flopping forward and back-ward, causing the runner to collapse after just a few steps. In designing *QWOP*, Foddy played with constraint—in this case on how players manipulate a humanoid to run—to develop a whimsically frustrating play experience.

QWOP brings out whimsy in different ways than *Hit Me*. Instead of having players use their bod-ies to create the playfulness, *QWOP* relies on awkward, intentionally difficult skeletal rigging and button control of the onscreen character. Most games make controlling player movement trivial—simply press the proper key, or push the correct stick, and the onscreen character moves. But *QWOP* plays with these ideas to create a truly whimsical play experience.

Figure 3.16   A screenshot from *QWOP*.

An example of conceptual whimsy is *Tenya Wanya Teens* by Keita Takashi and Uvula with the assistance of Wild Rumpus and Venus Patrol (see Figure 3.17). The game's silliness starts with its controller: a joystick next to a panel of 16 buttons with no identifying labels. The player is tasked with helping a little onscreen boy perform the appropriate task by pressing the correct button on the controller. So sometimes, this means the player makes the character cry when it should be bathing, or rock out on a guitar when the character should be sleeping. The game doesn't ask the player to physically move or act silly, but it does lead to all sorts of onscreen hilarity. Adding to this is the speed with which the game changes environments and tasks— nearly every 10 seconds, the character is presented with a new activity, and the player has to find the right button to perform the task.

Whimsical play is often about physical silliness. Spinning around on a merry-go-round and then trying to walk is whimsical play. Twister and the ways it asks the player to move their body around other players is whimsical play. As we see in *Hit Me*, a careful interplay of actions and goals can set up silly interactions. With *QWOP*, whimsical play can be produced through the careful application of constraint to player actions. Whimsical games like *Hit Me* and *QWOP* emphasize the role of the body, and differently from sports, focus on our physical foibles over our skillful grace. And with *Tenya Wanya Teens*, the silliness is conceptual, as the comedic design of the unexpected outcomes from the player's attempts to click the correct button lead their character to perform actions that don't match their setting. And in so doing, the designer has created whimsy through the interplay of actions, goals, and theme.

Figure 3.17   A game of *Tenya Wanya Teens*.

Role-Playing

For many people, games are a form of storytelling. Perhaps better stated, they are a form of story experience; as the player engages with the game, and through their actions, the story unfolds. There are multiple traditions of storytelling that wind through games, from the character-driven experience of tabletop role-playing games to the more cinematic storytelling associated with many AAA titles. Let's look at an example of both kinds: Leah Gilliam's tabletop RPG Lesberation: Trouble in Paradise, and Tale of Tales' first-person dark fairytale *The Path*.

Leah Gilliam's role-playing game Lesberation: Trouble in Paradise (see Figure 3.18) puts players in the role of a group of lesbian activists trying to establish a utopian society. The game's structure is much simpler than the average RPG. Players are given a set of cards representing objects—coffee mugs, Volkswagen minivans, microphones, rope, and so on—and verbs—rock, love, shout, know, and so on. Players lay their cards out face-up so that everyone can see what everyone else has. Players then take turns playing a card of each type to advance the story scene established by the game-runner. Players have to agree upon decisions as a group and can use other players' cards with permission. The game promotes discussion and consensus-making within a socio-political scenario.

Figure 3.18 A game of Lesberation: Trouble in Paradise. Photo by Leah Gilliam.

Lesberation: Trouble in Paradise uses the basic ideas and structures of role-playing games, but in a way that is accessible to a larger audience. No character sheets, no long rules manual, and no monster manual are needed to play the game. There are just a few simple rules for role-playing a group of activists in a near future scenario. We could pretend to be in those roles without a game, but the light structure of Lesberation makes the experience more enjoyable and facilitates the creation and interaction of the characters.

That is really what this sort of play is about: providing the structure within which stories unfold through role-playing. Jesper Juul has referred to this as **games of emergence**.[1] By this, Juul refers to a space of possibility that is in part defined by how its players enact the actions, objects, and playspace. Lesberation allows players to develop stories within a loose set of rules through which all sorts of possibilities can emerge, limited only by players' imaginations.

Tale of Tales' *The Path* (see Figure 3.19) is a very different kind of role-playing game. Rather than the character and the events being generated by the players, it is designed by the game's creators and experienced by the player. The storyworld of *The Path* is loosely based on the *Little Red Riding Hood* fairytale. Six sisters between the ages of 9 and 19 are on the outskirts of a forest. The girls' mother asks that one of them run over to their grandmother's house in the woods. The player picks one of the six sisters to inhabit on the journey. As the game progresses,

---

1   Jesper Juul, "The Open and the Closed: Games of Emergence and Games of Progression." www.jesperjuul.net/text/openandtheclosed.html. 2002.

players inhabit all six characters and experience the world through their eyes. This sort of role-playing experience happens inside a predefined storyworld, one authored by the gamemakers and unfolded by the player.

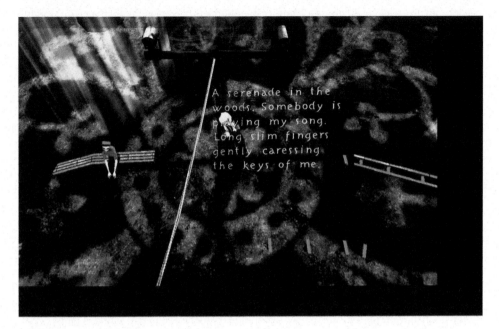

Figure 3.19 A screenshot from *The Path*.

This approach is much closer to movies in that a tighter storyworld can be constructed, with characters and situations designed by the gamemakers rather than by the players themselves. While this approach provides less open-ended play, it provides richer, authored storyworlds to investigate. Jesper Juul refers to this as **games of progression**—those in which the player makes decisions, but all possible outcomes are already defined by the game's creators. In *The Path*, players are free to choose to wander into the woods, but nothing they see or encounter exists without having been preauthored by the game's creators.

A similar example is Porpentine's text adventure *Howling Dogs*. Instead of using 3D representations of a space, the game is delivered entirely through text. Players navigate through Porpentine's surreal storyworld by clicking on text links inside the game. The story is set in a dystopian prison in which the player engages with virtual reality devices. The experience is heightened through its text-based narrative in the same way novels provide us with opportunities to imagine the worlds they present to us. Because of the fractured structure of the game's story, players are left to move through the space in a more impressionistic manner, seeking to construct an understanding of who their character is and why they are where they are. *Howling Dogs* drops us into a role that we must play through to begin to understand. Attempting to find a traditional story progression will only lead to frustration, but embodying the experimental nature of both the format—interactive fiction—and the storyspace provides for a deeply striking experience.

What we see in Lesberation, *The Path,* and *Howling Dogs* are three of the many ways role-playing can be experienced inside a game. Lesberation lets players generate their own stories by providing a structure and set of processes for collaboratively telling a story. It's a system that establishes the general rules for storytelling and lets players feed their story through these rules to create an emergent play experience. *The Path,* on the other hand, has a preauthored story that the player explores by moving through the gameworld. In *The Path,* players experience the game differently through each of the sisters, playing a series of roles that are defined by the game. It's like a machine that contains the threads of the story, delivering each thread as players experience each of the characters that delivers a progressive play experience. *Howling Dogs* is similar in structure, but instead it uses branching text structures to deliver the story experience and help the player piece together who they are. The player makes choices, and as they do so, they experience one path through the story. These three examples mark the different approaches to how role-playing can tell stories in games, as games of emergence and games of progression. And there are many ways in between.

Performative Play

Some games use performance as the core of the play experience. When they do, they're often as much fun to watch as they are to play; generating dramatic action and acting. A game of Charades is based on player performance, adding challenge by taking away some of the expressive abilities like speech to emphasize the qualities of gesture to give clues to the team. Hasbro's Twister provides yet another form of physical play: using a spinner to randomly select the color players must place their feet and hands on, within the colored dots on a floor mat. This creates a form of modern dance where the fun is all in the foibles of the body. Two videogames illustrate different kinds of performative play: Die Gute Fabrik's *Johann Sebastian Joust* and Dietrich Squinkifer's *Coffee: A Misunderstanding.*

The hybrid physical/digital game *Johann Sebastian Joust* (see Figure 3.20) generates improvisational performance through the physical interplay of players attempting to jostle each others' controllers. Players also need to listen to the game's classical music score to learn the speed with which they should move. When the music is slow, players also move slowly—carefully protecting their controllers. When the music speeds up, play becomes more frantic, with players making faster moves and larger gestures. To the spectator, the dance of the players to the music looks like mercenaries at a classical ballroom dance.

Figure 3.22   A game of *Johann Sebastian Joust*. Photo by Elliot Trinidad. Used with permission of the IndieCade International Festival of Independent Games.

Like a playground game, *JS Joust* is flexible, allowing for individual or team play. But it is also a videogame in the tradition of *Wii Sports*, where the Playstation Move Motion controller provides feedback and input into the game and is responsive to different musical styles and speeds. What *JS Joust* emphasizes the most is player performance—in terms of agility and strategy, but also in the sense that there is a dance that everyone is participating in. The interesting thing is that the players, who are deeply absorbed in keeping balanced while unbalancing everyone else, have little time to think about what they are doing or what they look like while doing it. So *JS Joust* is performative, but in a fairly unselfconscious way that spectators observe more than the players are aware of. Absorption becomes an important design tool for creating unselfconscious play, as it takes the player's mind away from their everyday focus on self-presentation and opens them up to an unselfconsciously performative play experience.

A very different example is Dietrich Squinkifer's *Coffee: A Misunderstanding* (see Figure 3.21). In this theatrical game, two players perform as online friends meeting in person for the first time at a fan convention. The players receive prompts for how to interact with one another via their phones from the game's moderator. How they interpret and enact the prompts is up to the players: will they work together to have an enjoyable experience? Will they be at odds and create a tense conversation? Will the conversation simply be awkward? To add to the challenge of maintaining a conversation, two audience volunteers are given a mobile device that allows them to choose key moments and topics in the conversation. As Dietrich describes it, "It's a combination of multiplayer Choose Your Own Adventure and improv theatre, resulting in a play experience that's every bit as awkward as the story it's trying to tell."[2] Dietrich points out an important aspect of this sort of performative play—there is a deliberate, self-conscious performance in this game that very much adds to the game's effect on players and spectators alike.

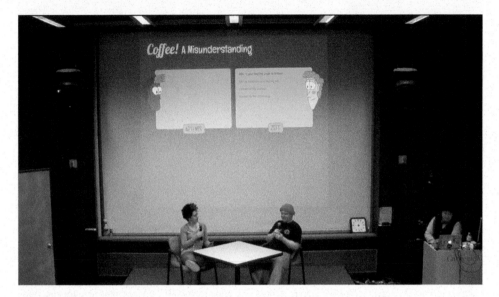

Figure 3.21 *A game of* Coffee: A Misunderstanding.

Games can often act like a score for player performance, generating dance, acting, and acrobatics emergent from the game's play. With *JS Joust*, we see a form of performative play that asks players to abandon themselves to the game in a way that enables performance within the game and for those watching the game. The more focused a player becomes, the more performative they are. *Coffee: A Misunderstanding* takes a very different approach, keeping players keenly aware of their actions and the potential for awkwardness and vulnerability. The game asks players to perform within the context and prompts designed, but the way players deliver their lines and the choices made by the audience volunteers add to the unpredictable playfulness of the experience.

---

2   From the description of the game on Dietrich Squinkifer's website (http://squinky.me/my-games/coffee-a-misunderstanding/).

Expressive Play

A related form of play is **expressive play**: play that expresses a feeling or concept, whether intended by the designer or derived from the player. This idea of artistic expression is usually associated with music, film, literature, and painting, but not games. However, increasingly, gamemakers are using games to express ideas and feelings. Two examples of this are anna anthropy's *Queers in Love at the End of the World* and Elizabeth Sampat's Deadbolt.

Queers in Love at the End of the World (see Figure 3.22) is a text-based game in which actions are presented in the form of hyperlinks. The player has only 10 seconds to play the entire game. In the final fleeting moments of the world, the player steals a kiss, tries to say something, looks at the sky…all within 10 seconds. And then the game ends. If the player chooses to restart the game, they can try to see all of the paths not taken—wonder how much can be done in such a short amount of time and experience worry, desire, and regret condensed into the short game-play. It uses only text and a countdown timer, but trying to read everything and make choices only emphasizes the urgency of the gameplay and of the narrative of a world ending. *Queers in Love at the End of the World* expresses much in such a short amount of time: how we often wrestle with how to express the way we feel about our partners, our feelings around life ending when there are things left unsaid and not done, and the fleeting quality of a moment. So the game is expressive both for anna and for the player in making their decisions and reflecting upon their meaning.

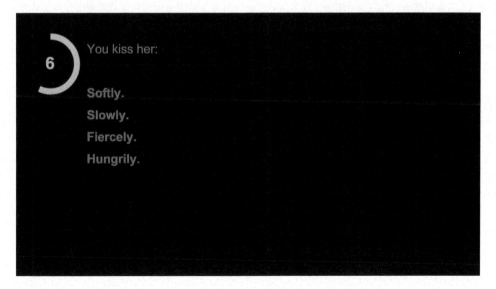

Figure 3.22 A screenshot from *Queers in Love at the End of the World*.

Elizabeth Sampat's Deadbolt is a tabletop role-playing game structured around personal reflection and conversation. Play begins with players filling out the key—a simple set of evaluations of the other players including who among the players is most intimidating, most beautiful, best known, least known, and so on. Once everyone has filled out the key, the players then open two envelopes: Signifier and the Question. Signifier lets the player know which player they will talk to first. The second envelope lets the player know what question will be asked. Conversations then begin around the prompts.

First, players are asked questions about themselves, and then about the other player. In the third round, players are given blank cards onto which they can write a comment or question for one of the other players. These cannot be viewed by the other player until the game is over. At that point, free from the structure of the game, the player can choose to engage with the other player who gave their comment or question. If a player is emotionally affected by the final card but doesn't want to speak about it, they can give the player who gave them the card a Deadbolt button.

Expressive play is a form of play that often subverts player choice in an effort to clearly express and share something about the human experience. In the case of *Queers in Love at the End of the World,* our choices are limited by the inexorable end of a 10-second timer. But choice-making isn't the place where expression resides in the game. Instead, it comes from anna's speculations. And in Deadbolt, players are given a framework within which they can reflect and express feelings about others and themselves. The game isn't about winning or losing, but simply about allowing oneself to be honest and reflective and to share those reflections.

Simulation-Based Play

The last kind of play we'd like to discuss is simulation-based play. *Sim City* and *Rollercoaster Tycoon* are well-known examples of this kind of game experience: some aspect of the real world is abstracted into a game, and players get to play "mayor" or "tycoon" within the abstracted interactive model. The Landlord's Game designed by Elizabeth Magie, which was the origin of a game we know now as Monopoly, is also an example of simulation-based play. Magie designed the game to demonstrate the economic principles of Georgism, an economic system proposed by Henry George. The primary focus of the game was to demonstrate how rents make property owners wealthy and tenants impoverished. Many of us can relate to the way this feels when we are inexorably losing a game of Monopoly to a greedy opponent or becoming that greedy property owner through the luck of a dice roll and some wisely purchased properties.

Two independent simulation-based videogames, Molleindustria's *The McDonald's Videogame* and Lucas Pope's *Papers, Please*, provide great examples of simulation-based games using the game design tool of **abstraction**—simplifying the complexity of real-world systems to be playable and accessible in a game.

The McDonald's Videogame (see Figure 3.23) is a satirical modeling of the McDonald's fast food restaurant chain and its impact on the people, animals, and environments that come in contact with the company. The game is made up of four interconnected playable models of the McDonald's ecosystem: a farming simulator that can grow soy beans or cattle; a meat processing plant; a McDonald's restaurant; and the McDonald's corporate board room.

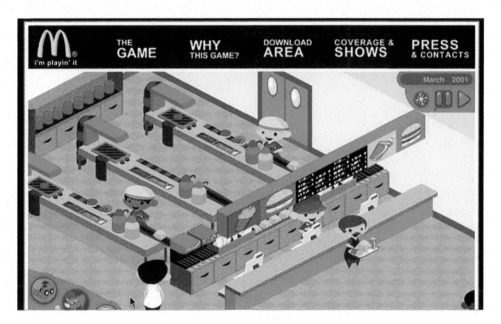

Figure 3.23 A screenshot from *The McDonald's Videogame*.

The game abstracts the complex systems at play at each level to emphasize the impacts McDonald's has on its supply chain and the interconnected nature of the company's business. The farming feeds into the slaughterhouse, which supplies the meat to the restaurants, which in turn produces revenue for the corporation. The game allows players to inhabit this process and play inside the systemic representation of the fast food restaurant. It does so to political ends, to use games and play to make a rhetorical point about the industry.

A different kind of simulation-based play is found in *Papers, Please* (see Figure 3.24). On the surface, *Papers, Please* seems like a political game. The player takes on the role of an employee in the Ministry of Admission inspecting passports in the fictional Arstotzka. Each day, the officer is given a set of notices about what to look out for as the applicants are being processed. For example, the player has to make sure that on some days only citizens of Arstotzka are allowed to enter, while on other days, those with valid visas can get in. Through the repetitive actions required to examine and stamp each passport, the game models the experience of someone in a similar kind of job. It also comments upon the seemingly arbitrary nature of government policies around issues that deeply affect people's lives. Instead of focusing on the larger systemic modeling, *Papers, Please* emphasizes the particulars of one small part of a larger whole, in the process placing the whole in a new light.

Figure 3.24   A screenshot from Papers, Please.

These two examples show different scales at which we can produce simulations. *The McDonald's Videogame* simulates a situation in a holistic yet stylized way, taking into account a large number of factors and presenting them in a simplified top-down model. *Papers, Please* scales things at a more human scale by putting the player into a more direct role of an individual. The whole can be experienced and contemplated, but in a more granular way. Both of them use point of view—from above or from below—as well as the game design tool of abstraction to help us understand the mechanics of a complex system.

Summary

We've looked at a wide range of play styles. There are multiple ways to think about designing games that can produce competition, cooperation, skill, chance, strategy, whimsy, role-playing, performance, expressiveness, and simulation. From a designer's perspective, these are the basic kinds of games we can create for our players to experience.

Ultimately, game designers should play all sorts of games, regardless of their own tastes. You never know when a randomizing strategy in a free-to-play puzzle game might come in handy for a cooperative role-playing game. The relationships between chance, strategy, skill, simulation, expressiveness, performance, whimsy, role-playing, competition, and cooperation can be recombined in different ways to create new play experiences—like a chef combines different ingredients and cuisines to create new dishes and fusions. The trick is thinking about games as a game designer. Instead of thinking about your own experience, think about what created that experience—what mix of competition or cooperation, of chance and skill, of role-playing or simulation shaped the experience and how these were used in the design of the game that generated it.

- *Competitive play:* A kind of play in which some players will win and some will lose. The kinds of competitive play are *player versus player, player versus game, asynchronous competition, symmetrical competition,* and *asymmetrical competition.*

- *Cooperative play:* Play experience in which players work together to achieve the game's goals. Cooperative play might include *symmetrical cooperation, asymmetrical cooperation,* and *symbiotic cooperation.*

- *Skill-based play:* Play that emphasizes player skill development in the pursuit of the game's goal. Kinds of skill-based play include *active skill* and *mental skill.*

- *Experience-based play:* A kind of play focused on providing players with an experience of the game through exploration, unfolding a story, or communal engagement.

- *Games of chance and uncertainty:* Games that ask players to develop strategies to allow for unpredictable moments or aspects of the game. Purely chance-based games remove decision-making from the player experience.

- *Whimsical play:* A kind of play that emphasizes silly actions, unexpected results, and a sense of euphoria by generating dizziness and a play experience that you need to feel to understand. Whimsical play is often based on *silly interactions, constraint as whimsy,* and *conceptual absurdity.*

- *Role-playing:* A game that generates stories through players inhabiting different roles and following a loose set of rules through which all sorts of possibilities can emerge, limited only by players' imaginations. Types of role-playing story generation include *emergent storytelling* and *progressive storytelling.*

■ *Performative play:* A theatrical form of play that generates dramatic action and acting and often includes a good deal of player improvisation. Performative play can generate *unintentional performance* and *conscious performance*.

■ *Expressive play:* A form of play that often subverts player choice in an effort to clearly express and share something about human experience. Expressive play might involve *authorial expression* or *player expression*.

■ *Simulation-based play:* A form of play that models a real-world system and presents a point of view (sometimes political, sometimes in terms of a player's perspective on the world) about that system to the player. Players might engage with a *top-down simulation* or a *bottom-up simulation*.

Exercises

1. Choose one of your favorite games and describe it using one or more of the kinds of play described in this chapter: competitive and cooperative play, skill-based play, experience-based play, chance-based play, whimsical play, role-playing, performative play, expressive play, or simulation-based play.

2. Take the game you described in Exercise 1 and try to apply another kind of play to it. What happens when a skill-based game becomes more whimsical? Or simulation based?

3. Turn a competitive game into a cooperative one. How will the rules of the game change? The goal?

4. Choose a game of skill and turn it into a game of experience, or vice versa. How does the game need to be modified to turn it from one type to another?

5. Redesign a game based primarily on chance and uncertainty (Candy Land, roulette) to rely less on chance and include more player choice and strategy. Try to play it with some friends. How is the play experience different?

CHAPTER 4

THE PLAYER EXPERIENCE

In this chapter we look at the kinds of knowledge players need to play games. We look at the five layers of player experience: sensory, information, interaction, frame, and purpose.

In the previous chapter we talked about the different kinds of play games can create for players. But to play the games, we ask more of our players than just using the actions to interact with the objects and other players inside a playspace. Game designers, particularly videogame designers, need to understand a little bit about cognition, a little about hand-eye coordination, a little bit about information and interface design, and a slew of other topics that help them design for people. As game designers work, they need to keep in mind what the interface designer Jef Raskin called "human frailties," or an understanding of the limits of what people can and cannot do, and what people are and aren't good at.[1] That's what this chapter sets out to do—help us take into account what we might call "player frailties." We'll think of the amalgam of all these ideas and approaches as player-centered design. This includes things like how players perceive the playspace, how much information the game provides and how players process this information, how challenge keeps them playing and developing their skills, and how the game's context impacts a player's experience such as where the game is and who is playing and watching.

Action Theory as a Framework

The most basic way to understand what a game asks of its players is to consider the principles of **action theory**. Action theory is a sociological concept originated by Talcott Parsons[2] as a way to understand the dynamics of what happens when people encounter a given situation. Action theory proposes the following cycle of interaction:

- *Beliefs:* A person has a set of prior experiences and belief systems that frame how they understand the world. Let's use three examples: being hungry, seeing a friend, and playing *Super Mario Bros.*

- *Reaction:* Given these beliefs, we encounter a situation and we form a reaction—I sure am hungry; look, there's my friend; oh no, it's a goomba.

- *Desire:* This reaction leads to a desire—I'd like to eat; I'd like to say hi; I'd like to jump over that goomba.

- *Intention:* This desire leads to the formation of a plan of action—I'm going to pick a sandwich and drink; I'm going to walk over and say hi; I'm going to run toward the goomba and then jump.

- *Action:* With an intention in place, the person then enacts the plan—orders the sandwich and a drink from a waiter; calls out the friend's name and waves as they walk toward them; executes the moves to attempt to jump over the goomba.

---

1   *The Humane Interface: New Directions for Designing Interactive Systems*, 2000.

2   Talcott Parsons, *The Structure of Social Action*, 1937.

- *Repeat:* With the action completed, we begin the cycle anew, with the outcome of the action causing a response from the situation that requires us to once more react, establish a desire, create a plan, and then conduct an action.

Within the cycle of action theory, we find so many important things to consider about our players: how they understand a situation, what they want from it, what they think they are able to do, what they are able to do, and how they interpret the outcome of their actions. This provides a perfect model for thinking about what we ask of our players anytime they play our games and fits nicely with the action-outcome unit discussed in Chapter 3, "The Kinds of Play"—whether it is the "bird's eye" view of their learning about your game, what they hope to get from the experience, and then the actual experience they have; or the more detailed process of each decision they make as they play your game.

The best way to think about this is as a layered process through which players interact with videogames. In his book *The Elements of User Experience,*[3] Jesse James Garrett outlines five planes of user experience: the surface (what we see and hear), the skeleton (the information within the surface), the structure (how that information is organized), the scope (the boundaries of what is and isn't contained within the experience), and the strategy (the purpose of the experience). We can transpose this model onto how a player experiences a videogame (see Figure 4.1):

- *Sensory (the surface):* What the player sees, hears, feels, smells, and tastes when playing the game.
- *Information (the skeleton):* Within the sensory layer, the information the player discerns about the game.
- *Interaction (the structure):* Given the sensory layer and the information, what the player understands they can do while playing the game.
- *Frame (the scope):* The player's understanding of the game's space of possibility informed by their experiences as a player and more broadly as a person.
- *Purpose (the strategy):* The player's goals for the game.

---

3 Jesse James Garrett, *The Elements of User Experience*, 2002.

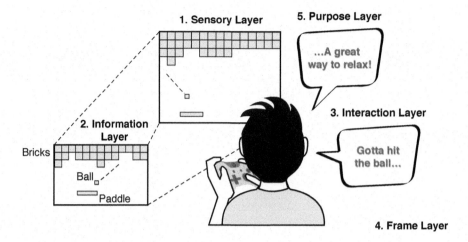

Figure 4.1   The layers of player experience.

The Layers of a Play Experience

These five planes provide us with a model for thinking about what game designers ask of their players. Instead of planes, we will refer to them as layers. This better illustrates the relationship between each—a sequential yet recursive process by which players interact with our games.

The Sensory Layer

Like any other human experience, play begins with our five senses. We see, hear, and feel video-games as the most elemental aspect of our play experiences. Understanding what it means to see, hear, and feel a game is therefore quite important.

Let's start with one of the more often-used components of videogames: the player's point of view. The dominant approach in AAA games is a three-dimensional world seen either through the player's eyes (a first-person perspective) or from just behind the player (a third-person over-the-shoulder perspective).[4] These approaches are so commonplace that it doesn't even seem like there were any decisions to be made about how players see a game. But one of the most

---

4   Want a full list of all the kinds of perspective? Read John's essay on perspective in *The Routledge Companion to Video Game Studies*, 2013.

important decisions in a videogame's design is how the player sees the game's world—2D side view, 3D first-person view, 3D third-person view, and so on.

Just as important is how the world is represented. Is it with super-simple graphics pared down to a few pixels? Or is it hyper-realistic, with every shadow and texture defined and refined? Or is it a game that uses no images at all, but simply text or sound? Together, the way the player sees the world and the way the world is represented have an impact on how the player perceives their role in the game, determines what they want to do, and interprets their progress toward the game's or their own goals.

A good starting point here is *Alabaster* (see Figure 4.2)—a 'fractured fairytale' and collaborative work conceived of by Emily Short with contributions by John Cater, Rob Dubbin, Eric Eve, Elizabeth Heller, Jayzee, Kazuki Mishima, Sarah Morayati, Mark Musante, Adam Thornton, and Ziv Wities, with illustrations by Daniel Allington-Krzysztofiak. *Alabaster* is a text-based game that draws on the conventions of books, or in the digital world, early text adventures like Infocom's

"He left when the moon was full - the rest is surmise," she replies flatly.

You could now ask if she is the King's daughter or ask what exactly she surmises.

> ask what she surmises
"And what do you surmise?" You are close to something here: you can sense it.

She makes a face. "I have difficulty being sure."

"But what do you think happened?" you ask. "Whether you're sure or not."

She answers slowly. "There is an old magic, blood-sundering. By it daughters are made not-daughters, and sons not-sons; husbands and wives no longer know one another. Family is negated. Family members become strangers.

"I don't think that the king died, or went into exile. I think he was made not to be the king any longer. But I *can't remember*. Nothing about that night save the red ring around the moon, and the drumming of the dwarrows that went silent by dawn."

You could now ask if she is the King's daughter or ask what became of the King.

> ask what became of the king
"What would have become of the King after this blood-sundering, if he became not-himself?"

"I doubt he would have gone far," she says. "He might still live nearby - in the village, in the palace itself. Who knows? The Queen might not even know him for who he is."

You wait. "Did anyone new come to the village around the time of the King's departure?" she asks.

You can answer questions with YES, NO, and MAYBE – though of course sometimes not all of those answers are appropriate.

>|

Figure 4.2 *Alabaster.*

Zork and, more generally, the field of **interactive fiction**. It is a playable story composed of text and the occasional image. Players take the role of a nameless woodsman tasked with bringing Snow White's heart to the Queen. Unable to bring himself to kill someone so young, beautiful, and seemingly innocent, the woodsman kills a deer and procures its heart. However, something about Snow White is unsettling. The woodsman begins to question his perception of her and whether, perhaps, she is not as innocent as she seemed. To truly know what the woodsman should do, the player must learn more about Snow White. So, from this point in the game, the player begins to ask questions and engage in a conversation with Snow White.

To move through the world and interact with Snow White and other objects in the game, the player enters simple commands into a text prompt, such as "ask", "tell", "north", and "kick", which turns these words into sentences like this one: "ask where there is safe haven." There's an incredibly rich number of responses from Snow White, authored by the many collaborators on the project.

In the case of *Alabaster*, the entire story unfolds through a series of still images and text. Outside the still images[5] that accompany each major **story beat**, the story unfolds in the player's mind through reading the descriptive text in the narrative. Because the player uses cardinal direction to move around, they are likely thinking spatially, and therefore about the setting of the action. But the majority of the gameplay occurs through conversation, and it is here that players try to understand the characters and their motivations and how the story will end.

Merritt Kopas's *Hugpunx* (see Figure 4.3) is an example of how 2D games provide players with a simple vantage point in a game and simplicity in terms of spatial interaction with the controls: for the most part, left and right. The game is quite simple in its premise: move from left to right to "hug" the green people and cats. Successful hugs result in happy, bouncy hug recipients. The implied camera in *Hugpunx* is alongside the playspace, almost as if it is attached to a tripod just in front of the playspace. There is no depth, as all action takes place in a single plane. The actions available to the player are therefore very simple—move left, move right, and hug.

In addition to the constrained movement, there is the simple, stylized representation of the game's world. *Hugpunx* uses a near-abstract pixel art style to represent the people, cats, and environment. There is no foreground, and there is no background. All of the imagery exists on a single plane on which the action takes place. This allows players to really focus on the interaction and goals of the game, as simple as they might be. *Hugpunx* uses its player point of view as a way to keep things simple, light, and focused. The decision space it presents is pared down to the essentials, with little extraneous information save the plants in the environment. But even these have a purpose; as they grow they help create a sense of excitement and chaos that builds as the game unfolds.

---

5   In this case, the illustrations are actually procedural, meaning they are composed with code, providing the player with many unique variations.

Figure 4.3 *Hugpunx.*

What happens when game designers want to provide more options for exploring the game-world and seeing it from multiple vantage points? Generally, this sort of experience comes through 3D game engines and 3D representations of the gameworld. Take Blendo Games's *Thirty Flights of Loving* (see Figure 4.4). It combines a 3D environment and a first-person perspective on the world with a blocky, flat-color, visual style to provide a unique play experience. The player takes on the role of an unnamed accomplice in a three-person team of…well, it's unclear what they are, as you'll see if you play.

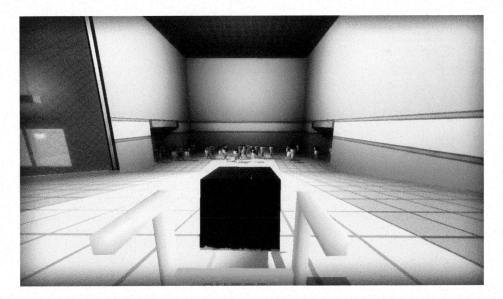

Figure 4.4 *Thirty Flights of Loving.*

Like all three-dimensional games, the primary actions through which you perceive the game world are looking and moving. *Thirty Flights of Loving* builds upon these in interesting ways, with most every other action implied rather than carried out. The player can open doors and pick up some objects, but the game really focuses on the idea of navigating and looking as the primary actions in a story-driven experience. The player inhabits a world that is three-dimensional, meaning you can move in all directions, through the x (left/right), y (up/down), and z (forward/backward) axes. This opens up all sorts of new information for the player to take in. But in *Thirty Flights of Loving*, the space is designed so that there are seldom more than two choices of where to go—back through the door the player entered through, or out through another door into the next space. This allows the player to focus on the environment they inhabit and creates natural changes in scene with every exit and entrance.

In *Thirty Flights of Loving,* the spaces players can explore tend to be either small and quickly examined or large but without a lot of extraneous information. So the player is able to quickly "read" the space and make choices about how to proceed. The visual style of the game— blocky, simplified representations of people, animals, objects, and spaces—is in line with the overall approach to players moving through and interacting with the world. The two go hand-in-hand.

The way a designer represents their playspace and how they let players move within it impacts what the player will do and how they will perceive the game and make decisions about what they want to do. The more the designer opens up the ways a player sees and moves, the more complex the interpretation of the visual information becomes.

This brings us to the last of our examples in player point of view and player perception, thatgamecompany's *Journey* (see Figure 4.5). Instead of being constrained to a single plane

Figure 4.5   *Journey.*

or having a tightly constrained space to move through, *Journey* presents the player with an expansive world through which they can explore.[6] The beautifully rendered world establishes the game's goal—reach the mountain visible in the distance. To do this, the player collects fragments of scarf that give her the power to float across distances otherwise too far to jump. By keeping the challenge straightforward, players can focus on exploring and enjoying the environment and the playground-like atmosphere of sliding down hills and jumping from ledges.

The game has a stylized yet detailed world full of sand dunes, snowy mountains, ancient runes, and detailed carpets and cloth. This is a big part of the experience of *Journey*—enjoying the lush world the player character inhabits. Despite all of the details and environments, players never get lost; in each section of the game, the goal—the top of the mountain—is seen in the distance. The use of the over-the-shoulder camera encourages the player to see themselves inside the gameworld, enabling them to experience their small scale in relation to the world, gauge their location when trying to land on elements in the game, and see their progress as the scarf trailing behind them lengthens.

Despite the fact that both of them are relatively easy games in terms of challenge, *Journey* and *Thirty Flights of Loving* are still pretty hard games for many people to play. There is a real accessibility issue with the implied camera and idiomatic interfaces we find with 3D games and the WASD keys-plus-mouse or the baroque, 15-plus buttons on console controllers we use to navigate them. The simulation of three-dimensional space is hard to wrap your head around, and getting used to the control mechanisms is even harder. Even *Alabaster*, with its seemingly simple text interface, still assumes knowledge of basic interactive fiction interaction schemes. On the other hand, the simpler mapping that happens in two-dimensional games like *Hugpunx* is much more accessible for a wider audience unfamiliar with the conventions of 3D games.

Alabaster, Hugpunx, Thirty Flights of Loving, and *Journey* help us see how the player's point of view and vantage point on a game impacts their play experience. They also show us how the visual style relates to this as both part of the experience and as a way of focusing our attention and decision-making.

This leads to questions designers might ask about player point of view and perception to guide their work: How do you want your player to take in information about the game world? And how does this relate to the player's experience of the world itself? Do you want everything to be clear and focused, with no distracting elements? Do you want the player's attention to be on getting around in the world? Do you want the attention on the world itself? Or on the goals? Or do you want the goal to be exploring the world? All these are considerations when deciding how to let the player see, sense, and move through your game.

---

6   The world is not completely open; there are moments in the game when the player must follow a path, and there are limits to the world's boundaries, but compared to the previous examples, players have much more freedom of movement.

The Information Layer

Here's a question: what is an assumption we too quickly make about the sensory layer of a videogame? The answer: that players know what they are looking at. There is a difference between seeing and understanding, which brings us to the information layer of the play experience. Within the field of information science, the working model for how people make sense of things is called DIKW—people first take in *data*, and from this build *information*, which leads to *knowledge* they can put into use, and eventually *wisdom* that allows deeper insight.

To turn data into information, we must first understand how we focus on the bits that are relevant and apply our **attention** to them. Related to this idea is the study of attention within cognitive psychology and how we respond to and process sensory stimulus. Game designer Richard Lemarchand's 2011 talk at the Game Developer's Conference titled "Attention, Not Immersion: Making Your Games Better with Psychology and Playtesting, the Uncharted Way"[7] identifies **reflexive attention** and **executive attention** as two forms of attention that define a player's understanding of what is currently happening in the game. Reflexive attention is from the back and side regions of the brain and is activated when loud noises, quickly moving objects, or anything novel is presented to us. Executive attention (sometimes called **voluntary attention**) refers to those things that we decide to pay attention to, such as looking at a health meter, for instance, or reading a sign in the road. Together, they help us understand the kinds of attention we are asking the player to give our game and how to keep track of the number of things we are asking our players to pay attention to.

Let's look at the beginning of *Journey* (see Figure 4.6) to help us understand this. The player first sees a character standing on a sandy hill. This is a series of data points—there is a figure in a cape, there is a hill, and it appears to be made of sand. The player can intuit that the character is probably the player character by virtue of the camera angle, the position the camera has onscreen, and other subtle but important cues. Once the player begins to move the sticks on the controller, they confirm that the figure is in fact their in-game representation. And as the player moves their in-game character, the sand-like material on the hill is confirmed to be sand by the way the character displaces it as they move. This process moves the player through data to information to knowledge—they now know the environment, who they are in the game, and how they move the character through the playspace.

This opening scenes in *Journey* utilize both our reflexive and our executive attention. As the game begins, the player hears an orchestral tone begin to rise and sees a field of shimmering sand. The tone activates the player's reflexive attention, as they use their executive attention to try to discern the image on the screen. A **jump cut** shows them a wider view of the scene, and more cuts lead to an image of the mountain, the sun, and a comet-like point of light moving across the landscape, all activating the player's reflexive attention with each cut. Once the

---

7   Richard Lemarchand, "Attention, Not Immersion: Making Your Games Better with Psychology and Playtesting, the Uncharted Way," GDC 2011.

Figure 4.6 The starting point in *Journey*.

game's opening animations complete, we are brought to the moment described earlier: our character on a sandy hill. Here the player uses their executive attention to begin to decipher where they are and how to move.

At this moment in the game, the player could go in any direction they wanted. But they are given a clue about the direction they should begin to move toward: the mountain visible on the horizon. They always know how to orient themselves, so they choose to move toward it as a goal. In theme park design, the mountain would be referred to as a "weenie," a term coined by Walt Disney in reference to a boyhood experience luring a dog home with a sausage, and used to describe an important aspect of his theme park's design.[8] A **weenie** is a large architectural element placed to be visible from many locations, serving as a visual magnet to orient and guide people toward a location. The designers of *Journey* and many 3D games use weenies to give players a visual reference point.

Part and parcel with transforming what players see, hear, and feel in the game is making sense of what is being seen, heard, and felt. Questions to ask about how players will turn all of this sensory data into information and knowledge include: Is every object in the game seen by the player, or are some objects hidden? Is the information easy to access, intentionally vague, or does it require lots of interpretation? How much information can players take in during gameplay? How much are we asking players to focus on, and are we providing the clues for players to know what information is relevant? All these questions relate to the **information space** of a game: the possible meanings a player can derive from a given game.

8   As referenced by Reece Fischer, "The Creation of Disneyland." *The Creation of Disneyland*. N.p., 2004. Web.
     14 Jan. 2013. http://universityhonors.umd.edu/HONR269J/projects/fischer.html.

Take chess (see Figure 4.7) as an example. In chess, the players can see every element in the game. The pieces on the board, their position, and the pieces that have been captured. This is called having **perfect information** on the game state. Nothing is hidden—except, of course, the thoughts of the other player. In chess, yomi (a concept discussed in Chapter 3) plays a big role in the strategic fun of the game as players try to imagine what their opponent might do on the next turn. As the player examines the chess board, they take in the position of both players' pieces, think about their short-term and long-term strategies for winning, and how they might get closer to capturing their opponent's king. They have to think about how each kind of piece moves, where their pieces are on the board, and which piece in particular to move on their turn to advance their strategy.

Figure 4.7   Chess.

That's a lot of information to think about around a single decision, isn't it? This is why chess works so well as a **turn-based** game. Players aren't in a rush to make their decisions since there isn't a time constraint on their actions (unless they are playing with a timer, of course). It is also why chess works just as well in person as it does via correspondence. What chess helps us understand is that everything a player sees becomes part of the information they have to process to make decisions about what to do next. Every time something happens in the game, the player has to analyze what changed, why, and how that impacts the state of the game.

Android: Netrunner (see Figure 4.8) puts players into an **imperfect information** space. In this two-player cardgame, players choose to be either the Corporation or the Runner, each with a different goal in the game. The Corporation has Agendas—cards that they must keep protected and hidden, either in their hand or face-down on the table in front of them. The Runner attempts to hack into the Corporation's hand or the cards on the table to steal enough Agendas to win the game. The Corporation wins by advancing agendas and applying resources to them before they are captured. Each player has data on the cards in their deck, though not of the order in which they will appear. Each player also has perfect information about the cards in their hand and that they have played. Both players have imperfect information about the other player's cards beyond those that have been revealed through play. However, some cards allow the player to peek at the other player's cards, and there is a way to keep some cards revealed, so the information space of the game fluctuates.

Figure 4.8 Android: Netrunner.

In addition to being an imperfect information space, Android: Netrunner is an **asymmetric information space**. Because each player is playing a different role, by a different set of rules and with different cards, each needs to try to understand the other's intentions and possible strategies as they are playing. It demands a great deal of understanding—one might say empathy—as players attempt to get inside the other player's head and anticipate their next move. It also certainly generates yomi, the attempt to guess what the other player is thinking, and what player A thinks player B thinks player A is thinking. Chess does this too, but in Android: Netrunner, the players think differently—as a Corporation or a Runner, depending on your *opponent*. And like chess, Android: Netrunner is a turn-based game; players can take time to think about and make their next move.

Basketball (see Figure 4.9) is a very differently paced game than chess or Android: Netrunner. Basketball is **real time,** forcing players to respond quickly to each other's moves, the location of the ball, and the position of players on the court. The information space is perfect—players can look around and see where everything of importance in the game is and what the current state of the game is, such as who has the ball.

Figure 4.9 Basketball. Photo by Laura Hale. Used under CC 3.0 SA Unported.

The challenge in the game is created by teams executing plays and improvising within them to surprise the other team and gain an advantage in moving the ball closer to the goal. Players feint moving in one direction and take off in another. Or they pass the ball to a player who just opened up because their teammate kept the defense from getting between the passer and the passee. So, while the information available to players is perfect, the real-time nature of the game makes it impossible to fully process all of the possible moves of the other team, making gameplay unpredictable, and ultimately, a lot of fun. Basketball is also a **symmetrical information space** in that all players have access to the same information about the state of the game—everyone can theoretically see who has the ball, where everyone else is on the floor, what the score is, how much time is left, and so on.

This leads to questions designers might ask about the information layer to guide their work: how much information do you want to provide to the player? What kind of attention will players use to make sense of and react to the information? Will it be reflexive or executive—thought out ahead of time? Will they have perfect or imperfect information? In a multiplayer game, will the information be symmetrical or asymmetrical? Will the game present information in real time, or will it give the player time to consider the information as they take their time to take a turn? How information is presented, how much is presented, and in what kind of time-frame all impact the player's ability to make choices and understand their next move.

The Interaction Layer

To really make sense of the information space, a player needs to understand how the information works together. In the Data-Information-Knowledge-Wisdom model, this is the step where patterns in the data create information, which in turn enables knowledge on which the player can make decisions and act. This means the player needs to have a working **mental model** of the game. There is often a gap between how something actually works and how players think it works. This runs the gamut from actions, objects, the boundaries of a playspace, and, most importantly, how broad and deep players understand the space of possibility of the game to be. When a player first plays a game, they are working off prior knowledge to help them interpret the information space. As they continue to play, they slowly develop a more specific understanding of your game until they are working off the information from their prior experiences in the game to develop their understanding of the game's space of possibility.

anna anthropy wrote an exceptional essay about the first level of *Super Mario Bros.* to think about how players learn to play a game.[9] In it, anna looks at the first thing players see in *Super Mario Bros.* A figure on the left side of the screen looking to the right (Mario), the ground, and an unbroken view of the sky above. The only thing the player can do—and it is clear from simply looking at the screen—is move to the right. As soon as the player moves Mario, they see the background moving, and a flashing brick with a '?' appears, along with an angry-looking creature. Players learn to jump, and in doing so, learn the primary action of the game: jumping. anthropy's close analysis of these first few seconds of *Super Mario Bros.* shows us just how ingenious Shigeru Miyamoto and Takashi Tezuka's design of the first level is.

Once a player understands what they are engaging with, they have to understand their role in the game and how they enact it. This takes us to **affordances**, an important concept in cognetics. As Donald Norman defines them, affordances are "the perceived properties of the thing, primarily those fundamental properties that determine just how the thing could possibly be used."[10] In other words, affordances are what we think things do before we actually interact with them. We see a tool with a handle, and we assume we can grip it. We see a book, and we assume we can read it. We see a joystick, and we assume we can use it to navigate something on a screen. These are the **perceptible affordances** of an object. Affordances also help us make what are called **correct rejections**—we can tell what something *isn't* used for as well.

---

9   anna anthropy, "Level Design Lesson: To the Right, Hold on Tight" from her website, http://auntiepixelante.com/?p=465, 2009.

10 Donald Norman, *The Design of Everyday Things*, pg. 8, 1988.

So we can guess a pillow won't work as a hammer or that an object in the background of a game isn't of the utmost importance.

There are two additional kinds of affordances: **hidden affordances** and **false affordances**. A hidden affordance is that which is present in an object but is not obvious from its appearance. You wouldn't realize you can drink from a hat, but you can; you wouldn't know a brick up in the air could be hit in order to release a coin, but it will, sometimes. False affordances are misinterpretations of what an object can do. We see a wax apple and think we might be able to eat it; we see a door in a 3D game but cannot open it.

In games, affordances help us understand the complex relationship between what players see, what they understand, and what they think they can do when playing a game. As players look at and listen to our games, they are also constantly assessing what they can and cannot do. The thing is, with videogames, players are almost always dealing with one or more levels of separation between the player, the game's interface, and the game's visual and auditory feedback. Videogames are played by looking at a screen and then interacting with the game via a separate game controller (fingers included). And even when there is a direct contact point, as on a touch screen, the gestures seldom directly map onto what happens onscreen. This introduces a gap between our perceptions—what we see on the screen and hear through the speakers—and our actions—the decision-making that results in button presses, stick movements, and finger gestures.

In this screen in *Braid* (see Figure 4.10) by Number None, Inc, the player character, Tim, has just grasped the key from a precarious position down in a pit with one of the enemies in the game.

Figure 4.10   The affordances of *Braid*.

In this case, the player has learned that the goomba is an enemy to be avoided because of their unfortunate encounter with it earlier in the game. Visually, it certainly has an expression that seems to indicate "stay away." And that is what the player has learned to do. The key's affordances are even more clear because of the player's previous experiences with keys in their life. They open doors and are meant to be picked up. So it makes sense in the game that the key is something to grab and use in doors. In this case there are several doors—one that we came out of, on the left, and a door with a big keyhole blocking the way to another door on the right. It's clear to the player that they should make their way over to the door with the big lock to use the key they have just picked up. This large keyhole provides the player with the perceptible affordance that the door can be unlocked with the key. Finally, as they have played, the player has learned that they can drop down into pits like this without getting hurt (as long as the enemies are avoided). But how to get back up? Well, yet another clue came to the player earlier in their play session. On the screen, a prompt to press a button on the controller to rewind time was given. After this one-time prompt, the player learned through trial and error how to rewind time. Being able to rewind time is a hidden affordance in *Braid*, one that we learn only through playing.

Beyond the peculiar reality that is videogame interaction, game designers also have to consider how people will engage with the interface of the game. Gillian Crampton-Smith proposed five characteristics of well-designed interactivity: clear mental model, feedback, navigability, consistency, and intuitiveness.[11]

Clear Mental Model

Crampton-Smith's five principles start with a clear **mental model**. In the context of videogames, this refers to the player's understanding of the basic elements of a game—the playspace, the rules that govern their actions and interactions with the objects (and other players, if there are any), and how all these relate to the stated goals (and those the players bring themselves)—build up to a coherent theme. Do players "get" how the game works?

This extends to the points of contact between the player and the game: the screen, the speakers, the control scheme and how it presents feedback. Is the feedback supporting the player's mental model of the game? Is it confirming player actions and providing qualitative evaluation of the impact on the game's state?

Besides confirming player inputs, is the game navigable? This refers to the player's understanding of how to move through the playspace but also how they engage the game as a whole. Do they know how to access important menus? Do they understand the full range of actions available to them and what impact they have on the space of possibility?

---

11 Articulated by Gillian Crampton-Smith in the foreword to Bill Moggridge's book, *Designing Interactions*, 2006.

Feedback

What helps players understand a game? "Reading" a game and performing within the players' understanding of the game's goals, rules, actions, and objects hinges on the quality of the **feedback** about their actions. Giving players feedback on a very granular level is important, as the loop between actions and outcomes we discussed in Chapter 2, "Basic Game Design Tools," is how players connect what they see, what they know, and what they do. Feedback is what allows them to assess what they are doing and how well they are doing it.

A particularly well-done feedback system is found in area/code's *Drop7*, a turn-based puzzle game in which players try to eliminate advancing columns of numbers by matching up the numbers of discs in a column or row with the discs found along the top. Every time the player successfully drops a disc to match a column or row, seven unique forms of feedback are provided: a sound effect plays, accompanied by a sequence of visual effects: the impacted row or column lights up, the disc rotates, a particle effect radiates out from the disc, the disc shrinks, the score received appears above the disc, and the remaining discs in the column animate down to the new position. All this works together to convey information to the player.

Despite so many levels of feedback, people new to the game can still have a hard time understanding what is happening. They may understand that a disc was eliminated, but they may not know why. Over time, through repetition, the player will likely begin to learn that a disc is eliminated when the number on the dropped disc matches the number in the row or column. But this can only happen through the repetition of receiving well-designed feedback. This comes back to the data-information-knowledge-wisdom progression of how players make sense of a videogame. The movement from information to knowledge comes by trying things out and building working mental models of the "laws" of a videogame's space of possibility.

Navigability

The final characteristic of well-done interactivity is **navigability**. In the most literal sense, this speaks to movement through space. Thinking back to our *Journey* example from earlier in the chapter, the mountain peak in the distance provides the most general sense of navigability—the player knows which direction to head. But navigability also relates to the smaller scale actions of knowing how to move through the information space. For *Journey*, this means knowing how to look and move. But what about the more abstract game *Drop7*? Here, the long-term navigability is knowing the game's goal (scoring the most points by keeping the discs from reaching the top of the screen), but also understanding the available actions and interrelationships between the numbered discs. And on the micro level, it's about knowing how to move and drop the discs into the playspace.

Navigability in games relates to players understanding their options within the game's space of possibility. And related, navigability relates to players being able to form goals, whether they are set by the game's designer or by the players themselves. For a game to have navigability, it must also have a clear mental model, provide feedback, be consistent in its response to players, and allow the players to develop intuitive understandings of how to interact with the game's component parts.

Consistency

For a player to understand the feedback received from a game, they need consistent communication. In the case of *Drop7*, **consistency** means the game responds to player actions in the same way every time—sliding and releasing a disc over a column always releases the disc; discs always fall until they reach the highest disc in that column; if the math adds up, the appropriate discs break and move through the seven forms of feedback. If the game responds differently at different times, it makes it difficult for the player to understand their role in the game. If, say, sometimes touching on the active disc makes it break, or it immediately falls upon contact or falls while the player's finger is still touching it, the player would be confused. Players need consistent responses from the game to be able to understand their relationship to the game.

Intuitiveness

Learning how to play a game is not a trivial undertaking. Making it as easy as possible for players to learn how to perform the actions and interactions of the game is important. This leads to the next characteristic of well-designed interactivity: **intuitiveness**. The more a game can become intuitive for players, the less mental and physical energy they have to spend to simply make the game go. Take basketball as an example. When players first learn the game, every action takes deliberate mental and physical focus—finding the rhythm of dribbling, getting the hang of how to arc a shot to go through the basket, sorting out how to move their feet to stay in front of the other team's players, and so on. Over time, through lots of repetition, players are able to develop an intuition about how to play without having to spend so much mental and physical attention attempting to perform basic actions. Once players gain an intuitive feel for the game, they are free to focus on their play experience rather than on the mechanical or mental interaction with the game.

In a game like *Drop7*, the discs behave in intuitive ways. They fall, following the familiar laws of gravity, and then they break, revealing what's inside—like the inside of an egg, a package, or any number of other things we are familiar with in life. If a disc has broken, it is then weakened and disappears. This, too, is intuitive based on our understanding of the circle of life as well as our possible familiarity with other, similar games like *Tetris*.

Failure

In addition to Crampton-Smith's five characteristics, there is one more important concern for the interaction layer—**failure**. Just because we can see and hear a game, can make sense of the information it is presenting us, and can determine an action we want to perform doesn't mean we'll perform it well. It also isn't a guarantee that it was the right action to perform or that we even really understood what we were seeing well enough to make a smart decision in the first place.

Players often make mistakes when playing games. This is a big part of how we learn them and, for certain kinds of play experiences, where the pleasure is found—overcoming the challenges of understanding and then performing within the game's space of possibility. As Jesper Juul notes in *The Art of Failure*, there are three kinds of failure stemming from the psychology-based concept of attribution theory.[12] We believe failures are individual flaws of the person who committed the failure (I flapped when I should have rolled in *Flywrench*), flaws in the thing itself (that procedurally generated level in *Spelunky* was impossible to get through), or flaws in the circumstance (the subway car jostled right as I was picking a tile in *Threes*, causing me to accidentally move in the wrong direction).

Juul's research into failure involved watching scores of players playing games and interviewing them about their experiences. For game designers, one of the most important findings Juul had in this work is that there are some failures that feel better to the player than others. And these are player failures—flaws in the player. Seem counterintuitive? If we think about it, it makes sense. A player feels better about the failure being their own because they believe they can improve their skills with more playing. A player who fails due to a flaw in the game—or a perceived flaw in the game—will likely quit playing the game entirely. As a designer, it is important, then, to recognize that incredibly difficult levels with only one solution may feel like a flaw in the game to the player if they don't perceive that the level is possible to beat. As Juul points out, failure often leads to players devising new strategies and trying new things in the game to succeed. So designing to embrace multiple strategies, is, well, a good design strategy. Take this with a grain of salt; some games, particularly puzzle games, may have only one solution, and some games may have little strategy or failure at all.

The Frame Layer

Play experiences do not take place in a vacuum. They are part of the lived experience, preceded by everything the player has seen or done before playing, and followed by everything else the player will do after. This is what we call the frame layer. All the time living, leading up to playing a game, creates a frame around how players perceive, experience, and build understanding. If someone has never played a videogame before, they might need some help understanding the basics of how videogames work. (Press this button, and the character on the screen will jump.) On the other hand, if someone is a videogame aficionado, they won't need an introduction to the basics. Players have come to expect that pushing a button, in fact, pushing the X button, probably gets their onscreen avatar to jump. Frame provides players with expectations, giving them reference points when they first encounter a game.

Beyond time spent playing videogames, time in the world frames how players expect things in the game to work. If a player sees a large anvil poised on the edge of a cliff, they might imagine

---

12   Jesper Juul, *The Art of Failure: An Essay on the Pain of Playing Video Games.* pp. 15–18, 2013.

that it could fall and crush whatever happens to get under it. This could come from their experiences in life with heavy anvils or their mediated experiences of falling anvils depicted in Saturday morning cartoons. Frames of reference for deciphering what the game is asking of players come from a variety of places: daily life, movies and television, books and stories, and, of course, games. In addition to understanding the basic physics of a precarious anvil, these frames might come from the player's own values, philosophies, and cultural contexts to help them interpret the information the game is giving them.

Let's look again at the game *Perfect Woman* by Lea Schöenfelder and Peter Lu (see Figure 4.11). The game plays off cultural framings of female gender roles, generating some unexpected juxtapositions of identities and interesting choices for players. Players are confronted with choices such as, once reaching the age of 60, becoming a foreign minister or a call girl. This choice can be further complicated by what they were before. If they were a street kid leading a gang, it may become impossible or very hard to be an MIT professor. As a child worker, an easy path may be found taking care of the player character's brother during the war or becoming a suicide bomber, but the player might want to challenge themself to be an eager student. Difficulty is based on how challenging it is to maintain and switch poses that match the player's onscreen female identity. *Perfect Woman* offers up both gender stereotypes and anti-stereotypes with a continued commentary on how our life choices provide us with varying levels of difficulty and struggle—all deftly modeled by asking us to contort our bodies to match with the woman we have become. It questions common framings of gender roles and asks players to open their minds to the diversity of experiences being a woman is in varying places around the world and stages of life—providing new frames of reference for female roles.

Figure 4.11 *Perfect Woman.*

Sometimes games surprise us and lead us to question the frames we place around them. An example of this is Brenda Romero's gallery game Train (see Figure 4.12), from her "The Mechanic Is the Message" series that depicts different historic events resulting in human tragedy. In Train, the player is presented with the task of transporting wooden player pieces from one end of the board to the other by cramming them into train cars. Some clues are given through the materials of the game. The board we are playing on is a broken window. The train tracks sitting atop this go only one way to their terminus. And the rules we are given are typewritten, with the last page still in the scroll of a vintage German typewriter. When we complete our task, the meaning of all of this is revealed, and what at the start seemed like an innocent game of transportation logistics is quickly flipped on its head. We won't give away this ending; but suffice it to say that you have just participated in something that you would never have imagined. At the end, our frame for the game has zoomed out to include what we know of history and led us to question the idea of following rules and orders and how our early framing of the game was naive.

Figure 4.12   Train. Photos by John McKinnon.

Games are interpreted through experiences and references that frame our understanding of them. *Perfect Woman* plays off of these frames, subverting our notions of female roles and life stages. And as we see with Train, they can also provide us with new frames around our understanding of history and human experience.

The Purpose Layer

This leads us to the final of our five layers of player experience and to the question, why? Why has the player decided to play this game? What do they hope to get from it? And what do they actually get from it? Players bring all sorts of intentions to their play experiences. In the three previous chapters, we spent a lot of time talking about goals from a game design perspective. But players have their own goals, too. The game designer Richard Bartle looked closely at players of early text-based multiplayer adventure games (called MUDs, or Multi-User Dungeons) to come up with four core player types: achievers, explorers, socializers, and killers.[13] While Bartle developed these against a particular kind of game, they provide a useful model for thinking more broadly about what players look for in a play experience.

Achievers

Achievers are interested in setting and obtaining goals in a game. Sometimes these players focus on the stated goals—win, collect all the coins, complete every optional mission. In this case, we could think of these players as "completists," as they want to experience everything the game has to offer. So in a game like Tale of Tale's *The Path*, an achiever would not only play all six characters (plus the unlocked seventh character), but also make sure to collect all 36 objects scattered throughout the game, but also 144 flowers found throughout the environment. Or in anna anthropy's *Queers in Love at the End of the World*, an achiever would play until they've moved through every possible combination of decisions within the story.

Sometimes achievers set their own goals for a game. This is where things like speed runs of Derek Yu's *Spelunky*, no-kill playthroughs of *Dishonored,* or permadeath plays of *Far Cry 2* fit. Other times, players set more intangible goals for themselves. In Dona Bailey and Ed Logg's *Centipede*, a player could attempt to clear out all the mushrooms, which is within the space of possibility of the game for sure but isn't an established goal. And then there are the legions of seemingly impossible things players have done with *Minecraft*, all of which were player derived.

Explorers

Explorers like to understand the full breadth of a game's space of possibility. So if an explorer plays *Proteus*, they want to walk the full expanse of their island or simply wander the woods in the University of Southern California's Game Innovation Lab's *Walden*, a game based on Thoreau's *On Walden Pond*. Where achievers often seek validation or measurement of their goals, explorers are content to simply understand the game more fully. Another way to think about this is focusing on coming to know the people, places, and spaces rather than the stated goals of a game.

---

13   Richard Bartle, "Hearts, Clubs, Diamonds, Spades: Players Who Suit MUDs" http://mud.co.uk/richard/hcds.htm.

Explorers also want to know the full potential of the actions and objects within a game. In other words, they are really interested in understanding the full breadth of a game's space of possibility. They want to know every possible direct outcome of an action, but also every indirect outcome. They want to know what happens when you spend too much time on the frozen pond in *Walden*, the underlying logic deciding the next tile in *Threes*, or the limits of swimming in the ocean in *Proteus*. They want to play *Spelunky* over and over until they have seen as many configurations of the environment, objects, and enemies as possible.

Socializers

Socializers are less interested in the actions and objects unto themselves than they are the other players. This category of players above all enjoy interacting with other players. They will do this inside the parameters of the designed communication channels, but also within the broader space of possibility of your game. Let's take a game like *Portal 2*. The co-op campaign is designed to encourage player communication—without it, completing the challenges will be really hard. So the game is designed to encourage socialization among all players. Similarly, Leah Gilliam's tabletop RPG Lesberation is designed to get players talking, planning, and acting as a unit.

Players who seek out socialization in games will find it in games that on the surface don't seem appropriate. Basketball, when played in a more casual manner, is a great way to hang out with friends. Dungeons & Dragons is a perfect way to spend an evening chatting and snacking while unfolding a legendary story. Local multiplayer games like Jane Friedhoff's *Slam City Oracles* similarly encourage people to spend time in one another's presence.

Killers

The last group in Bartle's model are the killers—the players who like to impose their will on other players. Sometimes this takes the form of help, but more often, it takes the form of attacking, thwarting, or otherwise disrupting other players' experiences. These are the players who not only want to win, but dominate the game. So in Dog Eat Dog, if killers are on the indigenous people's team, they will try to control the decision-making process.

Of course, killers also want to mess up other players. So in basketball, they want to keep the opponent they cover on defense from ever scoring. If they are playing *Johann Sebastian Joust*, they will not rest until they outdo everyone else—sometimes to the point of embarrassing the other players.

Beyond Bartle's Player Types

Each of these player types—achievers, explorers, socializers, and killers—might be tendencies players have as individuals, or they might represent the changing goals of a single player in one game as they continue to play. The important lesson for designers is to understand that not everyone will approach your game with the same mind-set. When designing, imagine how each type will approach your game and how these tendencies can be leveraged to strengthen your design.

Of course not all play experiences can be neatly captured inside Bartle's achievers, explorers, socializers, and killers. And not all designers create games thinking about the expectations or wants of different kinds of players. Particularly with more authorial games like Porpentine's *Howling Dogs* or Molleindustria's *The McDonald's Videogame*, players have a role in the game, but not necessarily in defining the kind of play experience they will have. Think of reading a novel or comic—we have no expectations that we can explore the novel in unexpected ways. Instead, we settle in for the experience the writer provides. The same can be said about certain play experiences. Playing *Kentucky Route Zero* is more enjoyable if we play to experience what the gamemakers created rather than trying to pigeon hole a particular play style into the game.

Summary

To really understand the design of a game, you have to consider what that game asks of its players. How does a game draw on a player's senses? What kind of (and how much) information does the game provide a player? How does a player understand their role in the game? What other life experiences and knowledge are likely to inform a play experience? What kinds of expectations will a player bring to their play experience? These questions are best understood by taking into account a series of theories drawn from sociology, psychology, information science, and related fields.

- *Action Theory:* The sociological understanding of what happens when people interact with things. People have beliefs that shape their understanding of things, which lead to reactions to what is going on around them, which lead to desires, around which people create intentions that lead to actions.

- *Layers of Player Experience:* Players move through five different interpretive acts when playing a game: the *sensory*, or what the player sees, hears, and feels; the *information*, or the data the player takes in about the game state; the *interaction*, or what the player understands they can do; the *frame*, or the broader interpretation of the play experience; and the *purpose*, or the goal of the play experience.

- *Attention:* Many things draw on a player's attention during gameplay. *Executive attention* is what we are intentionally focusing on while playing. *Reflexive attention* is caused by things that grab our attention away from our intentional focus like loud noises, visual distractions, and similar phenomena.

- *Information spaces:* Games have information spaces that we explore as players. *Perfect information spaces* are those in which everything to be known about a game is visible to the player. *Imperfect information spaces* are those in which some information is hidden from players either by the game itself or by other players.

- *Affordances:* The perceived properties of a thing that suggests to people what that thing is used for. Affordances break down further into four subcategories: *perceptible affordances*, or what we assume a thing does; *correct rejections*, or what we think it doesn't do; *hidden affordances,* or what a thing does that isn't obvious; and *false affordances,* or misinterpretations of what a thing does.

- *Crampton-Smith's five characteristics of well-done interactivity:* A set of five properties present in all good interaction design: mental model, feedback, consistency, intuitiveness, and navigability.

    - *Mental model:* The way a player perceives a game to work, both in terms of what they should do to play, but also what their actions mean within the game's space of possibility.

    - *Feedback:* The game provides reassuring feedback so that the user/player knows they have affected change in a meaningful way.

    - *Consistency:* Consistently and logically builds upon the commitment the player makes to learning and playing the game.

    - *Intuitiveness:* Allows the player to focus on the play experience rather than the mechanical inputs required to play.

    - *Navigability:* A clear and well-designed path through the play experience.

- *Failure:* There are three kinds of failure encountered through gameplay: *individual flaws* that are perceived as the player's fault; *flaws in the game* that are perceived to be caused by a bug or error in the game; and *circumstantial flaws* caused by an external force.

- *Player Types:* Richard Bartle's four kinds of players are *achievers, explorers, socializers,* and *killers. Achievers* are interested in obtaining a game's or their own goals. *Explorers* like to understand the breadth and depth of a game's space of possibility. *Socializers* play games to interact with other players. *Killers* want to impose their will on other players.

- *Beyond Player Types:* Not all games are designed to enable play styles within the space of possibility of the game. Particularly in authorially driven games, the purpose layer is simply having the experience planned by the gamemakers.

Exercises

1. Choose a simple game like tic tac toe or jacks to play. Use the principles of action theory to consider your play experience.

2. Choose a videogame and imagine what would happen if you changed the player point of view. If it's top down, how would the gameplay differ if it was side-view? 2D to 3D?

3. Pick a game and consider the mental model you have for how the game is played.

4. Watch people playing a challenging game. Create a log of all the moments of failure that happen. Categorize each instance of failure as either individual flaw, flaw in the game, or circumstantial flaw.

5. Pick a multiplayer game you like to play. Play it four times, each time modeling one of Bartle's four player types.

PROCESS

CHAPTER 5

THE ITERATIVE GAME DESIGN PROCESS

Making games is an iterative process that helps game designers understand and refine their games. This chapter introduces the steps in the iterative cycle: conceptualize, prototype, playtest, and evaluate.

The Origins of Iterative Design

Designing games is challenging—think no further than the concepts and principles introduced in the four chapters of Part I—the basic elements that make up games, the tools we have to design play experiences, the incredible range of play types, not to mention the things video-games ask of players. Compounding all this is the fact that game designers can't really "see" their designs until they are played, and their games can't be played until they are made.

This is where the iterative design process comes in handy (see Figure 5.1). Iterative design is a cycle of conceptualization, prototyping, testing, and evaluation. Iteration is an **adaptive process** whereby designers move through cycles of conceiving of an idea, creating a proto-type that embodies the idea, running playtests with the prototype to see the idea in action, and then evaluating the results to make the idea better. Adaptive processes stand in contrast to **predictive processes** in which the final product is well understood and can be produced without having to make changes to its design. Where predictive processes assume the designer is going to be right the first time around, adaptive processes leave room for error, but also new ideas that can improve upon the original.

An early version of iterative design comes from Walter Shewhart's work at Bell Labs in the first half of the twentieth century: the "Plan-Do-Study-Act" cycle.[1] Shewhart wanted a process that

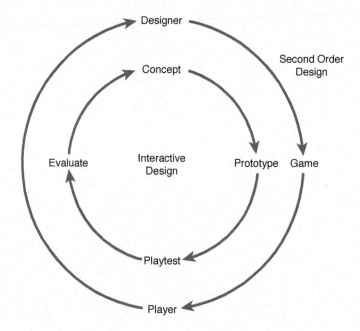

Figure 5.1   Second order design diagram nested in an iterative design diagram.

---

1   Andrew Walter Shewhart, *Statistical Method from the Viewpoint of Quality Control*. 1939.

increased the quality and consistency of Bell Lab's products and services. So he created a modi-fied version of the scientific method that would help the company improve upon those metrics:

- *Plan:* Identify the problem that needs attention.
- *Do:* Design a solution to the problem.
- *Study:* Develop statistical tools for analyzing the success or failure of the design.
- *Act:* Repeat the cycle if the results of the study find problems with the design solution.

Around the same time, the industrial and theatrical designer Henry Dreyfuss began to approach product design from a similar perspective.[2] Instead of focusing solely on the object, Dreyfuss wanted to take into account the person who used the telephone, vacuum cleaner, or typewriter he designed. His goal was simple but unexpected: understand the experiences his designs provided, and refine the design to better meet the functional needs of the end user. Dreyfuss's process involved a similar set of steps to Shewhart's (not a surprise, as Dreyfuss likely worked under Shewhart at Bell Labs):

- *Think:* Consider the cause of the problem, and then use brainstorming techniques to consider solutions.
- *Sketch:* Develop the most simple and efficient means of exploring the most promising solutions.
- *Show:* Share the sketches, whatever form they may take, with stakeholders (clients, potential users, and so on).
- *Evaluate:* Reflect on the responses from the designers, clients, and users to determine the effectiveness of the solution and to more fully understand the problem.

In both Shewhart's and Dreyfuss's models, the design process unfolds in an incremental, cycli-cal process. Where Shewhart relied on hard data to improve product consistency, Dreyfuss used the then-emerging fields of ergonomics and human factors to consider the functional, experiential, and emotional responses to his products.

A more recent influence on the iterative game design process comes from software develop-ment and Human-Computer Interaction (HCI). Both of these use approaches derived from Shewhart and Dreyfuss:

- *Requirements:* What is the function of the software or hardware?
- *Prototype:* Based on the requirements, create a functional prototype.
- *Review:* Have all stakeholders use the prototype and provide feedback.
- *Revise:* Based on the feedback, revise the requirements and plan.

---

2   Henry Dreyfuss, *Designing for People.* 1955.

It is from these three foundations that the iterative game design process emerges. While some people approach game design from a perspective of metrics and statistics, most gamemakers take a more intuitive approach. And while some use a more traditional predictive process, most embrace the adaptive methods of iteration that allow game designers to design and refine the game through successive iterative loops.

This is because, unlike phone infrastructure, typewriters, and ATM machines, games are experiences and expressions more than tools or functional products. Games are about the play-driven moment-to-moment events, while typewriters and ATMs are a means to an end. Game designers are therefore addressing a mix of gamemaker intention and player experience. As a result, the four-step iterative game design process (see Figure 5.2) is a little different:

- *Conceptualize:* Develop an idea for the game and its play experience.
- *Prototype:* Make some aspect of the game's design into a "playable" form.
- *Playtest:* Have players play the prototype to see what kind of experience they have.
- *Evaluate:* Review the results of the playtest to better understand and strengthen the game's design.

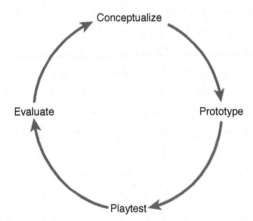

Figure 5.2 Iterative design diagram.

This is how the iterative game design process works: a series of steps toward the complete design of a game. Each loop through the cycle is an iteration on the design of a game: an incremental step toward better understanding the game being made so that the designer can work out the full design of the play experience. Sometimes an iterative loop will help the designer flesh out and tighten up the game's design; sometimes an iterative loop will point out problems that break aspects of the design. Either way, it's all part of the process toward a finished game.

The Four Steps

Let's look at each of the four steps in more detail: conceptualize, prototype, playtest, and evaluate.

Step 1: Conceptualize

In the beginning, there's just an idea (see Figure 5.3). And it could come from anywhere. Maybe it's a dream about unicorns jousting with dinosaurs. Or, it's something from everyday experience, like walking through the park or having a difficult conversation with a loved one. Maybe it starts with an idea for a cool action or an unusual use of a common game object. Maybe it starts with the need to explore or share a feeling that is difficult to put into words. In other words, a game concept can start from anything.

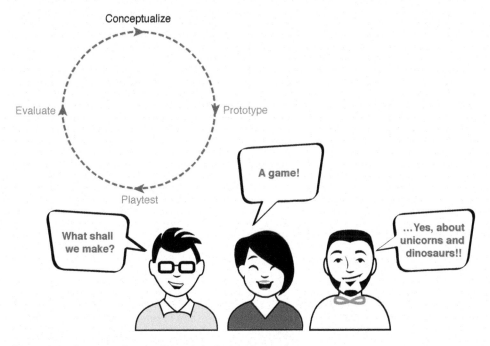

Figure 5.3 Conceptualize, the first step in the iterative cycle.

The conceptualization of a game begins with a number of different techniques to generate and shape ideas at the beginning of the game design process and continue to support the design through successive iterative loops. The main thing to keep in mind is that all that's needed is a kernel of an idea. It's not important to have every detail figured out. In fact, the thing to arrive at in this earliest stage is not an answer, but a simple, "How might we…" question.[3] For example, "How might we make a game where unicorns joust with dinosaurs?" or "How might we share the feeling of walking through the first snow of the year?" This question will become more refined with time and will generate even more questions. But at the start of the game design process, all that is needed is this one question.

Once a basic question is in place, the next step is brainstorming. Brainstorming is a process with specific rules meant to help participants explore all the possibilities around an idea or question. In fact, brainstorming is like a game—one that generates as many concepts as possible. And those concepts come in the form of even more questions, ones that begin with "what if…?" For example, "what if unicorns and dinosaurs joust while driving monster trucks along a rickety bridge?"

Another important point about the conceptualization phase is that there is a difference between a game's concept and a game's design. The concept is just that—an idea, a theory about what might make a good game. As we discussed in the Introduction to this book, game design is the creation of "blueprints" for a game. Turning an idea into a design requires that the designer structure the idea so that it can be used to produce prototypes, which are then playtested, the results of which are then evaluated to see what they say about the original idea. And from there, the process loops back around to conceptualize and the expansion, revision, or refinement of the game's design. Part of this process involves thinking through and answering more questions in the design process, including using **design values** as a way to identify the experiential and formal characteristics of the game.

We'll go into more detail on conceptualizing and designing in Chapter 9, "Conceptualizing Your Game," and design values in Chapter 6, "Design Values," but for now, the important thing to know is that a designer doesn't need much more than an idea and a question to get started creating a game.

Step 2: Prototype

The second step in the iterative game design process is turning the game idea into a prototype (see Figure 5.4). The best way to figure out how the game will look, feel, and act is to dive in and start making it. The faster the game moves from the pure ether of ideas and into a prototype, the closer the game will get to showing the kind of play experiences it can generate. The key to prototyping is to turn the most promising "what if…" question from the brainstorm, or a combination of "what ifs," into something tangible. That could be paper, quick and dirty code, even the designer's own body performing the actions of the game. The cool thing about prototyping is that it will help ideas get even more developed and might even lead to a discovery that

---

3   This question is from a method used by the design consultancy IDEO, and one we find incredibly helpful in the conceptualization stage of the game. "How might we" and other design exercises can be found on IDEO's DESIGN KIT project: www.designkit.org/methods/3.

would have never come up during the concepting phase. This is the point of the iterative process. Every step along the way initial ideas evolve—from a pie-in-the-sky idea about jousting unicorns to a fully designed game. It isn't necessary to figure it all out in the beginning; being open to the whole process and where it takes the game is the important thing.

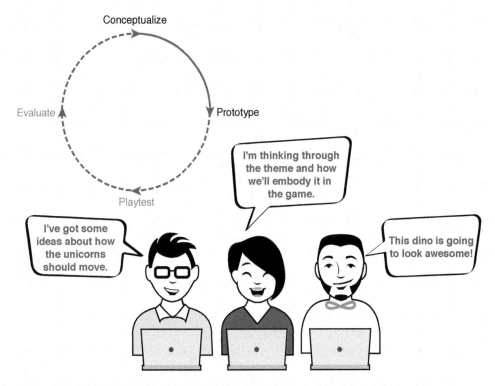

Figure 5.4 Prototype, the second step in the iterative cycle.

Prototypes should remain focused on the ideas and questions from the concepting phase, including the "what if…?" question. Prototyping requires a game designer to get more concrete. So, in the jousting unicorns and dinosaurs example, prototyping around "what if unicorns jousted with dinosaurs?" requires some understanding of what it means for these creatures to joust, where it would happen, and how players would participate. To keep things focused, the team might decide to prototype on paper by making little cutout unicorns and dinosaurs that they move around on a table. Or maybe they get some rough illustrations moving in 2D onscreen.

There are a lot of different kinds of prototypes, each suitable for different stages and questions. We'll go more into these and the prototyping process in general in Chapter 10, "Prototyping Your Game." For now, the most important thing to know is that the faster prototypes are made, the more quickly the game's design will start to take shape.

Step 3: Playtest

Once a game designer has a prototype made, they will want to playtest (see Figure 5.5). After all, a game designer doesn't really know what the game is until they test it. Playtests reveal what is or isn't working in a game's design. In other words, the playtest is the answer to the "what if…?" question the prototype asks. In fact, playtesting is the one step in the process that we end with answers, rather than questions. And not only answers in the form of seeing what happens when playing with a prototype that asks "what if unicorns jousted with dinosaurs…?" Answers to other questions as well, like, "Do players understand the goal of the game, and what they are striving for? Do players have the hoped-for emotional response? Do players get the game's message? Is the user interface clear or difficult to understand? And, is there clear feedback about how well the player is doing in the game?"

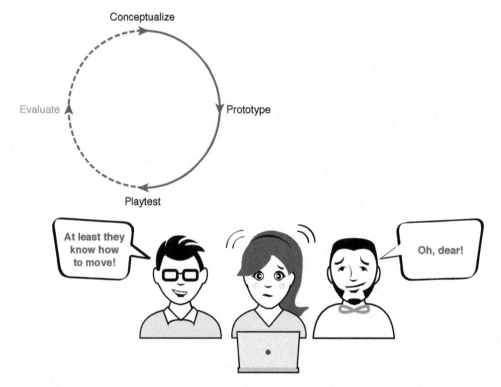

Figure 5.5   Playtest, the third step in the iterative cycle.

Playtesting is often the hardest and most revealing part of the iterative game design process. Often, what seems like a great idea that makes sense in a prototype falls apart when players get ahold of it. This might feel like a bad thing, but it's really a blessing in disguise. Seeing what fails in a playtest also sheds light on what is needed to fix it and make the game better. Failure is just part of the process. This is the most important lesson of the iterative process.

In the same way that a prototype can take different forms, there are many different types of playtests. Two of the most basic kinds are internal and external playtests. Internal playtests among the designers of the game are essential—and often the first kind of playtest the team engages in. External playtests are equally important and can involve friends, other game designers, the target audience, and more. No matter the kind of playtest, one of the most important things to do is capture the results. Whether simply listing the comments from playtesters or problems the designer observed, it's important to document the playtest to help in the next step in the iterative game design process: evaluate.

We look more closely at playtesting in Chapter 11, "Playtesting Your Game."

Step 4: Evaluate

Once a game designer finishes a round of playtesting, they evaluate the results to assess the game's design (see Figure 5.6). The art of evaluating the results of a playtest is taking what playtesters did and said and determining if and how the feedback necessitates changes to the game's design. For example, remember the dinosaur-unicorn jousting game? Let's say we observed players having a difficult time understanding how to get the creatures to pick up their lances.

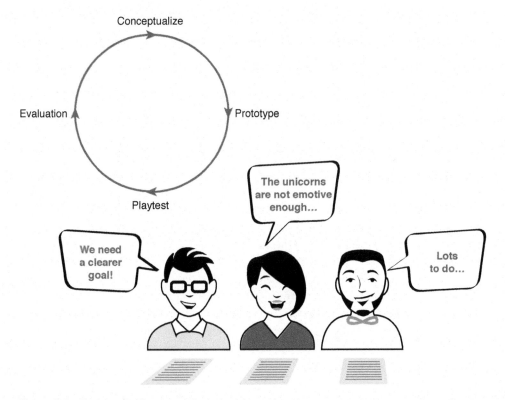

Figure 5.6   Evaluate, the fourth step in the iterative cycle.

Evaluating this observation involves more questions—this time along the lines of "why did play-ers have a hard time grasping how a unicorn jousts?" or "how might we make it easier for players to understand how to get their brontosaurus to pick up a lance?" Does the "How might we…?" sound familiar? It should—once you have reached this last step of the iterative process, you return to the same kinds of questions we began with in conceptualize. The borders between evaluate and conceptualize can be a bit fuzzy—hence the circular nature of the process!

The other part of evaluate involves taking some time to let the playtest results sink in while solutions begin to take form. Some designers take walks, some go running, some take a nap.[4] Others talk to other game designers and friends about the design problems they are working out. Still other game designers play games, watch movies, or read books and generally look outside of games for inspiration and influence.

Being a game designer is not about coming up with perfect ideas right off the bat. The challenge of game design is paying close attention to how other people engage with game prototypes and then translating that feedback into design revisions to be tried out in the next prototype. Some of the feedback from players will be pretty straightforward. Other feedback is more difficult to diagnose, like, "I feel like this game is too intense." It takes practice, kind of like a doctor hearing a patient talk about their symptoms and then from that, building up enough evidence to make a diagnosis. It involves not only listening to what the patient says, but observ-ing them and including all of that into the evaluation. In Chapter 12, "Evaluating Your Game," we look more closely at the role of evaluation in the iterative game design process.

A Repeated Process, Not a Single Cycle

Because there is no single motivation for creating games, no two games follow an identical iterative cycle. There are many paths the process can take, and they may loop through the iterative steps several times in different ways for different reasons (see Figure 5.7). The design of some games resolves quickly after three or four loops through the process. Other games take dozens of loops through the process. The most important thing to bring to the iterative game design process is patience. It takes time, but more often than not, the method brings great results. Iterative game design is a cycle that steers a game's design in all sorts of directions the designer may never have imagined. For game designers who want to create a particular kind of play experience, the iterative cycle helps them home in on delivering exactly what they have in mind. For game designers who are more concerned with expression, the iterative cycle helps them find just the right way to do so. For game designers who just want people to enjoy them-selves, the iterative cycle helps discover what players enjoy about a game. Ultimately, we iterate because we are making games, and to build them we need to prototype and playtest them to fully understand what they can do.

---

4   We know a game designer who ponders design problems by lying under his desk.

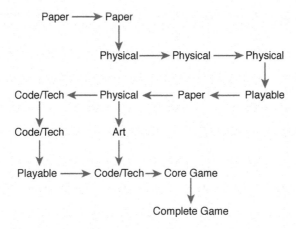

Figure 5.7 A theoretical path for the design of a game.

And, of course, there is life after game design. Indeed, the game design process is just the beginning, as a whole range of tasks remain—production, marketing, release, and then maintaining the game. We'll get into some of this in Chapter 13, "Moving from Design to Production," but mostly, we're focused on the design process in this book and not production.

Embracing Failure to Succeed

In addition to patience, another key to the iterative game design process is being open to failure. It is going to happen. In fact, it is really important that it happens. Early in the design process, failure can make visible the problems in a game and help the designer find solutions for fixing them. Even the best game designers fail early in the design process. Reiner Knizia, a boardgame designer with dozens and dozens of successful games to his name, once said that all his game designs were perfect until they were playtested.[5] That's the power—and the pain—of the iterative game design process. A game designer has intuitions about their game, but until they get all the way through an iterative loop, they just don't know what they have. That's why game designers want to find the quickest way possible through early loops in the cycle so they can fail early and often.

Failure is what helps us learn and make our games better. The key is to be aware that it will happen, and when it does happen, to address it as a team and identify possible solutions. The best way to leverage failure to improve the game's design? By failing fast, with purpose, early in the game design process. This means doing your best not to get discouraged by it and view it as a learning experience. Another way to put it is that your first time at anything will inevitably involve learning from failure. Remember the first time you played your favorite videogame?

---

5   Overheard at Practice 2012, a conference on game design hosted by New York University's Game Center.

When we play videogames, failure teaches us how the world works in the game. In game design, failure teaches us how to make better games.

The iterative design process can be used to support a wide range of creative intentions and play experiences. The next three chapters provide a set of useful tools for guiding the iterative process. Chapter 6, "Design Values," introduces an important tool for capturing the important factors in a game's design. Chapter 7, "Game Design Documentation," outlines the three main tools for capturing a game's design—design documents, schematics, and tracking spreadsheets. Chapter 8, "Collaboration and Teamwork," rounds out Part II with a discussion of important considerations around working in teams.

Summary

Don't worry about getting it right the first time. Making games is always an iterative process punctuated by failure and incremental improvement. Once you have conceptualized your game, you should move as quickly as possible to prototyping it. There's no need to worry about coding your game at the start; prototype it on paper, with your body, any way you can. The key is to get it as quickly as possible to the playtesting stage. Here you will actually see your played game for the first time and see it for what it really is. In most cases, there will be some things about your design that fail. This is where you evaluate the results of your playtest and return to your initial concept, including your design values, and begin the process again.

- *Conceptualize:* The initial idea and the subsequent ideas about the game explored in prototyping and development.
- *Prototype:* A form of some aspect of your game, or the entire game in a prerelease stage that helps you work through the design questions your game poses.
- *Playtest:* An answer to the question the prototype poses, and a moment when you or other people play your prototype and you observe and document the reactions.
- *Evaluate:* Reviewing the playtest observations and diagnosing the results into next steps or new ideas.

Exercise

Find a partner and in 10 minutes, design a game the two of you can play using your own bodies and anything in the room. You will have to move quickly, coming up with an idea, prototyping it, playtesting between yourselves, and then refining it. Make note of each step in the process. At the end of 10 minutes, write down the rules to your game and give them to two other players to playtest. How did they interpret the rules? Did they discover anything new about the game? Did they use any strategies that might break the game or point in new directions for the design?

CHAPTER 6

DESIGN VALUES

Most simply stated, design values are the qualities
and characteristics a game's designer wants to
embody in the game and its play experience. Design
values help designers identify what kind of play
experience they want to create and articulate some
of the parts that will help their game generate
that experience.

Designing games can be challenging in large part because of the way games work. Game designers have many reasons for creating games. Sometimes they want to share a certain kind of play. Sometimes they have ideas that are best expressed through a game. Regardless of the reasons, being able to fully realize the goals you have for a game can be difficult. This is because of the second-order design problem we discussed in Chapter 1, "Games, Design and Play;" the designer doesn't have direct control of how players will play; instead, they simply define the parameters within which players play.

One of the best tools to guide the creation of play experiences is **design values**, a concept we borrow from the scholar Ivar Holm[1] and the game designers Eric Zimmerman and Mary Flanagan. The term value here isn't referring to the financial worth of the game. Instead, design values are the qualities and characteristics you want to embody in a game. This can reflect your own goals as a creator, but also the experience you want your audience to have.

The broadest conception of design values is found in Ivar Holm's work with architecture and industrial design. Holm identifies five key approaches: aesthetic, social, environmental, traditional, and gender based.

- *Aesthetic:* Aesthetic design values focus on the form and experience.
- *Social:* Social design values focus on social change and the betterment of society.
- *Environmental:* Environmental design values address the concerns of the environment and sustainability. This has more obvious application to architecture and product design, but is also of importance to games.
- *Traditional:* Traditional design values use history and region as inspiration. In the context of architecture, this might apply to restoring a building to its original state or building in the local, traditional style. For game design, this might involve working within a genre, or reviving a historically important game.
- *Gender based:* Gender-based design values bring feminist conceptions of gender equality into the design process.

The first game-specific conception of design values comes from Eric Zimmerman's "play values," which he describes as "the abstract principles that the game design would embody."[2] At times, this sort of design value relates directly to the "mechanical" nature of the game and its play—the actions players perform, the objects used, the goal of the game, and so on. Sometimes design values are adjectives like fast and long and twitchy—descriptions of what the game will feel like while playing. Other times design values refer to the "look and feel" of

1   Holm, Ivar. *Ideas and Beliefs in Architecture and Industrial Design: How Attitudes, Orientations, and Underlying Assumptions Shape the Built Environment.* Oslo School of Architecture and Design, 2006.

2   Although Zimmerman uses the term "play values," our conception of design values is very much based on this idea. "Play as Research: The Iterative Design Process" www.ericzimmerman.com/texts/Iterative_Design.html.

the game. Sometimes design values are more about the kind of player the designer envisions playing their game in the first place. Other times, design values are reminders of context—the location the game is to be played, the technological parameters of the platform, and so on. These fit within Holm's aesthetic and traditional design values.

In addition to the kind of play experience the designer wants to create, design values can be derived from different personal, political, or cultural values as well—in other words, social design values. Social design values might reflect a desire to express an idea about the human condition, an experience the designer once had and how it felt, or a political position based on personal or collective values. A good example of this notion of design values as an embodiment of political, feminist, and personal values comes from Mary Flanagan and Helen Nissenbaum's project and book *Values at Play*.[3] Flanagan and Nissenbaum developed a framework and toolkit for identifying political, social, and ethical values in games and exploring how designers might express their own perspectives. These connect to Holm's social and gender design values but can as well extend to the environmental if we frame it more broadly.

Generating Design Values

Creating design values is a process of determining what is important about the game—the play experience it provides, who it is for, the meaning it produces for its players, the constraints within which it must be created, and so on. We've found the best way to get started is with a series of questions that explore the who, what, why, where, and when of a game. While not every game begins with all of these, the following are the general questions to discuss while establishing the design values for a game.

- *Experience:* What does the player do when playing? As game designer and educator Tracy Fullerton puts it, what does the player get to do? And how does this make the player feel physically and emotionally?

- *Theme:* What is the game about? How does it present this to players? What concepts, perspectives, or experiences might the player encounter during play? How are these delivered? Through story? Systems modeling? Metaphor?

- *Point of view:* What does the player see, hear, or feel? From what cultural reference point? How are the game and the information within it represented? Simple graphics? Stylized geometric shapes? Highly detailed models?

- *Challenge:* What kind of challenges does the game present? Mental challenge? Physical challenge? Or is it more a question of a challenging perspective, subject or theme?

- *Decision-making:* How and where do players make decisions? How are decisions presented?

---

3   Mary Flanagan and Helen Nissenbaum, *Values at Play in Digital Games*, 2014.

- *Skill, strategy, chance, and uncertainty:* What skills does the game ask of the player? Is the development of strategy important to a fulfilling play experience? Does chance factor into the game? From what sources does uncertainty develop?

- *Context:* Who is the player? Where are they encountering the game? How did they find out about it? When are they playing it? Why are they playing it?

- *Emotions:* What emotions might the game create in players?

This may seem like a lot to think about before designing a game. And it *is* a lot. But all these are important factors to consider at the beginning of the design process for a number of reasons. For one, design values establish the overarching concept, goals, and "flavor" of a game.

Just as important is the way design values create a shared understanding of the game. Most games are made collaboratively, and everyone on the team is likely to have opinions and ideas about what the game is and what its play experience should be. Design values allow the team members to agree on what they are making and why they are doing it. They also are an important check-in when great ideas come up but might not fit the game's design values. Continuing to ask, "does this fit our design values?" will help resolve team conflicts, and, even if it's a great idea, know whether it should be included in this game or a future project.

Example: Pong Design Values

Having examples to draw from can be really helpful, particularly when exploring a new idea or concept—that's why Part I, "Concepts," is filled with examples drawn from games. Now that we're moving from basic concepts into the design process, we're going to use a speculative design example to illustrate things—*Pong* (see Figure 6.1). We're going to pretend like we're designing the classic arcade game. To start, the design values are the following:

- *Experience: Pong* is a two-player game based on a mashup between the physical games of tennis and ping pong. It uses a simple scoring system, allowing players to focus on competing for the best score.

- *Theme:* Sportsball! Head to head competition!

- *Point of view: Pong* is presented from a top-down perspective, which takes the challenge of modeling gravity and hitting the ball over the net away from gameplay—focusing on the act of hitting the ball back and forth and trying to get it past your opponent's paddle. The graphics are simple and abstract, also keeping the focus on fast and responsive gameplay.

- *Challenge:* The game's challenge is one of speed, eye-hand coordination, and hitting the ball in ways that your opponent is not expecting.

- *Decision-making:* Decisions are made in real time, with a clear view of the ball's trajectory and your opponent's paddle.

- *Skill, strategy, chance, and uncertainty: Pong* is a game of skill, with some chance related to the angle of the ball when it is served and some uncertainty of how your opponent will hit the ball and thus in how you will counter.

- *Context:* The game is played in an arcade context, with your opponent next to you, enabling interaction on the game screen and in the real world.

- *Emotions: Pong* is meant to generate the feeling of being completely focused, grace, intense competition, and excitement.

Figure 6.1 *Pong*. Photo by Rob Boudon, used under Creative Commons Attribution 2.0 Generic license.

Case Studies

To help see how design values play out in real-world examples, following are three real-world case studies: thatgamecompany's *Journey*, Captain Game's *Desert Golfing*, and Naomi Clark's *Consentacle*.[4]

---

4   John writes about additional examples (including the writing of this book) in his essay "Design Values." www.heyimjohn.com/design-values.

Case Study 1: thatgamecompany's *Journey*

thatgamecompany's *Journey* (see Figure 6.2) was an idea Jenova Chen, the company's cofounder and creative director, had during his time as a student in the University of California's Interactive Media and Games Division MFA program. He had been playing a lot of Massively Multiplayer Online games (MMOs) but was increasingly dissatisfied with the inability to really connect with other players on a human, emotional level. At the time, well before thatgamecompany formed, the game concept was beyond his abilities to pull off on his own. Years later, after thatgamecompany had *Flow* and *Flower* under its belt, Jenova thought it might be time to take on the challenges of *Journey*.

Figure 6.2   *Journey.*

In his talk at the 2013 Game Developer's Conference about designing *Journey*, Jenova described the goal of designing a game that makes the player feel "lonely, small, and with a great sense of awe."[5] This was a design value: make a game that generates this kind of feeling in the player.

Jenova also wanted the game to involve multiplayer collaboration (in the case of *Journey*, two players). This led to a second design value for the game—being able to share the emotional response with another player and to have that act of sharing heighten the overall emotional impact.

---

5   For more, see Jenova Chen's Game Developer's Conference 2013 talk, "Designing Journey." www.gdcvault.com/play/1017700/Designing.

In addition to these initial interests, the game's design is informed by where it is played. *Journey's* design values were influenced by the fact that it was being made for the PlayStation 3. Sony asked thatgamecompany to make a single-player game, which influenced how the cooperative mechanic was implemented. It's seamless, and the experience doesn't actually rely on other players being online and playing with you. Players appear and disappear as a natural occurrence in the world. And, of course, a game created to be experienced in your living room is going to be more cinematic and immersive than a game you might play on your phone while waiting for the bus, so the PlayStation platform informed the visual style and gameplay.

Another design value for *Journey* relates to the emotional and narrative arc of the play experience. Jenova was inspired by Joseph Campbell's work on the Hero's Journey, which builds upon the three-act structure common to theater and film. Jenova and his team began by creating a landscape that literally and emotionally tracked the arc of a traditional three-act narrative. This was intended to create an emotional flow from the highs of players sensing freedom, awe, and connections to the lows of being trapped, scared, and alone, and finally, closure through resolution.

During the design process, the design team went to visit sand dunes for inspiration for the game's environment. While there, they noticed how enjoyable it was to move through the sand, climbing a tall dune and experiencing the anticipation of seeing what was at the top. This led to the idea of sliding in the sand, moving up and down the dunes with grace. This action fed well into the initial design value of creating a sense of awe as you move through the environments, and creating experiences that felt realistic—yet better than reality. Because on a real sand dune, unless you have a sled, it's not really possible to slide down them—but in *Journey*, you surf the sand as if it were a wave (see Figure 6.3).

Figure 6.3   The player character sliding in the sand of *Journey*.

To achieve all these goals, Jenova and the thatgamecompany team had to work through a number of problems around player expectations and the conventions of multiplayer gameplay. In early prototypes, the game included puzzles involving pushing boulders together, or players pulling one another over obstacles.[6] The goal was to create a multiplayer environment that encouraged collaboration. However, while playtesting, the team observed players pushing one another and fighting over resources. They soon realized that the kinds of actions allowed in the game and the feedback players were getting were all working against the collaborative spirit they were hoping to encourage. So they devised a solution that led to players being able to complete the journey alone as well as together, have equal access to resources, and have little effect on the other player's ability to enjoy the game. And when players tended to use the in-game chat to bully or otherwise act in unsociable ways, the team had to make some difficult decisions about how to support player communication without allowing players to treat one another badly. This meant removing "chat" and replacing it with a single, signature tone. All of these decisions were informed by the design values of meaningful connection and a sense of awe.

Having the design values for the game allowed the team to remain focused on its goals and understand what they were aiming for as they developed prototypes. It took a good number of cycles through the iterative process to get the game to meet its design values and the goals initially set by Jenova. This was in large part because he wanted to do things that differed from most other games—there wasn't a set formula or a precedent to work from. And so he and the thatgamecompany team had to experiment and try things out to craft, refine, and clarify the *Journey* player experience, and as they went, revisit their design values to make sure they were staying true to the team's goals. In the end, all of the hard work paid off. *Journey* went on to win many awards, including The Game Developer's Choice award for best game of the year.

Case Study 2: Captain Game's *Desert Golfing*

Desert Golfing (see Figure 6.4) is a deceptively simple game: using the tried-and-true *Angry Birds*-style "tap, pull, aim, and release" action, players hit a ball through a desert golf course of 3,000 (or more) holes. The game is deeply minimal in all ways: a single action for achieving a single goal (get the ball in the hole), yielding a single score (the total number of strokes) over an enormous number of holes, all with spare, flat color graphics and minimalist sound effects.

Desert Golfing began with a simple idea: make an "indie *Angry Birds*." For Justin Smith, the game's designer, this was shorthand for keeping all the pleasurable aspects of the "pinball stopper" action of *Angry Birds*, while removing a lot of the extraneous details that he felt detracted from the potential of this action. This was the first and primary design value for the game. It meant keeping the gameplay minimal, which kept a clear focus on the core action.

---

6   Jenova Chen and Robin Hunicke, IndieCade 2010: "Discovering Multiplayer Dynamics in Journey Parts 1–4." https://www.youtube.com/watch?v=0BLoTk6cmWk.

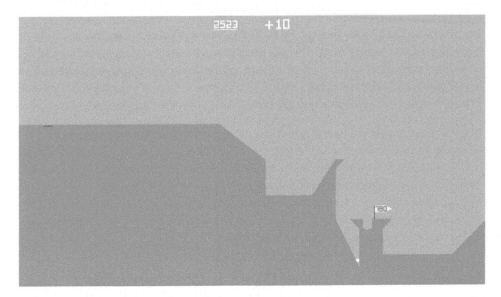

Figure 6.4 Captain Game's *Desert Golfing*.

Justin describes his design approach as "asynchronous"—he collects ideas in a notebook (jotting down things like "indie *Angry Birds*") and then when ready to work on a game, he flips through his notes to find ideas that connect. Justin always had an interest in sports games, and golf games in particular, which happened to lend itself well to the "pinball stopper" action. The interest in golf led to a thought experiment in which Justin imagined putting a golf game on top of thatgame-company's *Journey*. Though he didn't do that, it did inspire the color palette and environment of the game. This provided the next design value: the characteristics of the game's world.

Justin also thought about the minimum play experience and wanted players to be able to have a satisfying play session that was as small as a single stroke of the ball. This created the third design value: a deeply satisfying and discrete sense of pleasure from each action. This put a lot of importance on the "pinball stopper" action—the way it felt and how much nuance players could get from a simple gesture. Justin had to tinker with the responsiveness of the pull-and-release gesture, how feedback was visualized, and how the sound effects supported players' understanding of what they did.

Knowing he wanted a golf game, Justin thought about how he might generate the holes. He was much more interested and attuned to procedurally generating the holes with code than manually designing them. This led to the idea of creating a seemingly endless golf course in a desert and a fourth design value: a sense of infiniteness to the game. To achieve this, Justin had to develop a set of more concrete rules to procedurally generate the first 3,000 holes of the game. This came through a series of trial-and-error experiments as he moved through iterative cycles of generating levels, evaluating the results, and making changes to the rules controlling the golf hole generation.

The final design value related to how players shared their *Desert Golfing* play experiences. He wanted to allow players to organically find things they wanted to share and discover about the game. This led to a couple of things. One was the gradual shifting color palette. It created a sense of discovery that players wanted to share with one another. Similarly was a player's stroke total. Instead of creating leaderboards that would drive competition, Justin left it to players to find ways to share their scores. This led players to talk about this in person and through social media.

Desert Golfing is a great example of how design values can develop over time. Keeping a notebook for ideas and then returning to those ideas can begin the process of forming design values for a game, even from a simple notion, like an action or a setting inspired from another game. Justin Smith's process of establishing design values was also influenced by the things he was interested in trying, such as the procedural generation of each level. Ultimately, design values are highly personal, based on choices about what you want the player experience to be and what you are interested in exploring as a designer.

Case Study 3: Naomi Clark's Consentacle

Naomi Clark's cardgame Consentacle (see Figure 6.5) is an example of a game created in response to the designer's experiences with other media and playing other games. Consentacle grew out of a dissatisfaction with a particular strain of animé—Hentai, a genre notable for sexual acts that are often nonconsensual and violently portrayed, between tentacled monsters and young women. The traditions of the genre had the monsters in the position of power. Naomi wondered what might happen if she created a game in which both characters had equal power. The idea of a game where characters have equal power and engage in consensual activities formed the core design value for Consentacle, one that manifests in how the game is played, but also its politics.

Figure 6.5 Naomi Clark's Consentacle.

There was one other thing from Hentai that Naomi drew inspiration from: the idea of developing alternative genders—the tentacled monster's gender was ambiguous in Hentai animé. Naomi thought this worked as a perfect metaphor for queering gender, though at first she wasn't exactly sure what form it would take. Together, these provided the theme of Consentacle, which is a strong guiding form of design value: finding ways to embed or express a theme through a game's play.

With these ideas tucked away for a future project, Naomi began playing Android: Netrunner. Thanks to fellow game designer Mattie Brice, Naomi noticed that if you approached Android: Netrunner as a role-playing game, there was an intimacy to the interactions between the Corporation and the Runner. The Corporation was always vulnerable to the Runners, who in turn were continuously probing to gain information and points. It reminded Naomi of the dynamics of her game idea, Consentacle, so she decided to use this as a point of reference. This led to the second design value: exploring the inherent intimacy of collectible card game economic systems as a system for emotional engagement.

Naomi realized that a good deal of the intimacy came from the interactions around imperfect information spaces—the Corporation always had hidden information that the Runner had to think about and try to learn. Naomi began looking around for other cardgames and boardgames that used hidden information in similarly intimate ways. She began playing Antoine Bauza's Hanabi (see Figure 6.6), a cardgame in which players can see one another's cards, but

Figure 6.6 Antoine Bauza's Hanabi.

not their own. In Hanabi, players must collaborate to help one another make the right decisions. This led Naomi to her next design value: collaborative gameplay as an exploration of consensual decision-making.

With these components in place, Naomi quickly conceived of the basic play experience of Consentacle. Players—one a human, the other a tentacled alien—work together to build trust, which leads to satisfaction. This is done by simultaneously playing a card that, when combined, describes actions players can make around the collection of trust tokens and satisfaction tokens. In the beginner's version of the game, the players can discuss which cards they will play, but in the advanced version, they are not allowed to talk and must develop alternate means of communicating with one another.

With constraint being a big part of a game designer's toolkit, Naomi began to think about ways she could constrain the player's ability to collaborate in a fun way. This led Naomi to think about the ways players could work together without regular communication. She came up with the idea of using what she calls "collaborative yomi"—players trying to guess one another's actions in order to help one another, instead of the normal understanding of yomi as trying to best one another in a competition. This was the third design value for the game.

Because the game was seeking to encourage collaboration, Naomi decided fairly early on that she didn't want the game to have an absolute win/lose condition. This was the fourth design value for the game. With this in mind, Naomi began thinking about ways to give players feedback on how they did without declaring a winner or loser (which would push against the collaborative nature of the game). Naomi took inspiration from the quizzes in *Cosmopolitan* magazine that rate along a scale. So the game used a scale to evaluate the collaborative score as well as the spread of points earned by the two players.

Consentacle's unique gameplay is crafted around a set of design values reflecting real-world issues around consent. As she developed Consentacle, Naomi looked to games and other forms of media to provide insights into the design process, leading to interesting and ultimately unique solutions. Throughout the process, the design values in the game led Naomi's research. This is important—it is easy to get lost looking at other games and media for influence—but if you have a strong set of design values, your search will have direction and purpose.

Summary

As you can see from our *Pong* thought experiment and the three case studies, design values are helpful in guiding the design process. They are guideposts in the journey through a game's design. This is important because as you create your game and test it with others, you need a goal to work toward. Design values can also answer many of the questions that arise in the process of making a game. They function as tools for calibrating the team's understanding of the game they hope to create, and they keep everyone working toward a unified play experience.

Here are the basic questions of design values:

- *Experience:* What does the player do when playing? As game designer and educator Tracy Fullerton puts it, what does the player get to do? And how does this make them feel physically and emotionally?

- *Theme:* What is the game about? How does it present this to players? What concepts, perspectives, or experiences might the player encounter during play? How are these delivered? Through story? Systems modeling? Metaphor?

- *Point of view:* What does the player see, hear, or feel? From what cultural reference point? How is the game and the information within it represented? Simple graphics? Stylized geometric shapes? Highly detailed models?

- *Challenge:* What kind of challenges does the game present? Mental challenge? Physical challenge? Challenges of perspective, subject, or theme?

- *Decision-making:* How and where do players make decisions? How are decisions presented? Is the information space perfect or imperfect?

- *Skill, strategy, chance, and uncertainty:* What skills does the game ask of the player? Is the development of strategy important to a fulfilling play experience? Does chance factor into the game? From what sources does uncertainty develop?

- *Context:* Who is the player? Where are they encountering the game? How did they find out about it? When are they playing it? Why are they playing it?

- *Emotions:* What emotions might the game create in players?

Exercises

1. Take a game and "reverse engineer" its design values. Pay close attention to how the game makes you feel and how you imagine the designer might have captured those feelings in design values. Follow the list of design values from this chapter as a guide.

2. Take that same game and change three of the design values. Then modify it (on paper, or by changing the game's rules) based on the new design values. How do these changes affect the whole? How different is the play experience?

CHAPTER 7

GAME DESIGN DOCUMENTATION

To keep the iterative design process from feeling like an ever-shifting state of chaos, we use three kinds of documentation: design documents, schematics, and tracking spreadsheets. Design documents record the specific design decisions made about the game, including a game's design values. Schematics illustrate how the design is manifest onscreen to make the abstract ideas of a game partially tangible before being implemented in a prototype. And the tracking spreadsheet captures big-picture and moment-to-moment tasks necessary to design, prototype, and playtest a game.

If all that happened during the iterative game design process was literally conceptualizing, prototyping, playtesting, and evaluating, the process would more often than not lead to confusion and despair. Team members might end up with different understandings of the game, duplicate work might get done, or even worse, work might not get done at all. To help keep everyone on the same page, we use three interrelated documentation methods: **design documents**, **schematics,** and **tracking spreadsheets**. Each plays a different role in the iterative game design process. The design document functions as the overview for a game's design and includes guiding elements such as design values (see Chapter 6, "Design Values"). Schematics are like blueprints, showing the basics of how a game looks to help explain what it will be like to play and what needs to be built. And the tracking spreadsheet is like the to-do list that guides the team through the tasks of producing prototypes and running playtests. The rest of this chapter digs into the details of each of these three important documentation methods and introduces how they are used.

The Game Design Document

The game design document is a useful tool to help game designers turn ideas, inspirations, and design values into more structured designs. Design documents capture decisions and turn them into concrete plans for a game's design that serve as a reference for everyone on the team. Without a game design document, moving through the iterative design process can be confusing and hard to keep track of. The team, or even a gamemaker working alone, will be left to rely on memory and the not fully explored ideas that seemed so excellent in the spur of the moment.

Many people assume a game design document is a 500-page tome exploring every last detail of a game. If an enormous team is making a massive game, that might be the case, but for many indie games, the document likely won't be much more than 10–20 pages. Finding the right level of detail for capturing the design of a game can take time to master. Particularly when working with a team, more detail is likely better at first, and as the team begins to understand the game and develops a group working style, the level of detail needed will become clear.

Game design documents share properties with film scripts (see Figure 7.1). For many filmmakers, the script is the "playbook" from which a film is produced. It includes descriptions of the scenes, dialog, and situation prompts, along with information on character emotions and motivations. Without the script, the film crew would be left to sort out what to shoot, and the actors would be left to guess at what they were supposed to do in a given scene. Game design documents serve a similar role for guiding a game's design and the aspects of it that are created through prototypes. Without some form of documentation, teams would likely get details wrong and cause confusion, frustration, and lost time.

```
                    How is everything?   The oxygen ok?

                              MADELINE
                    Not bad at all.   I feel kind of trippy.   Must
                    be the gravity thing.

         She takes a step and sails forward about the distance of
         three large strides.

                              MADELINE
                    Oh God, is that what I think it is?

                                   MALCOLM (V.O.)
                                   (alarmed)
                    What?   What is it?

                              MADELINE
                    It's..
                              MALCOLM
                    What?   What is it?   Get back..

                              MADELINE
                              (starts laughing)
                    It's a footprint!

                                   MONTY (V.O.)
                    I knew it!   Aliens!!

                              MADELINE
                    No, it must be Aldrin's or Armstrong's!
                    Unbelievable!

         Madeline begins to skip happily across the surface of the Moon,
         with the cobalt blue orb of the Earth glowing in the background.
```

Figure 7.1   Sample film script page from Nina Chernik's film *My Moon*.

Game design documents are also like software requirement specifications, something briefly alluded to in the introduction to the iterative process. Software requirement specifications (see Figure 7.2) outline how a piece of software will function, including the goal of its use. Unlike film scripts, which document a linear film, software specifications cannot, in most cases, outline exactly how the software will be used, as users will do different things with it. Software requirement documents therefore tend to have both a systems-oriented approach whereby the "moving parts" of the software are identified and their interactions explained and a set of use cases that illustrate how users might put the software into motion. Software specs also tend to be very technical in nature, with details on how the software will be constructed. They can be part of game design documents as well, but they often are handled in separate documents more closely oriented to production.

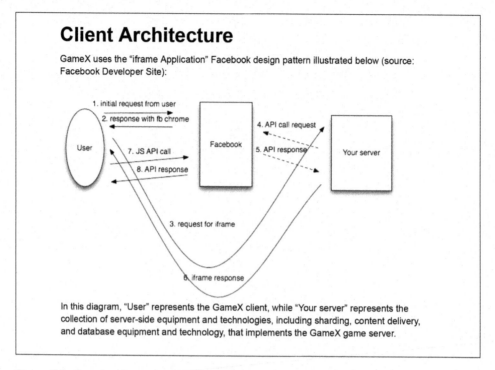

Figure 7.2   Sample software requirements page.

Think of the design document as a living document. Each time the team moves through the iterative cycle, it is important to return to the design document to keep it up to date and make sure it captures the current understanding of the game. This will likely lead to adding new sections and heavily revising or even throwing out other portions of the document. The most important thing, though, is keeping the design document up to date. This can seem like a time-consuming process, and sometimes it is, but it is still very important, particularly for more complex games or games with bigger teams.

There isn't a "one size fits all" solution to game design documents, as games have different focuses and needs. Sometimes the game may need something more like a film script (particularly story-driven and dialog-heavy games), while in other cases something closer to the systems-driven approach of software requirement specifications is more helpful. In most cases, particularly early in the process, there are some basic elements the team will want to include in its game design document, such as the following:

- *Working title:* Even if you aren't sure of the title yet, you are probably calling it by a name. Later on, the team can brainstorm titles and choose one based on what will communicate the idea of the game most effectively. And, of course, if the intention is to release the game, it must be a name that is unique and findable via online search, and if it is a commercial title, it should be available to trademark.

- *Description of play experience:* This is a paragraph that describes the basic elements and premise in language that would make sense to someone unfamiliar with the game. How is the game played, where, what is the game about, and how does the play experience feel? This is different from a use case, though that approach can be helpful earlier on before playtesting with people outside the team has begun.

- *Goal:* This should be a brief description of the game's goal(s). What are players trying to do through their play? This may be a zero-sum, winner-take-all outcome, it might be a collaborative outcome, or it may be a purely experiential outcome. Whatever it is, capturing it is an important part of steering a game's design.

- *Basic elements:* This is an overview of the important elements in the game. Think of it as a description of the system objects, or of the "moving parts" in the game. It may make sense to create a systems map to help visualize the relationship between the elements.

    - How many players are there?

    - What are the player goals in the game?

    - What are the main actions in the game—that is, what is the player doing to meet those goals?

    - What are the objects used?

    - What is the playspace?

    - What are the rules governing all of the above?

- *Annotated list of design values:* The annotated list of design values is where all of your design values are captured and shared. (See Chapter 6 for the full explanation of each of these.)

    - *Experience:* What does the player get to do?

    - *Theme:* What is the game about? How does the game present concepts?

    - *Point of view:* What does the player see, hear, or feel? From what cultural reference point? How are the game and the information within it represented?

    - *Challenge:* How does the game challenge the player?

    - *Decision-making:* How do players make decisions?

    - *Skill, strategy, chance, and uncertainty:* How are these elements used and balanced?

    - *Context:* Who is playing, where, and when? On what platform?

    - *Emotions:* How does the game make the player feel?

- *Interface and controls:* These are diagrams of what players see onscreen (if there is a screen), how information is organized and presented, and how the player interacts with the game. This will likely include schematics covered later in this chapter.

- *Game flow:* This is a flowchart supported by a series of schematics that show how the players move through the play experience.

- *Level design:* Should the game have levels, this information should be captured as well. For each, an overview description along with an annotated level map should be created.

- *Art direction:* The "look, feel, and sound" of the game. At first, this may be a moodboard with annotated photo and sound references. Later, it will include concept art and sample audio. Eventually, it will reflect the final visual and audio approach to the game.

- *Technical overview:* For some more ambitious games, a technical overview is a helpful tool to think through how the game will be produced. This likely won't start to take shape until a little ways into the design process.

Example: *Pong* Design Document

Continuing with our speculative *Pong* example, here's a fictional early stage game design document for the classic arcade game.

- *Title: Pong*

- *Gameplay description: Pong* is a two-player twitch-style local-multiplayer ballgame with a dose of strategic decision-making played in an arcade cabinet. The play experience transposes tennis and ping pong to a two-dimensional videogame. Players are positioned on opposite sides of a court from which they serve and volley.

  Play begins with one side **serving** the ball to the **receiving** side. As in tennis, volleyball, racquetball, and so on, a volley continues as long as each side hits the ball back to the other player, without missing it. Players can only move up and down (not left and right). The ball may bounce off the top or the bottom of the screen as part of legal play, but if a player misses the ball, it will exit on the player's side and the other player will receive a point.

- *Goal:* The goal of the game is for a player to reach a score of 11 before the other player.

- *Design values:*

  - *Experience: Pong* is a two-player game based on a mashup between the physical games of tennis and ping pong. It uses a simple scoring system, allowing players to focus on competing for the best score.

  - *Theme:* Sportsball! Head-to-head competition!

  - *Point of view: Pong* is presented from a top-down perspective, which takes the challenge of modeling gravity and hitting the ball over the net away from gameplay—focusing on the act of hitting the ball back and forth and trying to get it past your opponent's paddle. The graphics are simple and abstract, also keeping the focus on fast and responsive gameplay.

  - *Challenge:* The game's challenge is one of speed, eye-hand coordination, and hitting the ball in ways that your opponent is not expecting.

- *Decision-making:* Decisions are made in real time, with a clear view of the ball's trajectory and your opponent's paddle.

- *Skill, strategy, chance, and uncertainty: Pong* is a game of skill, with some chance related to the angle of the ball when it is served and some uncertainty of how your opponent will hit the ball.

- *Context:* The game is played in an arcade context, with your opponent next to you, enabling interaction on the game screen and in the real world.

- *Emotions: Pong* is meant to generate the feeling of being completely focused, grace, intense competition, and excitement.

- *Basic elements:*

  - *Players:* Two, represented by a rectangular paddle that moves vertically.

  - *Paddles:* Divided into eight segments that determine the angle at which the ball bounces.

  - *Ball:* A ball that reacts by bouncing in the opposite direction when hit, depending on what part of the paddle hits it (if it is hit by a paddle) and the angle at which it is moving. The ball speeds up with every successful hit.

  - *Walls:* Along the top and bottom of the screen, the ball may bounce off of them, and they keep the paddle from moving offscreen.

  - *Scoreboard:* A score on each side, goes up to 11. A sample scoreboard is 09 | 11.

  - *Scoring:* Points are scored as single points. Games are played to 11 and can be won by a single point (such as 11 - 10). Points are scored each time a player fails to return the opponent's volley.

- *Interface and controls:*

  - *Controls:* Each player has an **analog joystick** that controls the movement of the paddle on the player's side of the net. The analog joystick allows the player to move vertically along the baseline.

  - *The screen:* The court is seen from a top view. Players are positioned on opposing sides of the screen (left and right). There is a scoreboard along the top of the screen and a dotted line dividing each side.

- *Game flow:* The *Pong* game flow is illustrated in Figure 7.3.

- *Art direction:* Simplicity, white on black.

- *Technical overview:* Transistor-to-transistor logic. (It's 1972!)

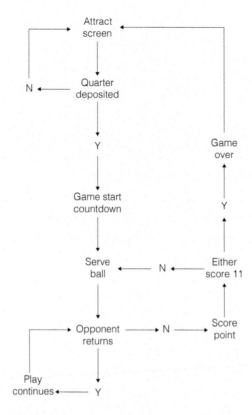

Figure 7.3 *Pong* game flow chart.

Schematics

Closely related to the game design document are schematics. Where the game design document focuses on detailed descriptions of the game's design, schematics use images to visualize the design. More often than not, these will work hand-in-hand with the game design document, and in some cases, they will be folded into or even replace it. The goal of schematics is to function as wireframes, storyboard, and blueprints of a game's design, showing how it will work, even if in abstract, cursory forms.

Game design schematics are like the wireframes associated with user-centered design of websites, apps and software (see Figure 7.4). Wireframes use simple geometric shapes and "greek" text to show what elements should be onscreen at any time. As the design becomes better understood, wireframes also represent how the user might move through the experience of using the website, app, or software. Schematics function like this for games. Early on, they capture what should be onscreen at any given moment. Over time, they begin to reflect the composition of core interface elements in the game. Eventually, they provide a guide for what happens during gameplay.

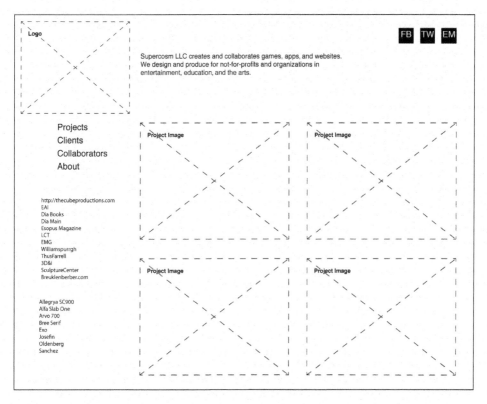

Figure 7.4 Sample website wireframe.

Let's take as an example what a wireframe for the classic arcade game *Pong* might look like (see Figure 7.5). The core elements of the game are represented—the two paddles, the net, the ball, the court, and the players' scores. This information is important in helping everyone understand the objects and playspace of the game. What the single wireframe doesn't represent, though, is how all of them interact. But when presented as a sequence, ideas about what happens when the game is in play can be expressed.

This raises an important question about wireframing a game—since the game state is constantly shifting and changing based on player experience, how does a game designer determine what should be represented? There isn't a one-size-fits-all answer, but a general rule of thumb is that key changes in the basic elements should be reflected. So, in our *Pong* example, what happens when a point is won, showing how the next point begins, or what happens when the game ends should be represented in wireframes.

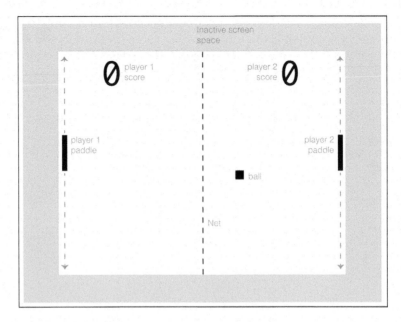

Figure 7.5 Fictional *Pong* wireframe.

Schematics are also like the storyboards used in filmmaking. Filmmakers use storyboards (see Figure 7.6) as an important tool for previsualizing the way the camera will capture a scene. They suggest placement within a space, the angle from which it will film, and should the camera move during the scene, an indication of the direction and speed. For many filmmakers, storyboards are based on the film's script. The storyboards visualize the setting and action

Figure 7.6 Sample film storyboard from Nina Chernik's film *My Moon*.

described in the script in a way that creates shared understanding among the film crew. For game design, storyboards serve a similar function—making sure everyone understands how the game will be represented onscreen (for those games that use a screen, that is). This is particularly useful for 3D games and games with more complex uses of the screen space.

A step past storyboards are animatics, a technique borrowed from animation. Animatics are simple sequences of storyboards that are used to indicate motion, pacing, and other important kinetic elements.

Schematics can also be like architectural blueprints (see Figure 7.7). Blueprints serve as the hyper-detailed plans from which a building is constructed. Beyond the details of the dimensions and materials, blueprints include information on how water and electric infrastructure are integrated. Blueprints are used to help architects and engineers communicate how a building needs to be built with the construction crews that do the actual construction. This sort of detailed drawing is also useful for game design, particularly once things get further along in the design process. Schematics can indicate things like the basic interactions of objects, or the pixel-specific dimensions of interface elements and other details important for the team to understand.

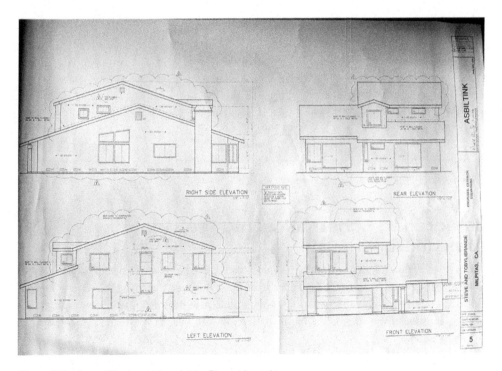

Figure 7.7   An architectural blueprint by Stone Librande.

In our fictional *Pong* schematics (see Figure 7.8), a production blueprint might be used to map out the dimensions of the game; the size of the paddles, ball, and net; and even typographic specifications. Because the ball bounces off the paddle in different angles depending on where on the paddle it lands, a schematic for *Pong* might also help communicate what angles each section of the paddles correspond to.

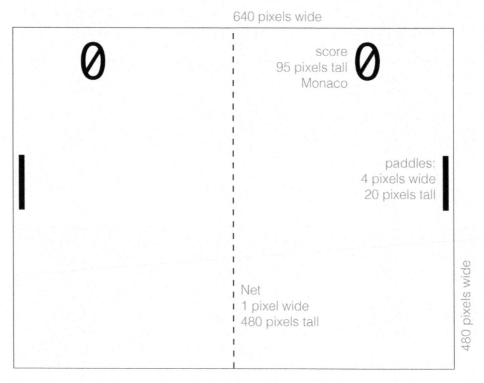

Figure 7.8 Fictional production blueprint for *Pong*.

Integrating Schematics into the Game Design Document

As detailed as they might be, the schematics produced for a game aren't always going to be able to stand alone to capture the full plan. More often than not, they need to be integrated into the design document to illustrate key points, but also to provide greater detail around what is captured in the schematics. Together, the two work well to capture the thinking around a game's design.

In other cases, a set of annotated schematics (see Figure 7.9) can replace the game design document. With our *Pong* example, the game is simple enough that this would probably work just fine. The basic information necessary can be added as notes supplementing the schematics. The team would likely want to still create design values, and the art direction process would still need to unfold, but these can happen outside the game design document structure.

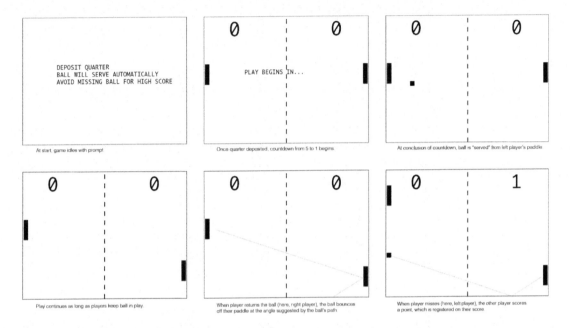

Figure 7.9 Annotated *Pong* schematics.

The Tracking Spreadsheet

While the iterative game design process provides an overarching methodology for designing games, there is still a lot left to sort out around both big-picture milestones and day-to-day tasks that take the team from concept to prototype to playtest to evaluation and back again. In our own game design practice, tracking spreadsheets are particularly helpful. Often, our team is spread out around New York (where we live), with one of our frequent collaborators living in Seattle. Tracking spreadsheets have the additional value of being accessible to everyone, so long as we keep them in a cloud-based repository.

To track our projects through this modified process, we use a spreadsheet made up of six sheets: overview, for discussion, task list, ongoing responsibilities, asset list, and completed tasks. This document structures our process and has the added benefit of providing an agenda for our meetings, keeping things running smoothly and on track.

Overview

The "overview" sheet captures the overall schedule for the game's design. This sheet plots out an ideal trajectory that the team can refer to and use as a guide throughout the game design process. We tend to organize the "overview" sheet in terms of prototypes, planning three to five prototypes ahead. As the iterative cycle unfolds, things change, and so too will the overview schedule. For each item in the list, we include a title, a summary, and then a group of things to do within that prototype phase. Noel Llopis suggests that the first step is being able to understand the scale of a given task (see Figure 7.10).[1] He breaks things down into four categories: **long-range, mid-range, short-range,** and **immediate**:

- *Long-range tasks:* These are the "guideposts" of the game's design, like getting to the first core game prototype or a feature-complete state. To come up with this list, take the design elements from the design document and turn them into discrete tasks.

- *Mid-range tasks:* These are the more significant milestones in the game's design and include things like a prototype milestone or completing the game's art direction for review. Long-range tasks are often made up of sets of mid-range tasks.

- *Short-range tasks:* These are the more substantial tasks that will advance the game's design. Things like a new set of style frames for the game's look or implementing a new mechanic for playtesting fit into this category. These tasks should be measured in days, not take more than a week or two to complete, and should be planned as part of achieving mid-range tasks.

- *Immediate tasks:* These are the quick tasks that can be done in shorter measures of time, like fixing a known bug or capturing a new design idea in the design document. This is the most plentiful type of task in any game design project. These in turn should be in service of reaching short-range tasks.

	CONCEPTING	PROTOTYPE 1	PROTOTYPE 2	PROTOTYPE 3
	complete basic viable idea	first playable	second playable w/ controller experiments	first core game prototype
	Paper Prototype Gameplay	Basic paddle and ball physics (parameterized)	Scoring system	core game prototype
design	v1 design doc + schematics	ball/wall/net physics (parameterized)	implement basic visual design	revisions to paddles, scoring, etc.
art/sound		Processing for protototyping	Swappable Paddles	implement sound design
code	platform research		placeholder sounds	Unity for prototyping
playtesting	projection research	Visual Design Concepts	openFrameworks for prototyping	
tech		Color Palette		controller prototype
			controller prototypes	projection prototype
		scoring system		
		paddle, ball, environment properties	Sound Design	Playtest w/ 20 people
		controller design	animation tests	
		internal playtesting	Playtest with 10 people	

Figure 7.10   Long-range task list.

1   Noel Llopis, "Indie Project Management For One: Tools"
     http://gamesfromwithin.com/indie-project-management-for-one-tools.

Organizing your "overview" sheet around long-range tasks, which break down into a set of mid-range tasks, which are made up of a series of short-range tasks, is really helpful. Assigning timeframes to the long-range and mid-range tasks helps the team have shared goals for getting things done.

For Discussion

This sheet lists all the current things the group needs to review and make decisions about (see Figure 7.11). Sometimes, the items on this list are new ideas or design plans that need to be worked through. Often, "blockers" are on this list: things that need to be addressed for team members to complete tasks. Once an item has been discussed, it moves to one of the other sheets. The "for discussion" sheet has three columns: topic, who wants to discuss it, and notes.

FOR GROUP DISCUSSION / DECISION	WHO SUGGESTED IT?	NOTES
2 prototypes: plan for playtesting	CM	
Controller Prototyping	BB	
Game Jam	CM	
Visual references	JS	
Repository update	AM	
Revised schedule	JS	
IndieCade application	CM	we will need to write a short description and include video and images
Who will update the Design Document?	CM	

Figure 7.11 For discussion list.

Task List

The "task list" sheet is where all current tasks are tracked (see Figure 7.12). These generally relate to the current phase in the iterative cycle and often form a prototype and playtest plan. We divide our task lists into two sections: short term and immediate. The immediate tasks should be grouped under short-term tasks to help the team understand the bite-size chunks of work to be accomplished. For both, there are four columns: tasks, person, time estimate, and notes. As tasks are completed, they are struck through. And at the end of the phase, we move them to the "completed tasks" sheet.

TYPE OF TASK	TASK	PERSON	TIME ESTIMATE	NOTES
Immediate	Paper prototype gameplay	AM	4 hours	
Immediate	Play and discuss paper prototype	ALL	2 hours	
Immediate	Revise design document	CM	.5 hour	
Immediate	Research engines	AM	2 hours	
Short	Prototype physics in Processing	CM	4 hours	
Short	Placeholder sounds - select	JS	4 hours	
Short	Placeholder sounds - implement	CM	2 hours	Dependency: JS selects
Short	Playable prototype - internal playtest	ALL	1.5 hours	
Short	Art direction	JS	4 hours	
Short	Art direction review	ALL	1 hour	

Figure 7.12 Task list.

Ongoing Responsibilities

This sheet tracks which team member is responsible for what as part of the game (see Figure 7.13). As roles change, so too does this sheet. It has three columns: responsibilities, who, and notes.

ONGOING RESPONSIBILITIES	WHO	NOTES
Answer twitter	JS	
Answer facebook	CM	
Screenshot Saturday	CM	Saturday
Development blog	AM	
Keep Design Document up-to-date	CM	Monday AM
Press followups	ALL	
Update timesheets	ALL	
Update repositories	AM	Sunday PM

Figure 7.13   Ongoing responsibilities list.

Asset List

The asset list sheet (see Figure 7.14) keeps track of all the pieces the team needs to make. This includes models, sprites, sound files, in-game text, and any other pieces necessary for creating more complete prototypes. Given the specificity of this sheet's content, it doesn't come into play until later in the process, once a game's design is stable enough for the team to have a solid idea of the pieces needed to produce prototypes. The asset list is organized by the prototype the asset is needed for (from playable to complete), and the stage the asset should be in for that prototype (for visuals, from wireframe to art to art+animation, and for sound, from placeholder to final). If there's a schematic for the game, the page number is listed so the artist can see how the art is used.

WHAT	SCHEM. PG	PROTOTYPE: PLAYABLE 1	PROTOTYPE: CORE	PROTOTYPE: COMPLETE 1
Scoreboard	1	N/A	Wireframe	Art
Intro Screen	1	N/A	Wireframe	Art
Paddle: Soft	2	Wireframe	Art	Art+Animation
Paddle: Metal	2	Wireframe	Art	Art+Animation
Paddle: Jelly	2	Wireframe	Art	Art+Animation
Ball: Soft	2	Wireframe	Art	Art+Animation
Ball: Metal	2	Wireframe	Art	Art+Animation
Ball: Jelly	2	Wireframe	Art	Art+Animation
Win Screen	3	Wireframe	Wireframe	Art+Animation
Player Panel	3	N/A	Wireframe	Art
Sound: Soft Hit	N/A	Placeholder	Final	
Sound: Metal Hit	N/A	Placeholder	Final	
Sound: Jelly Hit	N/A	Placeholder	Final	
Sound: Win	N/A	Placeholder	Final	
Sound Score 1	N/A	Placeholder	Final	

Figure 7.14   Asset list.

Completed Tasks

The last sheet, "completed tasks" (see Figure 7.15), records all the work done in the various phases. It is important, as it helps you reflect on what you've already done and questions you've asked as a team. Generally, it helps you avoid revisiting work the team has already done. If you are striking through tasks on the overview sheet or task list, they can finally be moved here to keep everything clean and organized.

COMPLETED TASKS	WHO	NOTES
projection tests	ALL	
visual research	JS	
materials selection	ALL	
Prototype physics in Unity	CM	
Prototype 2 paddles	CM/AM	
update design document	JS	
choose prototype sound effects	JS	

Figure 7.15   Completed tasks list.

Summary

While this chapter is called "Game Design Documentation," it's really about how to stay on track through the iterative design process. While documenting the process involves, well, making documents, it also is a way to ensure that everyone on the team is on the same page. If you are working alone, it ensures that you make progress and stay true to your design values. Documenting gives you clarity about what you are making (through the design document), how it will take form (with schematics), and what to do next (in the task list).

- *Design Document:* Contains all of the concepts, values, and a description of your game.
- *Schematics:* A map of the actual game screens, wireframes screens, or a storyboard of the game experience that helps you make tangible the elements you will need to consider for your prototyping process. These are often integrated into the design document.
- *Task List:* A list of long-range, mid-range, short-range and immediate tasks, issues for discussion, ongoing responsibilities, assets, and completed tasks for your game design process.

Exercise

1. Create a design document for a project you are working on or an imaginary project you would like to work on.

2. Develop a set of schematics for the same game.

3. Plan a schedule for the game, and produce a task list spreadsheet.

CHAPTER 8

COLLABORATION AND TEAMWORK

This chapter explores one of the more important aspects of iterative game design: collaboration. Topics such as setting up team rules, running meetings, and establishing roles are discussed. And perhaps most important, techniques for resolving differences and conflicts among team members are introduced.

Before diving further into the game design process, let's step back and think about the collaborative nature of making games. Both of us have been part of many collaborative projects throughout our careers, with teams ranging from 2 to 20 people. We've also overseen hundreds of student teams as they worked on collaborative projects. Through all of this, we've experienced many, if not all, the pitfalls and challenges of collaboration. That's what this chapter is about: the things you need to pay attention to when working in a group. It's about knowing who is doing what, how you'll work together, how to run meetings, how to identify and work through differences, learning to embrace failure as part of the iterative process, and the creation of team agreements to help structure how it all unfolds.

More often than not, games are made by teams. This isn't always the case, of course, particularly around smaller, or more personal games like anna anthropy's *Queers in Love at the End of the World* or Captain Game's *Desert Golfing*. Still, in the vast majority of cases, games are collaborative productions. So developing skills to work well with others is just as important as honing game design, programming, sound design, and art direction skills.

Roles and Responsibilities

One of the most important areas to consider is who is doing what. Traditional roles in game development revolve around game design, programming, interface design, visual art, sound design, project management, and testing. On larger teams, these break down even further—within game design, there might be a lead game designer, level designer, vehicle designer, and so on. But on small teams, the roles and responsibilities tend to mix: a designer who also programs; an artist who handles project management; a sound designer who works on level design. Even with overlapping roles, it is important to know who is doing what to avoid potential confusion and frustration.

Here is a simple explanation of the roles and responsibilities to take into account as you and your team design your game. Depending on the game, not all roles may be needed, but these are the basics.

- *Game design:* Most simply stated, game design is the determination of the game's goals, the play experience, and the objects used and actions performed by players to achieve those goals.

- *Programming:* The programmers implement the code that allows the game to be played. This includes the gameplay but also other things like communication with servers, hooking into controller protocols, and other processes that make the gameplay happen.

- *Art direction:* The artist creates what the player sees while playing the game. This can include the character design, animation, world design, splash and credit screens, and interface elements.

- *Narrative design:* The creation of the game's storyworld, should it have one. This can include a range of activities like writing backstory, developing characters, writing dialogue, creating scenarios to connect levels or scenes, and so on.

- *Sound design:* The musical score, environmental or ambient sounds, and event sounds that play during the game. On smaller teams, this role will include both the early-stage concepting and style development and the later-stage production of implementing sound.

- *Art implementation:* Separate from the creation of the visual and aural style is the implementation of these. This breaks down into a wide range of production tasks—animation, modeling, rigging, and sprite creation, for example.

- *Testing:* The process of planning, organizing, running, and documenting playtests of the game's prototypes.

- *Project management:* The day-to-day management of the schedule and budget, ongoing and upcoming tasks in the iterative design process.

- *Marketing/public relations:* Even on student and indie projects, it's important to keep in mind that talking about your game and helping it find an audience is a part of the process.

While these are the primary tasks of game development, they do not have to be isolated roles. Many developers, particularly on the small team projects this book focuses on, find it better to have shared responsibility for tasks. Local No. 12, our company with Eric Zimmerman, shares game design and project management tasks, and everyone provides feedback on all aspects of the game. From there, we have specific roles. Colleen leads the narrative, content, and marketing aspects of our projects, John the visual design, and Eric the game design documentation and playtesting process. On some projects, Colleen codes, while on others we bring in collaborators to handle this part of our games. On another project outside Local No. 12, Colleen and John share game design, while another collaborator develops custom controllers, and two others code. John does art direction, too, while Colleen does interaction design.

Alignment Versus Autonomy

On most teams, there isn't a "boss," and no single team member has final say over any aspect of the game. In some fields, project manager or producer roles are thought of as "the boss," while in many creative fields, the creative lead is considered to be in charge. But in small team game projects, that isn't always the case. Many small game teams prefer to strike a balance between autonomy in roles and alignment of team vision. For example, the art director will likely create style frames (a single image of what the game will look like) or screen mockups, but they won't necessarily have final say. In fact, given the way game design, art direction, coding, sound design, narrative design, and all other facets of making games overlap, it is important that the team gives feedback on important decisions in the process.

The more autonomy someone has in their role (or roles) on the team, the more likely they are to feel empowered and thus engaged and committed to the game project. The more aligned everyone is, the more in sync the team will be, but the less autonomy any one person has. This is the fundamental balance teams must find to keep the process healthy and productive for everyone. Henrik Kniberg talks about balancing these at the streaming music service Spotify.[1] At Spotify, they think about this as a pair of intersecting continua where they want to have clear goals for each project that everyone agrees on. Team members are then given autonomy to find ways to achieve the goals.

We have found consensus-based decision-making[2] to be the best approach for balancing autonomy and alignment. Individuals have areas in which they focus their energies, but important decisions are discussed and agreed upon by the entire team. An important distinction to draw here is between agreement and consent. While everyone may be okay with a decision, that doesn't necessarily mean everyone is in agreement. Being able to tell the difference is important to avoid latent tension in the group. It takes time and energy, but establishing consensus in which everyone buys into a decision is well worth the effort. This may seem like it would take an inordinate amount of time, but that is not necessarily the case.

The more clearly a team can establish its goals for the game, the more members can trust one another to autonomously work toward their success. Design values (discussed in Chapter 6, "Design Values") play a big role in this. If everyone knows what the team values about the game's play experience, then team members can feel open to explore the best solutions, processes, and implementations to meet the design values. This also requires frequent check-ins to see how everyone is proceeding on their portion and how the decisions team members are making impact the work of others.

Time and Resources

In the same way that many of these roles will be split among team members in different ways, the amount of time and energy required by each will vary over the design process. For example, the art direction and programming may not really begin to happen until the concept is gelled on some projects, while on others, things begin with art or code. It is also likely that roles will shift over the course of the project. At first, the project management may be handled by the art team, but later, once the game design is understood, project management may shift to the game designer when the project gets to core game prototyping. (The types of prototyping are introduced in Chapter 11, "Playtesting Your Game.") Being aware of the shifting demands on different aspects of the design process is an important part of keeping a team productive.

---

1   Spotify Engineering Culture (Part 1)" by Henrik Kniberg. https://labs.spotify.com/2014/03/27/spotify-engineering-culture-part-1/.

2   A great resource for how to make decisions through consensus is found here: www.consensusdecisionmaking.org/.

At times, this can mean the team needs to make changes to the overall schedule to accommodate other responsibilities and needs.

Time is a precious resource, as are labor and money. While many games can be made by "sweat equity" (labor invested in the project in hopes of future returns), there are inevitable expenses the team will encounter—software licenses, game controllers, travel to events to showcase the game, snacks for playtesters. It is important to recognize and respect the time, financial, and material resources team members can afford to give the project.

Team Agreements

Once team roles are established and time commitments are understood by everyone, the next step is putting together a team agreement. Team agreements spell out how the team is going to interact, how decisions are made, how ownership of the game is handled, and many other important elements of collaborations between individuals. This may seem overly formal for a small-team game project, but the fact is, team agreements really can help a lot when things go incredibly bad, or, even more, when they go incredibly well. While this aspect of the process is perhaps outside the game design and development scope of this book, it is nevertheless important as you identify team roles and responsibilities and will prove invaluable as you all embark on the process of making your game.

- *Goal:* What is the purpose of the team? Knowing why you have come together is one of the most important things to capture in the agreement. Is it to bring the game to market? To be the first product of a new game studio? To create a proof of concept to enter in contests or shop to publishers? To give away? To display at game events or in a gallery? To successfully complete a school assignment?

- *Team member status:* Defining what it means to be a member of the team is important. Does it mean you have voting rights? Does it require a certain amount of time? What happens when a team member decides to leave the project or put their participation on hold?

- *Ownership:* If things go really well (your game ends up on a featured carousel on Steam or as a featured game on the Apple App Store, as a favored game at festivals and conferences, in the Museum of Modern Art) or really poorly (team members invest time, energy, and resources into a game that is never finished or doesn't find an audience), the team will want to establish how ownership of the game is calculated. Is it an even split among team members? Is it based on time put into the project? What happens to an ownership stake if a team member leaves the project before, during, or after its completion?

- *Participation expectations:* Making clear the team's expectations of its members is important to avoid conflicts around everyone's participation. Sometimes this is measured by time estimates, sometimes it is based on simply carrying out the assigned tasks, and sometimes it is not measured at all. The important thing here is everyone understanding how they and their team members are expected to participate in the project.

- *Roles:* Depending on how a team operates, they may want to establish the roles the team needs and who will fill each. It is also important here to acknowledge the shifting needs of the project and roles that may shift as you move from iteration to production to game release.

- *Decision-making:* There are many kinds of decisions to be made when designing a game—the design values, what to prototype and test next, but also decisions about whether or not to bring in a new team member, to spend money on tools or assets, and so on. Having protocols for how the different classes of decisions are made is crucial. Break down decisions into creative, process, and business. For each, identify what agreement means—majority rules, two-thirds agreement, consensus, and more.

- *Term of agreement:* Understanding the timeframe under which the team operates is the last important detail. Is it within the confines of a course or school program? Is it something everyone agrees they will work on for three months? A year? Knowing how long the team agrees to work on the project helps everyone measure time and create milestones for the project. Equally important is having a plan for extending the agreement, and in some cases, bringing it to an early conclusion.

Collaboration Tools

One of the seemingly mundane but critical aspects of collaboration is creating and refining the way your team works together. There are times you need everyone's attention and times when everyone needs to focus on their work. Sometimes a decision requires a meeting, and sometimes it requires just a short chat between a couple of team members.

Related is knowing when and how the team will meet. It might seem obvious, but having a handle on this is critical to a game's successful design and development. Will the team meet in person? Online? A mix of the two? For us, we tend toward a blend, with most work done remotely, and meetings held in person or over videoconference software.

Having a solid set of tools to track collaboration is essential. There are a lot of really useful tools out there, each perfect for different teams. We use a variety in our work, and often what we use will depend on the project. These broadly break down into three categories: file sharing, task management, and communication.

- *File sharing:* One of the more important kinds of tools is file sharing—without this, teams will have a hard time keeping track of the game design documents, schematics, playtest plans (covered in Chapter 11), and other important materials. Tools like Google Drive and Dropbox allow for cloud-based document sharing and work well as a place to keep important files everyone on the team needs to access. A more robust class of file sharing for actual project codebases is found in version control software such as Apache Subversion (SVN) and Concurrent Version Systems (CVS). These are the tools that allow teams to have a shared repository for the living documents of a project—code bases, 3D models, art files, and more. They allow team members to "check out" a file so that they can work on it without others writing over their work.

- *Task management:* Equally important are tools that manage workflow. There are a lot of options, from the task spreadsheets described in Chapter 7, "Game Design Documentation," to the shared tools like Trello and Basecamp. All these are excellent ways to create and stay on top of the team's schedule.

- *Communication:* The final category of collaboration tool is around remote and asynchronous communication. While some teams will work in a shared physical space, many will not, so having channels for communication is important. Here as well there are many options—Slack, Skype, even Google Plus or Apple's Messages.

We suggest trying the simplest, most familiar, most popular, and least expensive tools you can find, and if they don't work for the team or you need other functionalities, going from there. Ultimately, choosing the right tools for your collaboration is all about what everyone feels most comfortable using and what people will actually use. For example, we have tried more specialized task management software several times, but we always return to simply sharing a spreadsheet. The key here is that using the tools is seamless and easy—and doesn't get in the way of spending most of your time working on your game.

Running a Meeting

It may seem like there isn't anything to say about running meetings, but the fact is that keeping them productive, focused, and conflict-free is no small task. Poorly run meetings can sidetrack the best-laid plans, or even worse, hurt team morale and the progress on a game's design. On one hand, meetings are time not spent working on the game. On the other hand, they are an opportunity to share ideas and progress and to ensure everyone is working toward the same goal. There are a lot of theories about running meetings—from informal standing meetings to Robert's Rules of Order[3] to consensus decision-making. They all work—or don't—depending on the team, the project, and the context in which the work is being done. If you would rather not focus on a particular methodology, plan for the basics of a productive meeting: goals, agenda, talking rights, decision-making, action items, and note-taking.

- *Goals:* What is the meeting about? What does the team hope to achieve? Having a set of conversation topics will make the meeting more focused and productive for everyone. Using the "for discussion" sheet list in your project management spreadsheet (from Chapter 7) is great for keeping track of your team's goals. These goals should be steered by the increasingly granular breakdown of long-range, mid-range, short-range, and immediate

---

3   Robert's Rules of Order was created in 1876 by Henry Martyn Robert and continues to be used and revised to this day.

tasks. For full team meetings, staying at a level of abstraction above immediate tasks is smart because it keeps the meetings from bogging down in details that don't pertain to everyone. For smaller meetings around specific short-range tasks, getting into detailed immediate tasks makes more sense.

- *Agenda:* With the goals in mind, the team should create an agenda for the conversation. This involves which topics will be discussed, in what order, and for how long. An agenda keeps the team on track and helps keep focus on the topic at hand.

- *Talking rights:* When a group of people with passionate opinions on a subject get together, it is often hard to get a word in edgewise. To help manage the well-intentioned enthusiasm of your team, establish a protocol for who can talk when and how that person communicates when they are done. Of course, there is a fine art to discussion and dialogue, but it is also important that everyone be heard and that the loud and forceful don't win out over the quiet and polite.

- *Decision-making:* How will the team make decisions? There are so many things to make decisions about when designing a game, but the most important are those around what to prototype, how to test it, and what to do next based on the outcome of the playtest. So establishing a process for how decisions will be made is essential. Here again, consensus decision-making can provide some guidance.

- *Action items:* A meeting without action items is just a conversation. Make sure everyone has a list of action items based on the discussion and decisions made during the meeting. These should be transcribed into the "task list" sheet discussed in Chapter 7.

- *Note-taking:* To help capture the discussion and decisions, someone should take notes. Using the agenda as an outline is a helpful way to do this. Moreover, rotating who takes notes is a smart way to share the responsibility from meeting to meeting. These notes should be kept in a place accessible to the whole team. Using a Google Doc that contains a running set of notes for all team meetings is a good idea since it allows the team to revisit previous meetings as necessary, as well as translating the notes to action items in the tracking spreadsheet, including any updates necessary in the design document.

The Soft Skills of Collaboration

Equally important to the successful design process are the "soft skills" of being a good team member. It is important for the team to recognize the shared and divergent values and goals of all team members. Some will value the freedom to manage their own time, while others are fine with a detailed schedule but prefer to work at night or only during the workweek. Some will have strong personalities, while others will be shy and quiet. Some will be on the project for the experience, while others might be because they really love the game's concept. One team member may prefer coworking, while others prefer asynchronous work. This team member may prefer daily meetings, while that team member may prefer no meetings but having a constant open chat session among the team for questions and discussion.

There is no single right way to run a team, and finding the right way for a team will take time, patience, and mutual respect. Listening to each other, being open to ideas radically different from your own, and giving credit to teammates are just a few of the most important skills to develop to work effectively in teams. And even if everyone works well together, learning how to resolve conflict is something that can test anyone's patience. This is where structures like meeting agendas, agreements, and even the iterative process come in handy. During some of the biggest conflicts on design questions, it's often the prototyping and playtesting process that we can fall back on to help resolve things and show the way.

Special attention should be paid to make sure everyone's opinions are heard. Since not everyone is comfortable speaking up on their own, it is helpful to pose questions to the group, give prompts to those who are more soft-spoken, and give opportunity for written feedback before or after meetings. Strategies like these can go a long way to make sure everyone's thoughts are taken into account.

Resolving Differences

Put talented, passionate people together, and you are bound to encounter differences of opinion, personality, methodology, and so on. This is inevitable. The trick is to find ways as a team to work through your differences and turn them into strengths, not weaknesses.

In their book, *WOVENText*,[4] Rebecca Burnett and her collaborators identify three core kinds of conflict in teams: **procedural**, **affective,** and **substantive**.

- *Procedural conflicts:* Procedural conflicts relate to the processes through which a team collaborates. Does someone feel unheard based on how meetings are conducted? Is the schedule too loose or tight? Do team members feel constrained by or uncertain of their responsibilities? Procedural conflicts are systemic in nature and can be worked on iteratively. Seek out solutions to the problems causing the conflicts, and implement changes to see if things get better for everyone.

- *Affective conflicts:* Affective conflicts are those relating to team members' feelings, which in turn relate to their goals, needs, and wishes for the project. As Burnett notes, affective conflicts often emerge from differences in values, which often derive from factors like gender, creed, culture, class, age, and sexual orientation. Dealing with this sort of conflict can be a real challenge, as it is often borne from deeply instilled ways of thinking and belief. The best way to avoid affective conflict? Be open to other points of view, develop active listening skills, and most important, be willing to reflect on the ways your own identity, beliefs, and behaviors impact those around you.

---

4   Rebecca Burnett, Andy Frazee, and Robin Wharton with Katy Crowther, Kathleen Hanggi, Jennifer Orth-Veillon, Sarah Schiff, and Malavika Shetty, *Georgia Tech WOVENText* version 2.1. New York: Bedford St. Martin's, 2012.

- *Substantive conflicts:* Finally, substantive conflicts are those relating to the game itself—things like what kind of game it is and what kind of experience the team wants to provide players. These are the "good" kind of conflicts, within reason. Best case, substantive conflicts come from team members' commitment to the game and wanting it to be the best it can be. Worst case, substantive conflicts come from team members' wanting to overly assert their own vision of the game. The best way to handle this sort of conflict is to return to the design values the team has established and to make sure everyone is still on the same page.

One of the benefits of the iterative design process is that it provides insight into the game's design in ways other methodologies do not. Instead of relying solely on the opinions of team members, well-done playtesting will illuminate the strengths and weaknesses of your game. This can help push through the substantive conflicts, so long as the team is willing to objectively learn from what playtesters show and tell.

Understanding Failure

One thing is certain about the iterative game design process: failure is going to happen. This is a good thing, particularly early in the process, as it helps strengthen a game's design. But there are also challenges that come with failure, as failures are often the cause for some of the conflicts that emerge during collaborations. Spotify's Henrik Kniberg talks about not worrying about whose fault a particular problem is but rather what was learned from the failure and how the issue will be addressed.[5] Keeping things constructive is always important. The iterative cycle is an excellent tool for constructively handling moments of failure. Looking back at the prototype and its playtest will often hold answers to these questions of what was learned and how it will be fixed.

Of course, not all failures are alike. Design researcher Jamer Hunt describes the kinds of failure we might encounter and which ones are most productive in the design process:[6]

- *Abject failure:* This is failure at its most final and devastating. For a game, this might be failure to meet your final goals or the team dissolving due to irreconcilable differences.
- *Structural failure:* A failure, often technological. For a game, this might be bugs that make the game unplayable or a platform change that renders the game broken.
- *Glorious failure:* A grand failure, or "glorious trainwreck"—a game that aims high and fails big, but in a way that provides valuable lessons or an exciting cultural moment.

---

5   "Spotify Engineering Culture (Part 2)" by Henrik Kniberg. https://labs.spotify.com/2014/09/20/spotify-engineering-culture-part-2/.

6   From Jamer Hunt's Fast Company article "Among Six Types of Failure, Only a Few Help You Innovate." www.fastcodesign.com/1664360/among-six-types-of-failure-only-a-few-help-you-innovate.

- *Common failure:* Everyday moments of messing up, such as the team not meeting deadlines or someone sleeping through a meeting.
- *Version failure:* Bugs and glitches that lead to incremental improvement. This is often why we see so many updates on the App Store.
- *Predicted failure:* This is the kind of failure we're talking about when we talk about iterative design. We all know there will be failures in our prototype that our playtesting will reveal. This is the "good" kind of failure we need to happen to improve our game.

Early in the game design process, structural, common, and version failures are expected and welcomed. Throughout the process, predicted failures are desired, as they create safe places within which the team can experiment with limited risk. Glorious failures are sometimes needed to learn important lessons from taking large risks. Sometimes they are formative for the next project. Abject failure? It's certainly the most foreboding of the kinds of failure. It's also important to know that all of the best designers have, in some way or another, been through this kind of failure. However, it can certainly be mitigated if the team is open to failing early on in the process and addressing those failures.

Summary

Making games is often a collaborative effort—and collaboration is an art in and of itself. Creating an environment and set of practices that ensure everyone is engaged, has a say, and is contributing their best ideas and work to the project involves planning and thought. Strategies to manage disagreements like consensus decision-making, writing team agreements, and using tools to help everyone track meeting results and action items will go a long way to ensuring that your game is the best it can be.

PART III

PRACTICE

CHAPTER 9

CONCEPTUALIZING YOUR GAME

This is the start of the journey to making a game. But what will that game be? There's nothing more daunting than a blank screen, but there's also no shortage of ideas, people, places, things, dreams, and other games to be inspired by. Conceptualizing your game starts with just a thought, but it doesn't end there. Using techniques such as brainstorming, motivations, and design values will help turn those ideas into a game design.

The first phase in the iterative game design process is conceptualize—developing an idea for the game and its play experience. At the beginning of the iterative design process, the focus is on generating the concept of the game. Once the first loop is complete, the conceptualize phase becomes more about refining and revising the game's design and solving design problems that become visible through prototyping and playtesting. This chapter covers a set of processes and techniques for coming up with the initial concept for a game and covers methods like brainstorming, which will be helpful in deepening and refining the game as it moves through successive iterative loops.

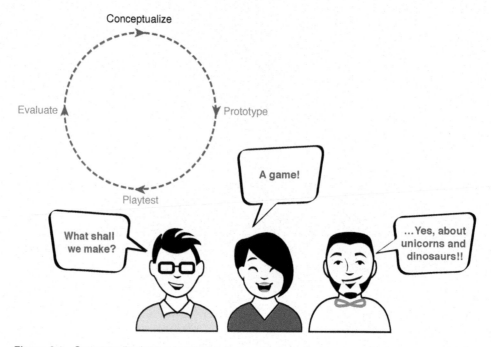

Figure 9.1   Conceptualization begins the iterative cycle.

Generating Ideas for Your Game

There are many ways to come up with ideas for games. They can come from life experiences, media, books, and even other games. Chris Bell was inspired to create *Way* after getting lost in a Tokyo fish market and communicating with an elderly Japanese woman through gestures and movement to find his way out.[1] Playing *Way*, you can see how this experience informed the game—it is all about nonverbal communication, using gestures to connect two players in a united goal. *Way* is a game that was inspired by an experience that meant something to Bell.

---

1   Chris Bell, "Designing for Friendship: Shaping Player Relationships with Rules and Freedom," GDC 2012. www.gdcvault.com/play/1015706/Designing-for-Friendship-Shaping-Player.

But it simply provided the kernel of an idea for the game. The game itself is about nonverbal communication, but it doesn't take place in a fish market in Tokyo. Ideas for games can come from many different places and be about anything you can imagine.

While there are lots of videogames with fantastic worlds filled with space marines, wizards, and tiny plumbers, there's much more we can make games about. In anna anthropy's book *Rise of the Videogame Zinesters*, she talks about how all kinds of people are making games about all kinds of different topics. She lists some of the things games can be about, many of them based on personal experience:

> **What to Make a Game About?** Your dog, your cat, your child, your boyfriend, your girl-friend, your mother, your father, your grandmother, your friends, your imaginary friends, the dream you had last night, the experience of opening the garage, a silent moment at a pond, a noisy moment in the heart of a city, the lifestyle of an imaginary creature, a trip on a boat, a trip on a plane, a trip down a vanishing path through a forest, waking up after twenty years of sleep, a sunset, a sunrise, a lingering smile, a heartfelt greeting, a bitter-sweet goodbye. Your past lives, your future lives, lies that you've told, lies you plan to tell, diary entries. Jumping over a pit, jumping into a pool, jumping into the sky and never coming down.
>
> **Anything. Everything.**[2]

As you can see from this list, games can be about stories from the personal to the fantastical and everything in-between. Ideas can certainly come from anywhere—and they can happen anytime. In fact, because they can come from all kinds of experiences, you might have an idea in the middle of the Tokyo fish market, on the beach, or in the shower.

Brainstorming

One of the best ways to generate and capture ideas is brainstorming. **Brainstorming** is a technique meant to fully explore all of the possible answers to a design question, coming up with as many ideas as possible. Techniques for brainstorming were first described by Alex F. Osborn in the 1953 book *Applied Imagination*.[3] There, he outlined the primary rules for brainstorming:

- *Quantity over quality:* The golden rule of brainstorming is to come up with as many ideas as possible—no matter if you think they're good, bad, or ugly.

- *Defer judgment:* Don't judge your ideas, or if you're in a team, the ideas of others. The point of brainstorming is to come up with lots of ideas—not to limit them through judgment.

---

2   anna anthropy, *Rise of the Videogame Zinesters: How Freaks, Normals, Amateurs, Artists, Dreamers, Drop-outs, Queers, Housewives, and People Like You Are Taking Back an Art Form.* pp. 137-138, 2012.

3   Alex F. Osborn, *Applied Imagination:* Principles and Procedures of Creative Problem-solving, 1953.

- *No buts (just ands):* Add on to each others' ideas (or your own). So instead of saying, "but there are no tubes to another dimension on a hike in the woods" say, "…and what if they lead to rooms full of coins and other goodies?"

- *Go wild:* Let your ideas be as wild and improbable as possible. It's easier to rein in a far-out idea than it is to try to breathe some fun and creativity into conservative ideas after the fact.

- *Get visual:* Drawing something can sometimes capture an idea better than words.

- *Combine ideas:* Once you have some ideas written down and drawn, mix them up, and look at how they combine. You could come up with something unique from the combination of different ideas.

There are many different ways to brainstorm, but the rules are always the same. It's important not to limit ideas in the beginning. You want to build on each others' ideas (by focusing on "yes, and…" and most importantly, to defer judgment. This can be challenging, as it's natural to try to sort out the most promising direction—but don't worry—that part is coming. The point of the brainstorm is to come up with lots of ideas to sort through later. Some brainstorming techniques work well with teams, while some are suited to individuals. Some are good for focusing on a single question, while other brainstorming methods help expand to many different possibilities. Some work well for the first pass at conceptualization, and others work best for later iterative cycles.

The goal of brainstorming isn't *just* generating lots of ideas. It is to help get the creative juices flowing, to get team members thinking and riffing off one another and to value everyone's ideas, no matter the role they might play in the design. It's also a great way to come to agreement as a team about what's important. It isn't the only way to get ideas going, but it is one we use in our work and one we use with our students. Here are a few brainstorming techniques we have found particularly helpful during the conceptualization process.

Idea Speed-Dating

Idea speed-dating (see Figure 9.2) is a way for groups to generate a lot of ideas for games, often unexpected and exciting ideas. It's best done at the very beginning of the game design process to come up with game concepts. It is also a productive way for teams to share all of their ideas and then collectively home in on the most promising ones.

To prepare, everyone should come with a game idea to share with the group. To get started, grab a timer, some 8.5"×11" paper, markers, and pushpins or tape. Each participant should write a game idea on a sheet of paper in one or two sentences—maybe "Unicorns jousting with dinosaurs." Once everyone has their ideas written down, the group should sit down in pairs to pitch their ideas to one another. For example, one person might present their unicorn and dinosaur idea, while the other might have something like "Soccer in complete darkness. The ball is the only source of light." Then together the pair should spend a few minutes coming up with a game idea that is a mash-up of the two ideas. This might be "unicorns and dinosaurs trying to gain possession of a light-emitting soccer ball in the darkness so that they can find their way home."

Figure 9.2   A group participating in an idea speed-date.

(Remember "yes…and?") This is a great way to build on the ideas of each other, coming up with new and unexpected concepts. Often, the newly mashed-up ideas are even more compelling than the original ones. The pair writes the idea on a sheet of paper, and those along with the original ideas are then looked at by the team and either voted on or chosen based on consensus.

We always suggest a form of distribution voting, where everyone has a set number of votes they can use as they like. Five is a good number, or you might modify this based on how many ideas have been generated and how many voters there are. Everyone adds votes to ideas by drawing a mark on the sheet for each of the votes they want to give that idea. It's okay for a participant to assign all their votes to one idea if they think it is most promising, or distribute them on different ideas. Once the votes are made, we suggest discussing the most voted items and coming to consensus as a team (covered in Chapter 8, "Collaboration and Teamwork"), or using this as a way to build small teams out of a larger group through ideas. This is how we divide our game design classes into teams at the beginning of a semester.

"How Might We…" Questions

Another way to brainstorm ideas is around a "how might we…" question.[4] This question is going to be the seed for the brainstorm. For example, "how might we model the fast food industry so that players learn about sustainability, obesity, and capitalism while still having

---

4   The "how might we…" question comes from an exercise that the design firm IDEO originated, found online as part of its design kit: www.designkit.org/methods/3.

fun?" Or, "how might we create a journey that generates a sense of awe and camaraderie?" The "how might we…" question opens up the brainstorm to all kinds of possibilities.

In the previous example, we could ask, "how might we design a game around unicorns and dinosaurs trying to gain possession of a light-emitting soccer ball in the darkness so that they can find their way home?" This example is too specific for early-stage ideation but can work well later in the game design process. A good "how might we…" question is not too specific and not too broad (for example, "how might we create a competitive game?"). We want the question to generate a variety of possible concepts, so we could refine our question to enable that: "how might we create a game about creatures finding their way home?" As you can see, with the "how might we…" method we have a general concept or design problem already, and we're using the brainstorm to consider the ways we can represent or solve it in a game. We're thinking through the details of an idea to various ways the game might look, feel, and play.

In some cases, a "how might we…" question can leave more up in the air in terms of the game-play and content. For example, "how might we create a game to help educate children about healthy eating habits?" Here we might brainstorm a game that is based around different kinds of gameplay, different themes, and stories, but all focused on the goal of educating young people about proper nutrition. Ultimately, the "how might we" method is a great way to use a question as the engine for your brainstorm, helping everyone focus on the same thing but come up with as many possible solutions as they can.

We like to use the silent method for "how might we" brainstorms (see Figure 9.3). To do this, make sure to have Post-it notes—the original square kind. They provide just the right amount of

Figure 9.3 Brainstorming materials.

room to write down or draw one idea—not two or three ideas per note, just one. This is important so that these ideas can be sorted later and put into clusters. Markers are also essential. You can't write too much with these, so it helps keep ideas to one idea on a Post-it. And the writing can be seen from far away—important when they are put up on the board to be discussed.

A silent brainstorm involves just that: silence. Set a timer for 10 minutes, make sure everyone has a stack of Post-it notes and a marker, and see who can come up with the most ideas. This is a great way to make sure that everyone's ideas are captured, and the slightly competitive element drives everyone to go for the brainstorming rule "quantity over quality." When the timer is done, everyone puts their ideas up on the wall and takes turns describing their ideas to the group. Ideas can be clustered into themes, new ideas developed from the combination of ideas, and ideas voted on, as in the idea speed-dating example. Finally, to make sure we don't lose all these ideas, we always document in a couple of ways. We take pictures of the grouped Post-its and transcribe them to a shared document.

Noun-Verb-Adjective Brainstorming

A final way to brainstorm is to develop nouns, verbs, and adjectives to brainstorm around (see Figure 9.4). This form of brainstorming is a way to take a concept, break it apart, and make something new out of it. Or take a more complex concept and break it down into components that can form the basis for a game. What you end up with at the end of the exercise is a much better understanding of the potential objects (nouns), actions (verbs), and emotions (adjectives) in your game. We often use this kind of brainstorming to break down a real-world system and

Figure 9.4 Cards from a noun, verb, and adjective exercise.

come up with ways to represent it in a game. For example, if we're designing a game to help children make good eating choices, we can take a moment to write down on separate index cards as many nouns, verbs, and adjectives that come to mind. For nouns, we might have broccoli, snack, parents, teachers, friends, grocery store, farm, candy bar…. For verbs, eating, jumping, talking, playing, craving…and adjectives, salty, sweet, hilarious, fuzzy, gigantic, sleepy…. We can then shuffle the cards and form combinations to create a "how might we…" question for a brainstorm: "how might we create a game to promote healthy eating with gigantic jumping broccoli?" We often add a few unexpected verbs and adjectives in there to keep things interesting. You can also spend a few minutes brainstorming a variety of noun-verb-adjective combinations or have more than one of each. The key to a noun-verb-adjective brainstorm is to help you come up with unexpected solutions to a game design problem.

To get started, grab some index cards in three different colors along with some black markers. Using the silent brainstorming process discussed in the "how might we…" exercise, everyone should individually think up and write down one noun, verb, or adjective on a corresponding colored index card. Once the brainstorm is complete, review as a group to see which everyone likes and which don't fit the collective vision for the game. More often than not, this discussion will generate more nouns, verbs, and adjectives—write those down, too.

Motivations

Once a game idea is formed, attention should shift to the game's focus. Is it all about the play experience and the main actions players get to use? Or is it more about exploring a narrative world? Is it a game meant to convey a feeling or idea? Or a game meant to simulate something in the real world? Journalists use the term *angle* to describe the perspective from which they are telling a story and their intention in researching and writing the piece. Similarly, understanding the angle you will take to craft your game will help you identify important questions to answer. A **motivation** is just that—the angle you are taking in the game's design. Motivations link the basic game design tools discussed in Chapter 2, "Basic Game Design Tools" with the kinds of play covered in Chapter 3, "The Kinds of Play" and help set the stage for your design values described in Chapter 6, "Design Values."

The main motivations are designing around the main thing the player gets to do, designing around constraints, designing around a story, designing around personal experiences, abstracting the real world, and designing around the player. We tried to be fairly comprehensive in this set of motivations, but just as game ideas can come from anywhere, there are certainly game design motivations beyond these. The key here is to design based on the kind of play experiences we want to create, unconstrained by genre, technology, or other preconceived notions of games, while at the same time creating a clear direction for setting the game's design values.

Designing Around the Main Thing the Player Gets to Do

Games allow us to do things we may not normally be able to do in real life, such as play a detective, an elven warrior, or an agile plumber. Or, for instance, they allow us the simple pleasures of surfing the sand dunes in *Journey*. It's not a direct model; it's an enhanced one that draws inspiration from the real-life event of running on the dunes and merges it with surfing and gliding to create a truly memorable experience. When designing around the main thing the player gets to do, the focus should be on the game's actions. There are many ways to think about player experience, but here are some of the key questions:

- *What does the player get to do?* Games are all about doing. What actions does the player get to perform, both mentally and physically?

- *What is going on in the game?* What actions are happening inside the game to make players want to perform these actions?

- *What are some adjectives that describe the play experience?* What do you want players to feel while performing these actions?

For *Johann Sebastian Joust* (or for short, *J.S. Joust*) (see Figure 9.5), the main thing the player gets to do is a big part of the entire experience of the game. Douglas Wilson, creator of the game,

Figure 9.5 *Johann Sebastian Joust*. Photo by Elliot Trinidad. Used with permission of the IndieCade International Festival of Independent Games.

describes it as a "digitally augmented playground game."[5] In *J.S. Joust*, players hold Playstation Move Motion controllers, attempting to jostle other players' controllers while remaining the last person standing. Bach's *Brandenburg Concertos* play in the background. When the music is slow, the Move controllers are more sensitive, forcing players to move very slowly, as if they are in slow motion. When the music speeds up, players can move more quickly, allowing them to try to jostle other players' controllers with more speedy movements. The main action that inspired Douglas to design the game? Not necessarily jostling controllers, although that is one thing players do in the game to achieve the goal of being the last player standing. It's actually moving in slow motion. This is the main action *J.S. Joust* is designed around—everything else being derived from that. As Douglas describes his approach: "my experience designing *B.U.T.T.O.N.* and *J.S. Joust* suggests a different starting point: find an activity that's already fun—say, roughhousing your friends, or moving in slow motion—and only then work to iterate a game system into the mix."[6] Douglas describes seeing a playground game where players were moving in slow motion and realizing that there was something inherently fun about it for players and for those watching them. Building from that simple, theatrical action, *J.S. Joust* is just that—almost as much fun to watch as it is to play.

Designing Around Constraints

In addition to the earlier question, "what can the player do?" is "what can the player *not* do?" Soccer, for example, constrains players' ability to touch the ball, using anything *but* their hands. Or Terry Cavanaugh's platformer *vvvvvv* (see Figure 9.6) doesn't let the player jump at all. Instead,

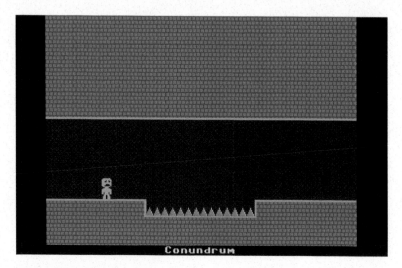

Figure 9.6　Terry Cavanaugh's *vvvvvv*.

5　GDC China 2012, "The Unlikely Story of Johann Sebastian Joust," Douglas Wilson.

6　"Designing for the Pleasures of Disputation—or—How to Make Friends by Trying to Kick Them!" Douglas Wilson, PhD dissertation, 2012.

the player has to switch gravity to get over even the smallest step. This is really a different take on the "what the player gets to do" approach, as it is about creating play by making the player work around the obvious way to achieve a goal. Part of the fun of games is how they generate interesting challenges by forcing us to overcome limitations on our actions or resources.

In addition to constraining players, our game's concept can benefit from constraint. Constraints are the designer's best friend. In fact, the famed product designers Ray and Charles Eames say that, "design depends largely on constraints."[7] Constraints can be an inspiration behind your game's design. In the early days of videogames, technology provided an incredibly influential constraint. Ever wonder why early Atari 2600 games used rectangular pixels over square ones? The answer is found in the relationship between the hardware and the television and how that information was processed. Designers those days used the limitations of the medium as inspiration in a variety of games, such as the horizontal rainbow colored bricks and paddles in *Breakout* (see Figure 9.7), which used the horizontal 8-bit graphics as a feature to define the shape of the bricks.

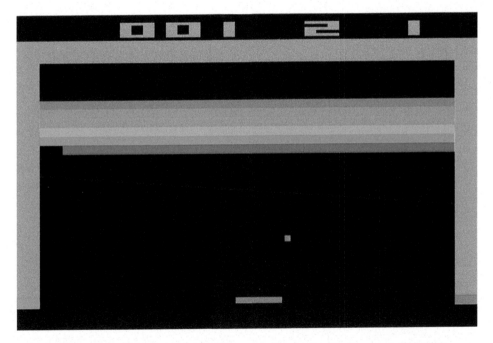

Figure 9.7 *Breakout*. Image credit: Fuyuan Cheng, used under Creative Commons Attribution-ShareAlike 2.0 Generic.

---

7   Qu'est ce que le design? (What Is Design?) at the Muséae des Arts Dáecoratifs, Palais de Louvre in 1972.

Technological constraints are also found today, but in addition, constraints are often used to limit the possibilities of technologies that are far more developed. *Canabalt,* described earlier in this book, was a design in response to the challenge of creating a game that used only one button. The game's designer, Adam Saltsman, describes his original idea, which was inspired by the concept of minimalism and developed at a game jam:

"As soon as I thought 'Super Mario with one button,' obstacles and level structures became obvious."[8]

Constraint, both in terms of constraining what players can do and providing interesting limits on our game's design, can generate creativity in overcoming them. Following are a few considerations we like to keep in mind when designing around constraints:

- *What does the game keep the player from doing?* How is the player's ability to overcome challenges limited? What do these limitations open up for players?

- *Where does the challenge come from?* What is pushing back against the player's ability to achieve their goals?

- *How do players make decisions—real time or turn based?* Limiting the player's time and ability to evaluate their options and make their next action is a great form of constraint.

- *Is the game competitive, cooperative, or both?* The goals and to what end players are interacting are forms of constraint.

- *What is the mix of strategy, skill, chance, and uncertainty?* Are there unpredictable elements in the game? What interesting choices can the player make? How skilled must the player become to achieve the goals of the game?

- *How does the player see, feel, and hear the game?* What constraints come through the player's ability to perceive the game? Is any information hidden?

- *How can we use constraint in our design process?* What are some ways we can constrain our choices as designers? How can we use limitations to our advantage?

Designing Around a Story

Another core consideration for a game might be telling an interesting story, or perhaps to be more precise in how games tell stories: developing a storyworld. Perhaps you are interested in developing a character through your game, or maybe you have an idea for a setting or historic moment to situate your game in. The Fullbright Company's *Gone Home* is a great example of designing around a story. Instead of trying to tell a story through scenarios resolved by characters through actions, *Gone Home* asks players to uncover the story by exploring an empty house. *Gone Home* tells a story, but in a uniquely exploratory and game-like way. The player inhabits the role of Kaitlin, a college student coming home from college to discover the family

---

house abandoned. The player then moves through the house examining objects, listening to tapes, reading letters, and otherwise learning about the family's story through artifacts.

Questions to ask if you are interested in designing around a story include these:

- *What is the game's theme?* What is the game about? Is there a point of view or moral to the story? In what kind of world does it take place? Is it inspired by a historic period?

- *What is the player's role in telling the story?* Is the player watching a story unfold, or are they an active participant? How do their actions advance the plot?

- *How many different outcomes or paths will there be through the story?* Do players progress through a predetermined set of story elements? Does the story branch? Are there optional moments in the game?

- *What are some adjectives that describe how the story will make players feel?* What emotional state will your story bring about in your players?

- *What are the important verbs in the story? What are the important nouns?* Can the story be abstracted down to key actions, or verbs, and key people and things, or nouns? Can these in turn be used to develop the game's structure?

- *What will the player be left thinking about after their play experience?* Are the ideas you hope to explore in the game coming through the story? If so, what will it lead the player to think about?

Designing Around Personal Experiences

Personal experiences can be a big inspiration for creating games, although interestingly enough, the personal story is not as prevalent in games as it is in mediums like writing and film. This may be because we are early in videogames' history and still developing a language and set of techniques to express ideas with games. That said, there are some pioneers out there making incredible games about personal experiences.

anna anthropy's *dys4ia* (see Figure 9.8) is a journal game describing anna's experiences with hormone replacement therapy. Players experience what anna experiences and thinks as they move through the different sections of the game. *Way* is an abstraction of Chris Bell's personal experience—for instance, the game does not take place in the Tokyo fish market and does not include Bell as a protagonist, but it is still inspired by that one personal experience.

Questions to ask if you are developing a game around personal experience include these:

- *How autobiographical will the game be?* Is this game a memoir of a particular experience you had? Will you include actual dialogue, places, and people? Images from your life?

- *Will the game be a more abstract representation of your experience?* Is the game meant to express a feeling or experience you had but displace it from the particular details of your own? What kind of representations, settings, and characters would help express the experience?

Figure 9.8 Screenshot from *dys4ia*.

■ *What are some of the verbs or actions you can include to help the player understand the experience and feel it for themself?* What physical activities are involved in the experience? What actions can express the conflicts or challenges in the experience? How will the player unfold the experience through their interactions with it?

Abstracting the Real World

Games are a medium defined by systems. As Donella Meadows states, "A system is a set of things—people, cells, molecules, or whatever—interconnected in such a way that they produce their own pattern of behavior over time."[9] Meadows' definition is used to describe the systems that underlay much of how the world works. Games are systems too and are well suited to modeling systems that exist in the real world. They are also abstractions. The world itself is a pretty complicated place—games take that complexity and boil it down into simple rules. When abstracting a system in the real world, we need to choose a player point of view, a core set of actions, and a way to provide feedback to the player about the impact of their actions.

---

9   Donella H. Meadows, *Thinking in Systems: A Primer*, 2008.

In Molleindustria's *McDonald's Videogame* (see Figure 9.9), Paolo Pedercini chose to show the system of fast food by leveling players up through different perspectives—from pasture to feedlot to restaurant to corporate board room. Each level has a different set of actions, constraints, and materials, but they all combine to contribute to the franchise's bottom line: profit. The modeling makes it clear how difficult it is to run a profitable company without cutting corners or implementing questionable policies. The abstraction serves to tell a story and represents a set of concepts Pedercini wants to highlight.

Figure 9.9   Screenshot from *McDonald's Videogame.*

Questions to ask when designing games that abstract the real world include these:

- *How does the system in the real world work?* What are the elements in the system? How are they connected? What are the dynamics of those connections? What are the inputs and outputs of the system?

- *What does the game say about this system?* How changeable is the system? What kinds of actions does the system reward? Is the system a reflection on a societal or a human problem?

- *How can player point of view and feedback help players understand how the system works?* Is the player an element in the system, or are they above it, in a bird's eye view? Do they have any control over how the system works, or are they subjected to the rules of the system? How does the game reward or penalize actions within the system?

- *What does the abstraction leave out?* Just as important is considering the things removed from the real-world phenomenon to create a simplified representation for the game.

Designing Around the Player

For many games, players are among the most important considerations. Who do you imagine as the audience for your game? What are they like? A great tool for fleshing out your player is **personas**. Personas, a tool developed initially by Alan Cooper in his book *The Inmates Are Running the Asylum*,[10] are fictional players that are based on the attributes we think our players will have. A persona has a name, age, job, education history, and other details, such as the kinds of games and other media they might like (or dislike, for that matter). Often, teams will create two or three personas to guide their design process. The first persona will be the primary one—the main player the team wants to design for. The second and third personas will be other players the team wants to keep in mind and who the team thinks will enjoy playing the game.

Whether you create personas or not, these questions are really helpful in understanding your players:

- *Who is playing?* This might be specific people, but it may also be a particular community or culture or most any other grouping of individuals.

- *Where are they playing?* Having a particular setting in mind is helpful, particularly if designing for installation, arcade, or other known space like a subway, a bus, at an event, and so on.

- *When are they playing?* Having a handle on a time period (such as daytime or evening) is helpful, but more important is what else players might be doing at that time—socializing, being alone at home, and so on.

- *What else do they play?* Having a sense of what kinds of games the ideal player engages with is helpful, too.

- *What else do they like?* Beyond games, what else does the player enjoy? Camping, cooking, or knitting? Films, comics, or music? Thinking about the other activities and mediums the player engages with will help think more broadly about the game.

All of these considerations around what the team wants to do with the game and the design motivations in making it take time to develop. Holding quick brainstorming sessions to work through these questions can be really helpful for generating ideas. Not only will it help focus everyone on each of these questions, it will provide a structure for discussions so that everyone's ideas can be explored and captured.

---

10   Alan Cooper, *The Inmates Are Running the Asylum: Why Tech Products Drive Us Crazy and How to Restore the Sanity.* New York: Sams-Pearson Education, 2004.

Design Values Capture Motivations

Once the ideation process has generated motivations for the game, it is helpful to try to capture these in an organized manner. Our favorite method is design values, which we introduced in Chapter 6. Design values help give structure by converting your motivations into actionable principles. Using design values to guide the process while iterating through the creation of the game is essential to keeping up momentum, focus, and clarity as the game develops. In a collaboration, it also helps the team hold the same ideas in their heads as they work on their parts of the game. In addition to being guideposts, design values are like the scaffolding for the game. They guide the shape of the game and make sure it doesn't grow in unexpected directions that take time and energy away from the core goals. It's easy to get sidetracked when designing a game. The overall process can follow a long and winding path, and the last thing needed is to spend time working on an aspect of the game that complicates or dilutes the vision. Design values help the game keep shape and maintain a direction that is strong and clear. Recapping from Chapter 6:

- *Experience:* What does the player do when playing? As our friend, game designer, and educator Tracy Fullerton puts it, what does the player get to do? And how does this make them feel physically and emotionally?

- *Theme:* What is the game about? How does it present this to players? What concepts, perspectives, or experiences might the player encounter during play? How are these delivered? Through story? Systems modeling? Metaphor?

- *Point of view:* What does the player see, hear, or feel? From what cultural reference point? How are the game and the information within it represented? Simple graphics? Stylized geometric shapes? Highly detailed models?

- *Challenge:* What kind of challenges does the game present? Mental challenge? Physical challenge? Or is it more a question of a challenging perspective, subject, or theme?

- *Decision-making:* How and where do players make decisions? How are decisions presented?

- *Skill, strategy, chance, and uncertainty:* What skills does the game ask of the player? Is the development of strategy important to a fulfilling play experience? Does chance factor into the game? From what sources does uncertainty develop?

- *Context:* Who is the player? Where are they encountering the game? How did they find out about it? When are they playing it? Why are they playing it?

- *Emotions:* What emotions might the game create in players?

Remember, design values are guidelines—they're not written in stone. Sometimes, as a game's design evolves, ideas can arise and values may shift around them. Whether collaborating or working alone, it is important to revisit design values. If things drift (and they probably will) ask yourself why, and decide if you need to change the design values to accommodate something discovered in the design process. But be careful. Often, we have new ideas as we're creating, and sometimes those ideas need to be set aside and worked on later, in a new game. Being able to distinguish whether you are drifting or moving forward is something that takes practice. A good rule of thumb is to ask how shifting a design value will strengthen the player experience of the game and what you want it to say.

Summary

The iterative game design process begins with an idea or maybe a lot of ideas. The trick is turning those ideas into raw materials from which a game can be created. The best way to begin this process is using brainstorm techniques, including these:

- *Idea speed-dating:* A process by which individuals quickly pitch a game idea to another person, who in turn pitches theirs. And from there, the pair generates a new idea that combines elements from both pitches. Once everyone in the group has pitched to everyone else, everyone votes on the strongest ideas.

- *"How might we…" questions:* A process by which a group explores questions to help them start designing their game. First, decide on a question. Silently brainstorm around this question by writing individual ideas on Post-it notes. After a set period of time, everyone puts their Post-its on the wall and explains them to one another.

- *Noun-verb-adjective brainstorm:* A process for identifying the "moving parts" of a game concept. Using three colors of index cards, write down all the nouns, verbs, and adjectives you can think of relating to your game concept. After a set period of time, everyone shares their ideas with one another.

At most any stage in the conceptualizing phase, it is helpful to think about the motivations for creating the game. There are six different considerations to take into account here:

- Designing around the main thing the player gets to do
- Designing around constraints
- Designing around a story
- Designing around personal experience
- Abstracting the real world
- Designing around the player

It is helpful to convert the motivations for creating a game into a set of design values, a subject covered in detail in Chapter 6.

CHAPTER 10

PROTOTYPING YOUR GAME

The second step in the iterative cycle is prototyping. Depending on where you are in your design process, this might involve paper and markers, tennis balls and spatulas, functioning code, even a playable version of your game. The key idea with prototypes is giving form to your ideas.

Once you have a solid game concept, prototyping is the next step in the iterative design cycle. Prototypes turn ideas and concepts into something concrete that everyone on the team can evaluate. Prototypes do this by making ideas, motivations, and design values into tangible forms that can be played. This process of turning ideas into something material is where we see if seemingly excellent ideas are in fact excellent. Prototyping often flushes out issues and unintended or unexpected results—which is exactly what should happen. That is the goal of the iterative approach, after all—leveraging failure early in the process to put your design to the test to make sure it is capturing the design values and goals for the game and providing the intended play experience.

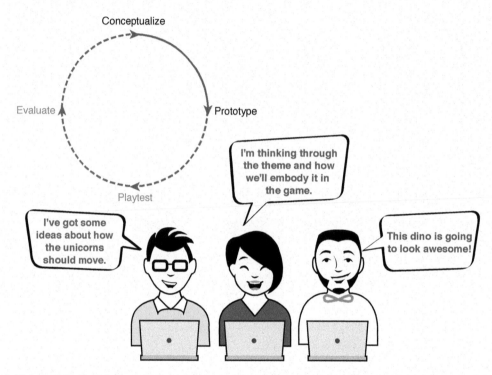

Figure 10.1 Prototyping is the second phase of the iterative cycle.

Prototyping often involves creating multiple prototypes to test how well they function and how easy they are to use. The concept originates with industrial design, where the focus is on the performance of an object. Take a vegetable peeler as an example. Prototypes will explore how the handle fits in the hand, how balanced it feels when in use, and how well it peels a variety of vegetables. The designer would have ideas about how to make the perfect peeler, which they put to the test in a series of prototypes that let them see their ideas in action.

Prototyping games is similar, but also different in some important ways. Instead of appearance, shape, or function, game designers focus on play experiences. And these are driven by the actions players take both inside the game (their character or interaction with the environment, objects, and other players) and outside the game (the controller, the screen, and so on). So just as the peeler is modeled and refined to feel right and make the task of peeling vegetables easier, prototyping a game is trying to give form to the game designer's ideas about how the game feels to the player, the experiences the game provides the player with, and how that makes the player think and feel. That's one of the main differences between game design and many other forms of design. Instead of making something easier to do, games emphasize fun, challenge, or mood over ease of use—which sometimes means making things harder instead of easier.

This is one of the great things about games—they are about creating play. An important thing to keep in mind: games can be a form of expression, too. Not all games need to be "fun," but they do need to create interesting choices for the player and engage the player in an experience. To do this, we need to prototype so that we can see if aspects of our game are indeed providing the experience we imagined they would. Game designers heavily rely on a process of prototyping and playtesting to actually see what they're making. So one of the main questions prototypes investigate is whether the game provides the in-game experience and emotional and intellectual response the team hopes to provide, whether that be an intuitive, fun, or challenging play experience.

Prototypes Are Playable Questions

One of the important things to consider when setting out to make a prototype is what ideas and goals need to be evaluated. One of the better ways to do this is to pose questions about the aspects of a game's design that need to be answered. Is the primary activity enjoyable? Are players understanding the game's theme? Is the color palette working stylistically and functionally? Prototyping should always be driven by questions like this so that you can keep the game's design moving forward. This is the transition from conceptualization to prototyping—taking the goals and design values generated during conceptualization, and creating prototypes that explore open design questions that will be answered through playtesting.

Early in the process, getting from an idea to a prototype as fast as possible is important to really see ideas in action. Later, it might take a good deal of time to get from design revisions to a new prototype. The important thing is to remain focused on the most efficient way to give form to the questions about the game's design.

As things proceed through the iterative design process, prototypes will probably take multiple forms. Early on, prototype with paper or physical objects like dice, index cards, or maybe existing code libraries and old models and visual assets. The point here is to try out some of the main actions and overall structure of the game to determine if there's something with potential to engage players. Some game concepts and approaches require getting digital early in the process. Even then, structure and player actions should be the focus. The old adage, "perfect is the enemy of done," applies to game design and perhaps should be refined to "polish is the enemy of iterative game design," at least in the early stages. There are a couple reasons for this: the more time spent getting something just-so, the longer you have to wait to see the answers to the questions embedded in the prototype. Just as important is avoiding emotional invest-ment in ideas early on—the more time spent polishing, the more likely it is the ideas will start feeling "good" and the harder it will be to think about them objectively. We know this goes against almost everything taught about making things. But trust us, the quicker a prototype is created, the sooner it can be tested, and the sooner the game can be refined and made better.

Keeping the number of changes made to the game's design to a minimum while working on the prototype is important. Because changing a rule—or a single variable—can generate all kinds of emergent phenomenon in the game, it's important to playtest before making too many signifi-cant changes to the game. (Playtesting is covered in Chapter 11, "Playtesting Your Game.")

Remember to keep referring back to the design values while prototyping. Design values may shift or change during the process, but be aware when they might change, and be sure to dis-cuss with the team and then integrate it into your documentation—because the prototyping and internal playtesting process might reveal a new design value.

Eight Kinds of Prototypes

Just like there are different motivations for creating a game, there are different types of pro-totypes and goals behind them. When designing around story, start with writing. If designing around the main actions of a game, start trying to perform the actions physically, or write up some rough code to figure out how it feels. In fact, there are so many ways to prototype and so many forms to prototype in, it could be the subject of its own book. But we'll attempt to outline the primary ones in this chapter: paper, physical, playable, art and sound, interface, code and technology, core game, and complete game.

Paper Prototypes

Paper prototypes are the most abstract of prototypes. They aren't necessarily abstract in the sense of not representing things, but instead in the sense of being very schematic and high level, representing the game in a simplified form. If you are designing a videogame, paper prototypes can be a bit like pretending to play a videogame with little paper cutouts—which is all they need to be most of the time. Paper prototypes are often the first step in giving form to a game concept. Sometimes they involve schematic drawings, sometimes they are paper cutouts, and sometimes they use little pieces of paper, tokens, and other small objects. The main goal of a paper prototype is starting to see the game, even if it isn't really playable.

A game that we are working on with a working title of *Ping!* is derived from a moment we had playing ping pong in our office together and is an homage to the classic game *Pong*, but with a strategic twist of adding different kinds of paddles with different abilities. Early in the conceptualization process, we realized we needed to home in on what the nouns (or objects), verbs (or actions), and adjectives (or emotions) of our game would include. We started with what we experienced in a regular game of ping pong and then added some of the nouns, verbs, and adjectives we were thinking about for our model of it. We then listed each one using color-coded index cards to help us keep things organized. Once we had the cards, we reviewed them to see which we wanted to keep and which we wanted to remove in our videogame. We also took the opportunity to discuss some new nouns, verbs, and adjectives that we thought we ought to include in our game. This exercise made starting our paper prototype much easier, as we had strong lists of the objects, playspace, and actions we wanted to try out. You might recognize the noun-verb-adjective exercise from the previous chapter—it's no coincidence that it's also a great way to identify elements to prototype on paper.

We had questions we wanted to answer about our basic concept that would be easier to answer through testing them with a paper prototype. Producing a paper prototype was a great way to turn the abstract ideas we'd developed on our noun, verb, and adjective cards into something more than ideas. Further, it would allow us to ask and answer some basic questions about our game: does the basic idea here make sense? What are the elements we need in the game? How will they move and interact?

We used the simplest materials we could and didn't worry about things looking good. So we grabbed regular printer paper, some construction paper, scissors, and a few magic markers to make a quick paper prototype (see Figure 10.2). We created a series of paddles and balls for the game and then used our fingers to move things around and imagine what the game would feel like. The paper prototype also forced us to develop rough preliminary interface sketches, which

Figure 10.2 Creating a paper prototype.

further advanced our understanding of the game, including things like where the score would be placed, how scoring would be calculated, and other important details we hadn't considered up to that point.

As we worked on the paper prototype, we quickly iterated on ideas around the size of the balls, the size of the paddles, possible ways to create a more dynamic play experience for our players. Making this prototype helped us think about how some of the paddles might look, how we show the paddle that's being used, and really basic stuff that we wouldn't be able to think through without a paper prototype, such as where the ball should come in. We figured out that it should be either auto-served from the center with some kind of angle on it or served from one or another of the paddles. The paper prototype really helped us figure things out about screen layout and how objects in the game might move. Sometimes that's the main use for a paper prototype.

As in the previous example, a paper prototype doesn't need to look pretty. In fact, in the beginning, when thinking through the basic play experience, putting energy into what the game looks like isn't always helpful. Just use rough sketches. Again, the goal is getting something together quickly so the ideas behind the game can be evaluated.

Different games will require different kinds of paper prototypes, so having a basic toolkit of elementary school art supplies is the best bet: paper, magic markers, scissors, glue, tape, rulers, some dice, and game tokens (see Figure 10.3). Paper prototypes are good for asking basic questions about your game. What are the elements onscreen? What is the playspace? What objects do players engage with? What actions do players perform during play? How will the experience make players feel?

Figure 10.3 An array of prototyping materials.

Physical Prototypes

Physical prototypes are all about trying to capture the way the game actions will play out. Instead of trying to represent what the game will look like onscreen, as we did with our paper prototype, physical prototypes are attempts to quickly iterate on how the game feels. Physical prototypes can model the kinetic aspects of a game. They can also model how players engage with the rules of the game, particularly when the game has a skill-based challenge or challenge that involves moving spatially.

One of our favorite multiplayer arcade games, *Killer Queen*, by Josh DeBonis and Nik Mikros, was designed first as a physical field game. We'll call the physical version Killer Queen Field Game (see Figure 10.4). It's an interesting example of a physical prototype because Killer Queen Field Game is also its own exciting, standalone game. It was developed for the Come Out and Play Festival[1] in 2011, with the goal "to bring people together to play and to have a good time."[2] That it did, with the field game being played and shown at a wide array of game festivals in the United States and abroad.

Figure 10.4 *Killer Queen* and Killer Queen Field Game. Photo by Lindsay Dill.

Killer Queen Field Game is played with 2 teams of 10 players. One player on each team is the Queen, which is akin to the role of quarterback in football. Other players are the Workers. They can run around and gather food (represented by rubber balls). One way the team can win is by bringing that food back to the base basket and filling it up. Or the team can use the food to become soldiers, and then they can kill other players, including the Queen. They can also win

---

1 A game festival focused on outdoor games and games in the streets.

2 Indiecade East 2014, "Swords and Snails: The Killer Queen Story," www.youtube.com/watch?v=Fe6eUncuXFM.

by killing the enemy Queen three times. The Workers can move the snail, or its analog in the field game, the bomb. The third way to win is to bring the snail home or push the bomb to the opponent's base. All of the rules and win conditions in Killer Queen Field Game are the same in the videogame edition. The field version allowed Josh and Nik to develop the rules and test and refine it based on how teams devised strategies. It also gave them the opportunity to see how teams managed and coordinated movement and physical skill—running from where balls were deposited on the field to bring them back to the base, while avoiding killers with foam swords. All of this physical prototyping and testing of the game at various festivals led to a well-honed sport emphasizing deep strategy.

This was Josh and Nik's third physical game together, in a set of games that emphasized playful spectacle. After touring with Killer Queen Field Game, they decided that lugging all of the game elements (foam swords, bats, dozens of rubber balls) was becoming taxing. Because they already made videogames professionally, they decided to try to develop the game into a videogame so that it was more portable. The irony is that *Killer Queen* (the videogame) turned out to be a huge arcade game, with a large enough cabinet to accommodate 10 players. Most of the rules developed and tested in the field game were translated to the videogame, with the addition of actions inspired by the classic Williams Electronics arcade game *Joust*. Now, rather than running on a field, teams flew or jumped from platform to platform collecting food, moving the Snail (the Bomb in the field version) to home base, or trying to parry with their sword and kill the Queen.

Killer Queen Field Game is an example of how physical games (and prototypes) can be converted into videogames. Through iterations of the game at different events, Josh and Nik developed a deeply strategic game with the kind of spectacle their games were known for. Even if your physical prototype is not as fully iterated on or developed as Killer Queen Field Game, it can serve to illuminate player strategy, physical constraint, and even the feel of the game and game physics and kinetics. Remember the *Journey* example about sliding up and down the sand dunes? That could also be considered a form of physical prototyping. It really depends on the kind of play experience you are designing.

Playable Prototypes

The playable prototype is usually the first digital prototype and might even form the base for the final game. Early playable prototypes are all about trying to model the core game activity players will do. Remember, games are about what players *do*, so this means focusing early digital prototypes on the game's actions. The key is to keep it rough and ugly here. Use simple shapes and colors to represent elements in the game, and focus your time and energy on the actual play experience. This early image of a prototype made to model the multiplayer aspects for *Journey* is a great example (see Figure 10.5). It looks nothing like the completed game and is played from a completely different camera perspective, but it helped the team find answers to their questions about player interactivity in the game.

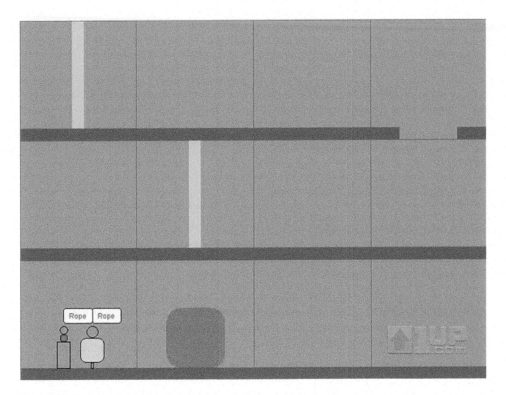

Figure 10.5   An early playable prototype for *Journey*.

As with most forms of prototyping, finding the fastest way to give form to ideas is the goal
with playable prototypes. Sometimes this means using unexpected methods. Local No. 12, our
company with Eric Zimmerman, is working with programmer Peter Berry on a mobile word
puzzle game called *Losswords*. In it, players create and solve word puzzles. Early on, to see if
the basic actions and goals were enjoyable, we wanted to make a playable digital version (see
Figure 10.6). Instead of putting the time and energy into coding a back end and interface, we
decided to use Skype's chat function to make a low-fidelity playable prototype. One of us
played the game logic, while the others took turns creating and solving the word puzzles. To do
this, the game logic player sent each of us a text message in Skype with a passage from a book.
Our task, as players, was to find the words inside the words and send back a version of the text
with the words we found. The game logic player then scored each of us based on a few criteria
(number of words, length, rarity) and told us the results. This was a simple test, and while it
didn't have all of the elements of our final game design, it gave us a sense of how the core
game would play. Because *Losswords* is a text-based word puzzle game, using Skype's text chat
functionality made sense as a way to quickly find out if the game was engaging. This method
allowed us to create a playable version of the game after an hour or so of planning rather than
days and days of programming.

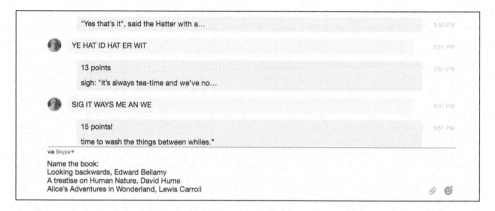

Figure 10.6 A playable prototype of *Losswords* created using Skype.

The key to the playable prototype is to keep your eye on your design values and not forget what you are trying to embody in your prototype. When you have a prototype you think works pretty well, check in on the design values. How well does your playable prototype express those values? Keep working on it until it does, or revise your design values if you find something in your prototype that will improve the experience. As we said before, design values are an important guide to the process, but when you are prototyping, you're going to discover some new, exciting elements for your game. The key is not to get too carried away and have a discussion about whether editing your design values will help you improve the overall play experience of your game.

Early playable prototypes make real the design ideas about the actions the players carry out in the game. This type of prototype is really important because if the actions the players are doing over and over aren't fun, the game won't be fun. Most games go through a dozen or more playable prototypes in the process of developing and refining the main actions, objects, and playspaces of the game.

Art and Sound Prototypes

Another form of prototyping is art and sound prototypes. The playable prototype may not have final sound or art, using simple placeholders. However, art and sound prototypes can be developed in tandem to explore ideas around the visuals and the sounds of the game. These are more like traditional art direction approaches found in graphic design, application development, and animation. Art prototypes focus on things like the color palette, the typography, the illustration or modeling style—all the things that fit under the "look and feel" of a game. Often, one member of the team is working on the playable prototype while other team members are working on art prototypes.

For Tale of Tales' atmospheric game *The Path* (see Figure 10.7), Auriea Harvey and Michaël Samyn started with the theme and a feeling for the sound and art before developing the actual gameplay. They began with the theme of *Little Red Riding Hood* filtered through a horror lens. The music of Kris Force and Jarboe provided inspiration as well—beginning with the atmospheric effects of their music on other projects, and ending with a soundtrack they made specifically for *The Path*. The feeling of the music, the theme, and the design of the six sisters in the game provided inspiration and guided the entire design process. As Auriea explains,

> When we had to decide which character to make first, I said it immediately, "Ruby is the one!" Through working out her character and style we solidified what all the characters would be…. Before her, we had no idea what we were making. Ruby helped us figure all of it out.[3]

Figure 10.7   *The Path.*

---

3   Auriea Harvey, "The Making of Ruby" from *The Path* development blog, http://tale-of-tales.com/ThePath/blog/2008/10/03/the-making-of-ruby/.

Early on, an art prototype may be no more than moodboards—a collection of images taken from comics, film, art and photographs that serve as reference points to what the team wants the game to look like. The development of the characters in *The Path* is a great example of this. The development of Ruby involved plenty of sketching and visual research (see Figure 10.8)— looking to film and other media as inspiration. Later, an art prototype may include some animation and even some interactivity so that you can see how the visual style will feel in play.

Like the art prototype, a sound prototype might simply be existing music or sound effects that are put together like a moodboard to help the team decide on the tone of the music and sound. Sound and music deeply affect the mood of the game, so it's important to consider them as part of the early stage of game design rather than an afterthought. For *The Path*, the music of Kris Force and Jarboe served as constant inspiration, and ultimately, they became collaborators on the game, composing an original score. As the sound elements are defined, trying out different soundtracks and sound effects can greatly change the play experience. Sound brings a game to life, so integrating it into playable prototypes can really change the response from playtesters.

Figure 10.8 Art prototypes for *The Path*.

Interface Prototypes

Interface prototypes address the way the player interacts with the game. Is there a heads-up display? Is there a custom controller or an unusual use of a traditional controller? Interface prototypes explore ideas relating to how a player directly engages with the game.

With our game *Losswords*, the interface *is* the game (see Figure 10.9). By that, we mean that all of the actions in the game are represented by directly manipulating elements onscreen. The gameplay involves two modes. One mode is finding words inside words and selecting them so that they will drop out of the text and become fragments, generating a fragmented word puzzle for a friend to solve. The second game mode involves solving these puzzles by putting the word fragments back into the right places, trying to score high enough so that you can capture the book for your library. As Peter was writing basic game logic, we had plenty to prototype in terms of the screen layouts, how players would navigate to new puzzles, and how the word selection and movement of word fragments would work. Early on, we developed schematics for each screen to develop the player experience and logic of the game before beginning to build anything. We had interface schematics, screen by screen in image-editing software, and we used presentation software to replicate how players would move through the game's screens. These interface prototypes also served as the scaffolding for the art developed for the game.

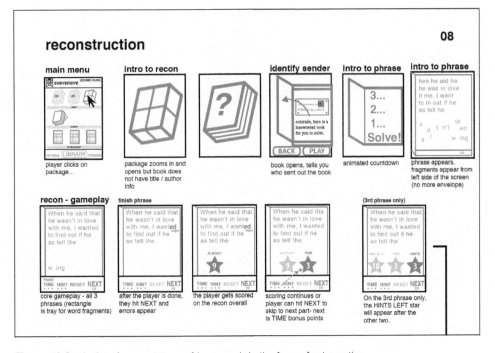

Figure 10.9 An interface prototype of *Losswords* in the form of schematics.

Note that interface prototypes don't necessarily involve coding anything. They can be created simply by using image-editing software or presentation software to figure out the interface components and how they work. Also note that the game schematics—described in Chapter 7, "Game Design Documentation," might line up with, or be the same document as, the interface prototype, as it did with our *Losswords* example.

Code/Tech Prototypes

As you move through early prototyping by considering the gameplay, art, sound, and interface, you might also need to begin testing technologies and beginning to write code. Once you have developed the playable prototype, you will also want to consider technologies for the larger game. Maybe you want to see how the basic code performs on a couple of machines, for example. Or perhaps you want to check the input/output to a server. This sort of prototype is a code prototype. Code prototypes are likely to be internal prototypes as well, to work out infrastructure necessary for more complete tests of your game.

For the game *Perfect Woman*, Peter Lu and Lea Schönfelder started off building the core technical aspect of the game: using the Kinect to capture player body positions and match them to the onscreen character (see Figure 10.10). Peter had worked on a Kinect-based game before, *Cosmicat Crunchies*, so he had a pretty good idea of the Kinect's capabilities. His experience of trial and error trying to push the Kinect's facial recognition capabilities showed him the limits of

Figure 10.10   A tech prototype for *Perfect Woman*.

the technology but also what it was good at. Many technical prototypes expose the strengths and weaknesses of the technology and help inform the game's design through the constraints of what that technology is able to do. For *Perfect Woman*, Peter wrote the code and Lea developed the art and narrative. Within just a few days, they had a working prototype of the gameplay, with the Kinect registering body position and transcribing that to a 2D model of one of the in-game characters. While many technical and code prototypes don't use final art, *Perfect Woman* did simply because Lea had already developed it, and it was easy enough for Peter to drop it in. The technical prototype didn't include all of the scenes or any of the actual game logic, but it did include the core gameplay of matching poses to body position. Connecting the Kinect to Unity and getting this core action to work was the main task at this point. Another aspect of these first few days in the development process was to tweak the code so that the mapping of the movements between the player and onscreen character were smooth, avoiding too much lag between the player and character movement.

From the *Perfect Woman* example, we can see that there are two primary functions for a technical or code prototype. One is to see if the core actions or aspects of the game are possible given the constraints of the technology. This involved Peter implementing and testing a Unity library for the Kinect and trying it out. Because he already had some experience with the Kinect in his earlier work, this aspect of the prototyping process went fairly quickly. The second function for a technical/code prototype is to develop the core gameplay, changing the code to arrive at the right feel for the interaction. Peter did this by changing the smoothing and speed with which the in-screen character reacted to Kinect input to address the quality of lag between them (since the lag was impossible to completely get rid of, based on the nature of the Kinect technology).

Technical and code prototypes can also help home in on the best game engine to use or on the right input devices or physical elements (if any) for the game. In some cases, the game might use a piece of technology that is new or unfamiliar. In this case, trying it out early on to get a good sense of whether it will be appropriate to the game is key. New technologies, such as the release of the Kinect 1.5 for *Perfect Woman*, can be hyped beyond what they are actually capable of. Testing them to see what their capabilities and constraints are will inform the gameplay—digital game design being a constant dance between what's possible with the technology and what's in the designer's imagination.

Core Game Prototypes

Once things start coming together around the playable prototype, it is time to move toward a core game prototype: a prototype that includes the core game experience.[4] It is different from the playable prototypes in that it isn't just focused on one or two aspects of the game: it

---

4   Some developers use the term "alpha" instead of "core game prototype." We stay away from this language due to its origin in software development and because it relates more to production than design.

brings all the core parts together to see how the whole feels and plays. At this stage, adding some basic art and sound design can be helpful to identify how they will be integrated into the experience. Also, it's time to include rough placeholders for some of the game content, writing, and any intro sequences or tutorial elements.

This also means you will want to create additional core game prototypes once your team has worked through the feedback from your playtesters. As with everything else, you want to remember the role of prototyping: giving form to your ideas and asking the right questions so that you can test them via playtesting (which we discuss in further detail in Chapter 11, "Play-testing Your Game"). Determining the right prototypes to keep your game advancing toward a complete design is important. This often means creating additional playable, art, and code prototypes that will inform the core game prototype. Work smartly and efficiently. That's the goal with a play-based game design process.

In Jane Friedhoff's *Slam City Oracles* (see Figure 10.11), Jane was trying to create the feeling of sensory overload she experienced playing games like Vlambeer's *Luftrausers*, but also in riot

Figure 10.11   An early prototype of *Slam City Oracles*.

grrrl moshpits. She quickly came up with some ideas involving two players bouncing around in an environment filled with objects. Instead of worrying about what it would look or sound like or even what the goals might be, Jane decided to create a prototype of the core action of the game. She created a core game prototype that represented the player characters as circles and the objects in the world represented by squares. There were no game goals, just the basic player abilities to smash around and the physics to create the bedlam of the two characters smashing around into objects. Because the basic pleasure of bouncing around and smashing into things *was* the core play experience, that was all Jane needed to really get a sense of whether her game was providing the play experience she intended.

Complete Game Prototypes

After a couple of rounds of core game prototypes and playtests, you are likely ready to move onto a complete game prototype. A complete game prototype includes all aspects of your game: menus, start screens, all the actions and objects in place, and the game able to be played through from start to finish. With the other kinds of prototypes, we emphasize making quick prototypes that aren't perfectly built. With complete game prototypes, work fast and remember that it doesn't need to be perfect until the production phase (discussed in Chapter 13, "Moving from Design to Production"). That said, paying attention to how things come together with more of an eye toward the final build of the game helps.

Kevin Cancienne's *Dog Park* (see Figure 10.12) is a great example. In this four-person local multiplayer game, players perform as dogs, running, cavorting, barking, jumping, and wrestling,

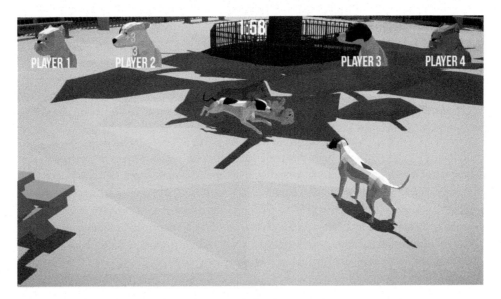

Figure 10.12 A complete game prototype of *Dog Park*.

each trying to have the most fun. Fun is measured by how many different moves and combos players perform, such as jumping over other dogs. Kevin worked on a complete game prototype for the months leading up to its premiere at NYU Game Center's 2014 No Quarter exhibition. The exhibition gave Kevin an excellent opportunity to see how players responded to the full game in a context conducive to local multiplayer games. Given that players would encounter and play the game without instruction, it was important for Kevin to make the game as complete as possible. But he also knew this was just a prototype, so he did not worry about writing elegant code or super-rigorous bugtesting (even though he did a lot of bugtesting). The goal was to see the full game design realized and played so that he could assess the overall state of the game, his goals for it, and players' reaction to it.

Documenting Your Prototypes

When creating prototypes, you want to capture the questions and ideas you are exploring through each. For each prototype, you want to have a clear reason for *why* you are creating it. You want to make sure to document the questions your prototype is exploring. You also want to record *what* you are doing to answer those questions. This may be written, or it might just be photo or video documentation. And you need to make sure you capture *how* you did it, so you can re-create the prototype if you need to. This form of documentation might be written, or it might be photos or videos. It really depends on what you are doing.

This is where the documentation introduced in Chapter 7 comes into play. Prototype notes and versions should be kept somewhere everyone can get to them, and issues that come up and need to be discussed must be captured in the tracking spreadsheet under "for discussion." Once it's been discussed, any changes to the design should be captured in the design document. Remember where you put your design values and recorded your ideas about the game? You want to document the ideas you haven't yet put into your prototype so that you have a to-do list for things to consider adding to the prototype. This is especially important when you're working in teams—to have one central document containing all of the design decisions you've made. Ultimately, it's the growing, live document of your iterative process.

In addition to the design document, the game schematics will embody many of your prototyping questions. In fact, in interface-heavy games, the schematic might *be* the interface prototype. Finally, you will want to keep track of all the to-do's that come up throughout the prototyping process. This is also where the tracking spreadsheet comes into play, in keeping up with the goals and tasks for producing the prototype. We really like to use a combination of the prototype, our design document, the schematic, and a task list to identify the kinds of tasks—or to-do items—involved in making our next prototype.

There is so much going on during the prototyping process that it is easy to lose track of what you've done, why you did it, and what you should do next. To help keep up with all this, documentation is super important. This doesn't necessarily mean writing lengthy design documents or creating super-detailed schematics, but it does mean being careful and meticulous to capture the why, what, and how of your prototypes.

Summary

Prototypes come in all kinds of forms, from physical, to paper, to digital, and hybrids in-between. Each prototype is trying to make tangible an aspect of your design concept, whether it be the way something moves, the way it looks, or the way it feels.

Prototyping shows us what our game will look and sound like and helps us figure out how it will be built. Prototypes can start quite simply, with very little or no technology; examples are paper prototypes, physical prototypes, art prototypes, and even interface prototypes. The first digital prototype is called a playable prototype, although one might start with a code/tech prototype to test out technology. Core game prototypes and complete game prototypes are developed as the game assets are created and after playtesting the first playable prototype.

- *Paper prototypes:* These are great early-stage means for making ideas concrete. Paper prototypes use paper to represent onscreen elements in a game. They help think through what needs to be onscreen and how the various objects interact within the playspace. Most importantly, they define what the player's role is in the game.

- *Physical prototypes:* These are helpful tools for working through how a game feels to play. Physical prototypes involve enacting aspects of the play experience in real life to help think through the play experience.

- *Playable prototypes:* These are functional, playable prototypes that allow players to experience the main actions in the game. These tend to be rough, often not including graphics, sound, or even goals. The point of playable prototypes is to investigate the core actions players perform in the game.

- *Art and sound prototypes:* These prototypes shift attention to the sensory elements of a game. The focus is on exploring the visual and aural style, and sometimes, the production processes for creating these.

- *Interface prototypes:* These explore the ways the player interacts with the game. This can include screen-based information and player action feedback systems, but also the actual mechanism by which the game is controlled.

- *Code/tech prototypes:* These prototypes explore technical aspects of the game, like whether or not it will play smoothly on certain kinds of devices or computers and whether or not the pipeline for integrating assets is working well. It can also help understand technologies that are new to the team, like special controllers or input devices.

- *Core game prototypes:* These allow the investigation of the core play experience. They move beyond the rougher playable prototype by including the full set of actions available to players, integration of goals and win and lose states, and other important aspects of the game. It is also wise to include basic art and sound in a core game prototype so that their impact on the play experience can be evaluated.

- *Complete game prototypes:* These are prototypes that embody the full play experience of the game. As such, they are the best way to fully evaluate the game's design.

Ultimately, you are giving form to your ideas and making something playable. However, how do you know if it's the right form and if it's fun? Well, our prototype is a playable question, and as we'll see in the next chapter, the playtest is the answer.

CHAPTER 11

PLAYTESTING YOUR GAME

The playtesting moment in the iterative cycle is where you find out the truth about your game's design. It's when the questions posed in the prototype are answered, often in ways that are unexpected. Just like there are many types of prototypes, there are many types of playtests, each based on getting your game closer to what you are hoping it will express.

If prototypes ask questions, then playtests provide the answers. Sometimes the team members ask and answer the question themselves. Sometimes playtesters from outside the team provide the answers. Sometimes playtests are super short, but other times they unfold over days, weeks, even months. It all depends on what questions are being asked through the prototype and what kinds of answers the team is seeking.

Figure 11.1 Playtesting is the third phase of the iterative cycle.

Playtesting lets us see what's working and what's not. Each time through the iterative cycle, different questions are posed by the prototype, and different answers are collected through playtesting. Early on, we're seeing if our game will even run, if the components work together and the dynamics between them are in balance. Sometimes playtests let the team see whether the design values guiding the game's design are embodied in the play experience. Later-stage playtests might focus on how easy or hard it is for players to understand how to play the game and gauge their progress, or they might test technical aspects of the game.

Often, particularly early in the iterative game design process, that answer isn't always what's expected. In fact, that's why playtesting is such an important step. Playtesting can reveal cracks in the design that players can exploit to their own advantage, aspects that are unclear or easy to misinterpret, parts that are too easy or too difficult, and a wide array of emotions different from those hoped for. Games can generate many different kinds of emotions and responses from players—often more than the designers imagined and more than is the scope of this book. For more on this, we would recommend Katherine Isbister's book *How Games Move Us: Emotion by Design*. It is a look into how games influence emotion, from the perspective of science and human psychology. *It* shows the depth of experiences games can evoke and how different games do this. Playtesting provides us with a method to witness and document these different responses—all answers to the questions our prototypes pose.

Six Kinds of Playtests

In the same way there are a lot of ways to prototype a game's design, so there are a lot of different kinds of playtests to run for those prototypes. There are six kinds of playtests that we use in the game design process: internal tests, game developer tests, friend tests, target audience tests, new player tests, and experienced player tests.

Internal Playtests

The first kinds of playtests are internal playtests. In other words, playtest it yourself or with your team. Internal testing takes two forms: for quick loops and reviews with the team, and then as a way to make sure the prototype is ready for playtesting with people outside the team.

As a designer, anytime a question arises about the game's design, a playtest should help find a suitable answer. Even with prototypes investigating aspects of the art, sound, code, or interface, there is still room for playtesting. Internal playtesting begins before we might even think of it as playtesting; every time code is tested during prototyping, that is an internal playtest.

Another form of internal testing happens with core and complete prototypes. Making sure the prototype functions well before asking others to spend time playtesting is important. This often catches bugs and basic gameplay problems without having to involve people outside the team. Just as important, internal playtests of playable prototypes provide the opportunity to review the game design as captured and investigated in that prototype.

With *Ping!*, our ping pong meets *Pong* game project, we did a lot of internal playtesting among the team (see Figure 11.2). Before we even got to our first coded prototype, when we were working on the paper prototype for *Ping!*, we were doing internal tests as we moved the paper elements around and making quick iterative loops as we went. This is one form of internal testing.

We also did a lot of this kind of playtesting with *Ping!*'s physical components—how to angle the projector and how projection looked on different materials, trying out the feel of different controllers and tweaking the code to get just the right kind of physics in the game. During our code prototypes and again in early playable prototypes, we created a series of custom controllers for the game to see which had the right combination of intuitiveness and the retro aesthetics we

Figure 11.2   Internal playtesting of a paper prototype.

desired for the game. We first tested these separate from the game, taking turns manipulating the slides and knobs, and then again attached to a playable prototype.

Our internal playtesting continued with more detailed aspects of the playable prototype (see Figure 11.3). For instance, we tested and tweaked the speed of the paddles and the ball. Once we liked where we had those, we began to iterate around paddle abilities, like making it grow or shrink when you scored. As we played around and playtested, we finally ended up with an interesting option: one that actually made your paddle shrink or degrade when you hit the ball and grow when you scored against your opponent. This felt like something that could actually happen in the world of the game—the player starts with a nice big paddle, but it gets smaller (in effect, weaker) every time the player hits the ball. It added an interesting level of challenge to the gameplay. This idea later came into our first playable prototype in the form of interactions between materials. We used the different physical aspects of the ball to affect the paddle, and depending on the combination between the two, one or the other would shrink or grow.

We did all of this playtesting in a day—often tweaking some variables and changing the code and playtesting right after. We sometimes call this "live coding"[1]—manipulating the game through the code and seeing right away how it changes the dynamics of play. One piece of advice about this kind of rapid iteration: don't change too much at once. Instead, change only one thing at a time so you can get a better sense of how that change impacts the overall game.

---

1   Live coding usually involves some kind of performance. It originated around computer music communities in the early 2000s. Our version is more oriented around rapidly prototyping and playtesting within the team to quickly home in on aspects of gameplay.

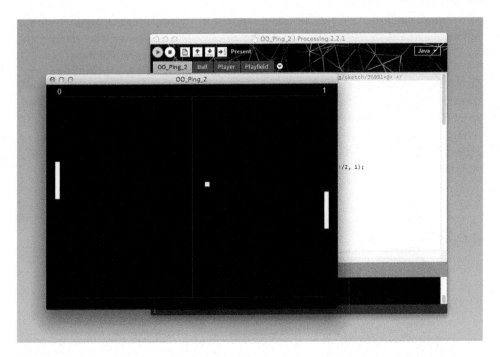

Figure 11.3   Playtesting an early playable prototype.

Sometimes the line between prototyping and playtesting can blur, as you can imagine from these examples. But the key with internal playtests is that the entire team takes time to play and share feedback on the game—even if it's happening live and in the moment.

Game Developer Playtests

The next kind of playtest is with fellow game developers: people who understand the game design process. This type of playtest can happen at most any stage in the game design process, whether the prototype explores ideas or play. We think this is one of the best ways to get targeted feedback and to generate ideas around problems. Of course, game developers tend to be quite opinionated about games and can often give feedback about the version of the game they would make instead of the version there in front of them. Keeping in mind the design values for the game is really important when taking developer feedback on playtests, as they help the team stay aligned with its goals and to filter through the constructive feedback for the game's design. You may even want to share your design values with your game developer testers so they know the principles guiding your design.

Game developers are great playtesters early on in the process because they have a trove of knowledge about games and can provide very detailed feedback. Maybe the team wants feedback on how one aspect of the game is coming together, in which case it is useful to bring in colleagues for a playable prototype. Or maybe the team wants feedback on how the visual design is working out, so running a playtest with some art director or graphic designer friends will benefit the game. Some coding challenges? Maybe a coder friend comes by to playtest a code prototype.

Early in the game design process for *Ping!*, we playtested an early playable prototype with our game designer friends Anthony and Naomi (see Figure 11.4). (In fact, Anthony loved the game so much, he joined the development team!) From this playtest we learned some important things about game feel and gameplay, and even more importantly, we learned of some new references and precedents for our game, including Bennett Foddy's *FLOP*, a floppy version of *Pong* hidden in the PlayStation game *Sportsfriends* that we found really informative.

Figure 11.4 Playtesting with our game developer friends Anthony and Naomi.

Game developer playtests are great gut checks on the game and how well it is coming together to meet the agreed-upon design values. But be sure to take game developers' feedback with a grain of…well, design values. Sometimes designers give feedback that is very solution oriented rather than simply reporting on their experience. They might suggest making certain changes to the game that pull it away from the kind of experience you are trying to generate. So do keep the design values in mind when considering feedback from other game designers.

Friend and Family Playtests

Another form of playtest is with friends and family—people with whom the team is comfortable sharing an in-progress game. Friend playtests can happen at most any stage. They are great for seeing how others respond to aspects of your game. But beware those friendly faces and kind words…. Your friends and family want you to succeed, so they likely will have only positive things to say about your game. With friend playtests, what people do or express is often more important than what they say, so pay close attention to what they are doing in the game, where they seem to be having the most fun, and where they seem to be having problems. And watch their facial expressions—these are often more honest and useful than what they will have to say.

With Local No. 12's cardgame The Metagame (see Figure 11.5), we ran a fairly early playtest with a close friend's family to see how people outside our game design communities responded to the game. We wanted the game to appeal to a wide range of players, so we thought a family gathering would make sense. We had people from 13 to 70 years old playing together, giving us a perfect range of ages for our pop culture–focused game. We were interested in seeing how people at the younger and older ends of the group reacted when they encountered things they didn't know. By playing with the family of a close friend, we were able to have just the right distance from the players to assess the game's content.

Figure 11.5 The Metagame.

Target Audience Playtests

Once the game's design has progressed to core game and complete game prototypes, it's time to bring in a wider range of playtesters. It can be helpful at this stage to find people who don't know anything about the game or have limited familiarity with it, and most importantly, are in the target audience for the game. People who enjoy the type of play experience the game provides will help you see if the game's design is creating the intended play experience.

Chris Hecker's two-player *Spy Party* is a great example. Early in his design process, Chris began to seek out "early adopters" for the game. He would get a booth at game conventions, and he created a community website. This attracted players interested in the game, allowing Chris to develop a group of players with whom he could playtest his prototypes. Because the audience was eager to play the game, Chris was able to get lots of invaluable feedback on the game's design from fairly early in the process, not so long after he had a first playable prototype. This also gave Chris an excellent gut check for design decisions—if his target audience playtesters enjoyed new features, art, and other aspects, then Chris knew he was heading in the right direction. And if they did not respond well, he was able to learn this early on and to work to find new solutions.

New Player Playtests

New player playtests are those that involve people new to the game. They are best for core game and complete game playtests to help see how new players will learn and enjoy the game. It is important to run between five and seven of these to try to see the full range of responses players will have. Less than five, and you might not get enough variation, and more than seven, and you are spending too much time on these tests. Keep in mind that a player is only a new player once, which means finding new people to playtest is an ongoing task.

Playtesting with new players will often shed light on the game that can be exploited in unexpected ways to a player's advantage. As Kevin Cancienne was showing a prototype of his four-player game *Dog Park* (see Figure 11.6) at IndieCade, an independent game developer's

Figure 11.6   *Dog Park* being playtested. Photo by Daniel Latorre.

conference, one player found an exploit in the rules: that barking incessantly would always win in terms of accumulating fun points over any other activity. Kevin and his friend decided to try to stop the barking player from barking, making their dog characters go over and wrestle the barking dog to submission. They proceeded to run and chase each other all over the dog park. As they were doing this, Kevin had the sudden realization that what they were all doing in the game was exactly what dogs would actually do in real life—the game encourages the exact thing that Kevin was hoping for—giving people a chance to play like dogs. So instead of over-correcting the exploit by completely removing barking from the game, he simply calibrated the number of points barking would give players. So barking is still a powerful strategy, but it can be overcome by the kinds of things dogs do to another dog whose behavior is annoying—chasing them, and wrestling them.

Experienced Player Playtests

Experienced player playtests are those where playtesters play a prototype over a longer period of time. Because of the nature of this sort of playtest, it is necessary to give experienced players some time—maybe a few days, maybe a week, maybe a few weeks. It will vary from game to game. Longer-term playtests like these are great for helping really see how the game design translates into play experiences. This kind of longer-term playtest can also show how changes in the game have impacted the experience since these playtesters will likely be around through various stages of the game's development. Playtesting with experienced players can begin at the point there is a playable prototype, and to be effectively "experienced," should continue through to complete game prototypes because these playtesters need to be able to give feedback on the whole experience. For longer-term playtests, it's a good idea to set up regular emails (to prompt players to check in), website-based forms, or multiple in-person sessions if the game is multiplayer.

Chris Hecker's work to develop a pool of target audience playtesters for *Spy Party* also allowed him to develop a group of experienced playtesters. This allowed him to focus on the core game and see what happened when players devoted time and energy to developing skills and strategy around the game. This sort of information is invaluable for games that emphasize player skill and goal-oriented play, but also for experiential games.

Matching Prototypes to Playtests

There are many different kinds of playtests—and playtesters—to use at every loop through the iterative cycle. Each one will provide different answers to the question that the prototype asks, based on their experiences, their relationship to you and the design team, and the kind of prototype they are testing. In fact, certain prototypes work best with certain playtesters.

Different prototypes lend themselves to different kinds of playtests (see Figure 11.7). This is because different kinds of playtests are better at evaluating different things:

- Paper prototypes are best suited for internal and game developer playtests.
- The same goes for physical and code prototypes.
- Art and playable prototypes might open up to also include friends and family.
- Core game prototypes can open up a bit more to include target audience playtesters.
- Complete game prototypes are the most open, involving all types of playtesters.
- Finally, experienced playtesters can be matched with almost any kind of prototype and might be playtesters from the beginning. How else will they become experienced?

playtesters / prototypes	internal	game developer	friends & family	target audience	new players	experienced players
paper	x	x				
physical	x	x				
code/tech	x	x		x		
art	x	x	x			
playable	x	x	x	x	x	x
core game	x	x	x	x	x	x
complete game	x			x	x	x

Figure 11.7   Matching prototypes to playtests.

Preparing for a Playtest

There is a lot more to running a playtest than just grabbing a couple of friends and letting them play the game (though that does work sometimes). Eric Zimmerman and his collaborator, the architect Nathalie Pozzi, talk about playtesting for their gallery games being both demanding and cruel.[2] As Nathalie puts it, playtesting, particularly for early prototypes, is asking people to try out something its creators know is broken or incomplete. Eric describes early playtests like a dinner party where some of the food may be unappetizing or completely uncooked. Playtests ask a lot of everyone—most importantly the playtesters. To make the most of playtesting, make sure the prototype is ready and the team is prepared to capture the answers that come out of the playtest.

Picking a Time and Place

The basics of preparing for a playtest are picking a time and date, a location, and of course, playtesters. Setting a time and place that will accommodate playtesters but also provide the atmosphere conducive to evaluating the prototype isn't trivial. For example, while a loud cafe

---

2   We interviewed Nathalie and Eric about their prototyping experience as part of our video series, Iterate: Design and Failure. http://www.designandfailure.com/nathalie-pozzi-and-eric-zimmerman/. 2015.

or bar may seem ideal, it will quickly undermine the playtest if the game requires focus and undivided attention.

Planning the Playtest

Something that will help focus playtesters' comments is a playtest plan—knowing how to introduce the game, what playtesters need to know to understand the current state of the game, and whatever info they need to know to play are all things to sort out ahead of time.

This means the team should meet before the playtest to identify what, exactly, everyone wants to learn from the playtest. A good place to start is revisiting the questions that led to creating the prototype in the first place. With *Ping!*, once we had our first playable prototype, we had a few questions we wanted to answer:

- How easy is it for players to manipulate the paddles?
- How long are they able to volley?
- Are certain materials and settings more fun than others?

These are the kinds of questions that we just couldn't answer ourselves. We had been playing the prototypes all along and had lost the feel for how easy or difficult the game was. This is a common occurrence when developing a game. You need others to test it to keep the difficulty within reason and game interactions clear to new players.

Capturing Feedback

Just as important is having a plan for capturing the feedback. Will team members observe the players or even play along with them? Will sessions be videotaped for later review? Will screen-grabs or video be captured if it is a screen-based prototype? Who will observe and take notes?

Much of what happens during playtests is nonverbal—a laugh, comments during gameplay, white knuckles during a particularly difficult challenge, bored glances at a cellphone. All these are important clues in the playtest and where videotaping can be quite helpful.

Running a Playtest

Once a prototype is ready to go, it's time to playtest. This is often a pretty surprising, and sometimes a pretty traumatic, experience. But it's also one that game designers become used to after a while. One of the most difficult things to do in a playtest is to sit back and pay attention to the playtest itself—and not try to intervene too much. It's so hard to watch players fail to understand something in the game that seems obvious. In essence, it's painful to watch them fail. This is exactly what we're looking for—points in the game where things are unclear, too difficult, or just downright broken. To keep playtests smooth and focused, we've identified four things you should always do in a playtest: introduce, observe, listen, and discuss.

Introduce

First off, you should **introduce** playtesters to what they are about to experience. Tell them more about the state of the prototype. Make sure they understand where the project's focus is right now. For example, if the art isn't final or the win condition isn't implemented, let playtesters know. This helps them understand better what they are playing and what they should comment upon.

Observe

The second is **observe**. When we observe the playtest, we're looking for all kinds of things—body language, what players are actually doing onscreen, what they say when they are playing, how much they want to play, and in the case of our game, what players say to each other.

And here's where we need to emphasize something. Observing doesn't mean talking, helping, or coaching. Keep interactions with playtesters to a minimum. In fact, try not to interact at all when they are playing—even when they are struggling. This is easier said than done. It's hard seeing playtesters fail because something in the game is unclear or play the game in a way that is totally unintended. Sometimes those surprises can be great to see—players helping strengthen the game's design. And sometimes it is horrible, with the natural instinct being speaking up and intervening. Resist this impulse, as it defeats the purpose of playtesting. The goal of playtesting is watching to find just these kinds of failures and not to stop them from happening. So fight the impulse, keep quiet, and just write down what the playtesters are doing and what is and is not working.

Listen

The third thing to do is **listen**. This is different from observing. When we listen, we might be listening to our players talk aloud as they play. A good thing to do to understand what is going on in the player's head is to ask them to actually say out loud what they are doing. A player can tell us why they are making certain choices, how the game is making them feel, or if there's anything they are unsure about.

Discuss

The final thing to do during a playtest is to **discuss**. Make sure when scheduling the playtest to leave time to discuss the game with your playtesters. In the discussion, the kinds of questions to ask are not "yes/no," or leading questions like "did the game feel fun?" Ask open questions like, "How did playing the game make you feel?" or use open prompts like, "Tell me how you figured out the game's goal." The goal here is looking for the playtester's reactions to the game, not feeding them yours.

For certain playtests, in particular with target audience playtesters, have a discussion before or after the playtest about the playtesters' own game preferences, who they are, and any other questions you might have to help you understand their point of view as they play your game.

So that's it. **Introduce, observe, listen,** and **discuss.** Those are the four steps for running a playtest.

After a Playtest

There is so much going on during the playtesting process that it is easy to lose track of what you've done, why you did it, and what you should do next. Playtesting is the most critical part of the iterative game design process because it is the time when you gain deeper insight into the ideas explored during conceptualization and answers to the questions posed in your prototype. To help keep up with all this and to get the most out of each test, documentation is important. In the previous chapter we went over the why, what, and how of documentation of prototypes; now it's time to focus on the who, when, where, and feedback of our playtests.

Who was playing? Make sure to record the playtesters' names and a way to contact them in case additional questions come up. When and where are important to note because they provide pertinent information on the context within which the game was playtested. Feedback is the most essential thing to document. This is why we playtest in the first place: to see what playtesters do and think about the game. To make the most of playtesters' time and efforts, pay careful attention to their experience.

We capture the most basic info like when we tested, who the playtesters were, which prototype we were testing, and who is taking the notes.

- *Gameplay:* This is where we collect notes relating to the play itself. Did the players enjoy themselves? Were they having problems? What worked? What didn't?

- *Visuals and audio:* These are notes on the presentation layer of the game. Were there reactions to sound? To any of the visual elements of the game?

- *Bugs:* Were there any bugs that popped up during the playtest? Making careful note of what happened and what the playtester was doing that caused the bug is important for being able to go back and fix the bug.

- *Comments:* If playtesters say things that are revealing about their experience, try to write these down along with a note about what triggered the comment.

- *Observations:* Sometimes playtesters give feedback without saying a word—the furrow of a brow, a smile, or a laugh while they play. Playtesters also give feedback through their play. Watching what is happening onscreen, or if it is a nondigital game, what happens on the board or in their hand of cards, is also revealing.

- *Ideas:* Any ideas that come to mind during the test should be written down to avoid forgetting them. These are ideas about what to add, how to fix issues, and ways to enhance and improve. Catch them all.

In addition to written notes, consider taking pictures and video of the playtest using screen capture software for recording the play sessions. The team can then go back and review these additional materials after the playtest session. But make sure to use notes to cross-reference with the video recordings to find relevant bits of footage rather than getting caught up re-watching hours of footage! We suggest adding exclamation points and noting the time or level so that these bits of footage can be easy to cue up and review.

As with all of this documentation, be sure to share it in a place where the team can access and review it. In the evaluate phase, any responses to the playtests will be added to the design document and reflected in schematics and task lists. (See Chapter 7, "Game Design Documentation," for more details on this kind of documentation.)

The Difference Between Input and Feedback

Before moving on, it's important to recognize some arguments that have been made against the iterative process. One of the stronger stances against iterative design comes from the critic and designer Mattie Brice.[3] As Mattie points out, the player-centric iterative cycle can lead to the designer changing or smoothing out their original message to suit players. For gamemakers interested in creating challenging works, this can be problematic because it can water down the intended expression and experience of a game. Lana Polansky takes up a similar argument, noting that the player-centric approach can lead to gamemakers taking it easy on players.[4] Further, by treating the player as central, gamemakers unintentionally have created a situation in which players often expect to be coddled and given what they want. Together, Brice and Polansky point out player-centered design has its problems and limits.

There are also certain kinds of games for which playtesting is not really possible. Mattie draws an apt analogy in her essay, drawing a comparison to asking a romantic interest to give feedback on an early draft of a love letter. This would let the cat out of the bag, so to speak, before the letter writer has their thoughts fully formed.

Mattie and Lana's thoughts on the role of playtesting bring up an important distinction between input and feedback. When game designers use the process to get player input on a game's design, it is likely that the game will change to more fully suit player interests and tastes. This is

---

3   Mattie Brice, "Death of the Player," *Alternate Ending.* www.mattiebrice.com/death-of-the-player, 2014.

4   Lana Polansky, "The Customer Is Often Wrong (Fuck the Player)," *Sufficiently Human.* http://sufficientlyhuman.com/archives/599, 2014.

different from getting feedback, which the game designer takes into account but doesn't necessarily act upon. Jonathan Blow, the designer of *Braid* and *The Witness*, has an interesting relationship to iteration and playtesting. For Blow, videogames are an expressive medium through which he has particular things to say. He isn't interested in getting ideas from his playtesters, yet he still playtests. Instead of looking for ways to better entertain his players, Blow playtests to make sure his games provide the play experience he intends. So playtesting becomes a tool for calibrating his expression rather than a method of giving players what they want.

The thing is, almost every creative medium has its own version of playtesting as feedback mechanism. For poets and writers, it is called workshops; for playwrights and screenplay writers, it is called table reads; for artists, it is called critiques. In these situations, the person creating the poem, play, or painting solicits feedback from their peers. This may come in the form of notes on where the work falls short of the intended goals, and it may come in the form of input, or suggestions, on how to change the work. Feedback points out the problems, while input suggests changes that may or may not be in line with the creator's intentions. The point is, no matter what field of perspective an artist or designer brings to the creative process, there is almost always room for feedback, and at times, input, so long as the creator knows what to do with it.

Summary

Playtesting is where your team gets answers to the question that your prototype asks. It's also where you are likely to see your playtesters struggle and your game fail to provide the play experience you want. This is exactly what you need to make your game better. Playtesting early with your team, fellow game designers and friends will help you see what's working and what isn't with your game. Later playtesting with your target audience, new players and experienced players will help you refine your game and turn it into something great. Remember to introduce, observe, listen, survey, and discuss with your playtesters and to record the results so that you can remember and discuss them with your team—which leads us to the next step in the iterative cycle: evaluate.

The six kinds of playtests include the following:

- *Internal tests:* Playtesting the game yourself or with your team. Internal testing takes two forms: for quick loops and reviews with the team, and then as a way to make sure the prototype is ready for playtesting with people outside the team.
- *Game developer tests:* Playtesting with fellow game developers: people who understand the game design process.
- *Friend and family tests:* Another form of playtest is with friends and family—people with whom the team is comfortable sharing an in-progress game.

- *Target audience tests:* Once the game's design has progressed to core game and complete game prototypes, it's time to bring in people who enjoy the type of play experience the game provides—in other words, the target audience.

- *New player tests:* New player playtests are those that involve people new to the game. They are best for core game and complete game playtests to help see how new players will learn and enjoy the game.

- *Experienced player tests:* Experienced player playtests are those where playtesters play a prototype over a longer period of time.

There is more to do than just decide what kind of playtest is needed for the current prototype. Planning is important in making the most of the playtest opportunity. There are a set of steps that help make a successful playtest:

1. Picking a time and place
2. Planning what is to be evaluated
3. Deciding how to document the playtest

Once the playtest begins, there are four key steps:

1. Introduce
2. Observe
3. Listen
4. Discuss

Depending on what is being playtested, there are a number of things to observe and document:

- Gameplay
- Visuals and audio
- Bugs
- Player comments
- Player behaviors
- Tester observations
- Ideas generated during the playtest

CHAPTER 12

EVALUATING YOUR GAME

Evaluation is where you consider your game's design, interpret the outcome of your playtests, and make decisions about how to refine your design plans. This directly flows into the first stage: conceptualization. You are reviewing the questions and answers (both expected and unexpected) and then making decisions about how to improve your game, including what kind of prototype will be next in the process.

Evaluation is the final, and sometimes most challenging, step in the iterative cycle. This is where all of the feedback from playtests gets examined by the team. If prototypes pose questions that are answered through playtests, then the evaluate phase is when those answers are reviewed and turned into actionable ideas for design revisions. The answers from the playtest, however, aren't always clear. Think of yourself as the doctor, the game as a patient, and the playtest session the symptoms the patient reports to you. Playtester feedback is what the game is saying to you about the alignment between your design values and your player experience. The team's observations of the playtest, and what the playtesters do and say, are the evidence considered to diagnose your game's design. Just like the medical profession, it takes time to accurately diagnose problems, and treatments can run the gamut from "take two aspirin and call me in the morning" to complex surgery.

Figure 12.1   Evaluating is the fourth phase of the iterative cycle.

Reviewing Playtest Results

To get started with evaluation, think back to the questions posed in the prototype. Was the prototype exploring the play experience? If so, the evaluation should be focused on that aspect of the game. If the prototype was an exploration of art, code, or other elements around play, then make sure the evaluation focuses accordingly. The important thing here is to focus the evaluation on what was present and under evaluation.

Next, consider the answers that emerged from the playtests. This isn't always as easy as it might seem. With the prototype, playtest notes, and documentation in hand, the team should review what happened during the playtest. This can happen in a couple of ways: individually review and collectively discuss, or collectively review and discuss. However the team decides, everyone should focus on thinking about issues in a structured way, focusing on what, where, why, and the takeaway.

- *What:* Instead of thinking in broad terms—it was awesome, players had fun, the game was too hard, and so on—break down feedback and observations from the playtest into small moments that highlight the good and the bad of the game, its design, and how that was implemented in the prototype. Focus on what actually happened, not your or a teammate's analysis. Did a playtester not know how to use a particular action? Did the players consistently laugh or get frustrated at a particular moment? Focus on the evidence, and not yet the team's interpretations.

- *Where:* An important aspect of evaluating playtest feedback is knowing the context within which the moment was observed. Sometimes knowing the specific moment within the gameplay is important. Was the player trying to achieve a particular goal? Were they dealing with a particularly challenging moment in the game? Other times, problems arise around aspects of the game not yet implemented, like someone complaining about the plainness of the game when art direction hasn't been implemented.

- *Why:* For each of these moments, diagnose why you think it happened. If the player didn't know how to use a particular action, was it because the control scheme wasn't explained? Did the game not provide the experience hoped? Or did the action work in an unexpected way? Try to understand the underlying causes of the feedback on the prototype.

- *Takeaway:* The most important thing in reviewing the playtest is coming to a consensus on what the playtest reveals about the game's design. Getting to a specific comment like "the paddle controls are too loose," "players seem to jump instead of climb," or "the object-oriented storytelling is not introducing the secondary characters well" is what to aim for. This requires a certain degree of diagnostic skill for converting player feedback into decisions for revising the design of the game. Again, this is a lot like what doctors do when reviewing a patient's symptoms. The feedback may be evidence of something, but the underlying cause still needs to be diagnosed. This diagnosis is especially important when players suggest a specific design change, like, "I think you should make the score bigger on the screen." Instead of just translating this into the design task "make score bigger," try to understand why the playtesters suggested that. This is like a patient coming into the doctor's office saying, "I have a sprained ankle." The patient is diagnosing themselves, but the doctor needs to understand why the patient thinks they have a sprained ankle and look at all of the evidence before the doctor makes a diagnosis. What are the symptoms? It could be that the playtesters are saying that they don't see the score changing—or that they think the score is important and that in the fast pacing of the game they miss it. A bigger score might not solve the problem. Instead, other forms of feedback about player performance might make more sense, such as a screen between matches emphasizing the score and player achievements.

Think of yourself as a doctor of game design. There are various ways to consider this feedback from a design perspective. But most importantly, think about it in relation to your design values. This could be an opportunity to bring your game more in line with them. If the team is not careful, this process can turn into a scene from the TV program *House*, where Hugh Laurie's character berates and talks over his colleagues. So be careful about keeping things constructive during the evaluation process.

What to Think About

Some of the most important aspects to evaluate about a game's design are the places where design values translate into player experience. Being able to think about how players are or aren't getting the intended experience often has to do with a combination of the implementation of basic game design tools and the mechanisms by which players engage with the game. Thinking through each of these is important during the evaluation of the prototype and playtest. Before starting this review, it is important to think back to the design motivations and related design values established for the game. Taking the time to refresh the team's hopes by looking back over the design values will help focus the team's evaluation of the playtest.

- *Actions:* Do the players understand what they can and cannot do when playing the game? Are the controls intuitive or easy to learn and master? Are players able to develop skill around the core actions of the game?

- *Goals:* Do the players understand the game's goals? Are players creating their own goals in addition to or instead of? How is the game communicating the goals? Are the goals supported by the actions, objects, playspace, story, and so on?

- *Challenge:* Is the game providing the right degree and kind of difficulty or push-back? Does the game keep players engaged? If the challenge comes from the subject, is it coming through during the play experience?

- *Information spaces:* Are players able to make sense of the information provided by the game? Is there too much information given the pace of the play experience? Too little? Are players missing out on essential information?

- *Feedback:* Is the loop between player actions and the game's response clear? Can players interpret the outcomes of their actions with confidence?

- *Decision-making:* Are players able to make decisions about how to pursue their goals and have the experience they seek?

- *Player perceptions:* Does the way the playspace is represented support the intended play experience?

- *Contexts of play:* Is the place where the game is played having an impact on player experience? How about the time of day? What else is going on around the play session?

- *Takeaways:* Is the game conveying the intended message, concept, or experience?

- *Emotions:* What emotions arise during play? Do they correspond to those hoped for?

Interpreting Observations

Once the team has captured the key observations of the playtest, it is time to think about what these observations say about the game's design. This breaks down into two key categories: strengths and weaknesses, or even better, intended and unintended strengths and weaknesses. Often, players will respond to things in the game that you hadn't anticipated or even intended to be part of the play experience. Take careful note of these moments for analysis. Intended strengths hopefully relate to the design values but may directly contradict them. Keeping them in mind as you discuss what you saw is very helpful, as it gives you another marker for evaluation.

Sometimes player responses that seem negative are actually what you were hoping to achieve. Maybe players said the game is too hard, which was intentional, or maybe they lament it is too short, but that was by design. With innovative design, there can often be a tension between player expectations and the design motivations and design values of the game. This particularly comes into play around genre conventions and the expectations players develop around how games will play. Bending and breaking convention is a hallmark of experimental and innovative game design, but it can also be a sign of poorly conceived design. Finding the right balance between intentional innovation and design oversights is a real challenge. Design values are always helpful in reminding the team of what they hope to achieve with a game and whether or not player expectations are inline or outside the focus of the game.

We taught a course in game design to a group of high school students once, and after a playtest, one of them said their playtesters "played it wrong." Of course, that's one way of looking at the weaknesses in your game that are surfaced in a playtest, but if they played it "wrong," it's likely that there's something in the design that needs to be addressed. Or, it could be that the way players played it is right, and perhaps more intuitive and fun than the way it was designed to be played. Either way, these revelations in a playtest are invaluable. This sounds counterintuitive—players exposing weaknesses is gold—but it's true. When it becomes apparent something is not working, you can fix it. A playtest helps give clarity about what works and what doesn't. And it shows the path for improving the game.

As with the strengths of the game, look for intended and unintended problems. Some of that will be anticipated, but there will inevitably be concerns previously not seen. And that is a good thing, as it is always better to find out while problems can still be addressed. Taking the time to focus on the strengths and weaknesses in your prototype will help get to the next step: refining the game.

Conceptualizing Solutions

We have all this feedback now. How do we turn it into actual changes we want to make to the game's design? This is where we return to conceptualize, the first step in the iterative design cycle. Many of the techniques are the same as outlined in Chapter 9, "Conceptualizing Your Game"—brainstorming, checking in on design motivations, and design values—but the context is different. With a full cycle of prototyping, playtesting, and evaluation complete, we now have seen some aspect of our game through our players' eyes. We have experienced what works and what doesn't in the game's design, or at least the aspects of it captured in the prototype. Because of this, we have much more specific feedback to interpret, and we might need more time to identify what we need to change in our prototype. So we recommend a six-part approach to making decisions about revisions to your game, whether it be early in the design process or later in the playable prototype phase: review, incubate, brainstorm, decide, document, and schedule.

Review

To make sure everyone knows what issues are being worked on, a two-step review process is always helpful. First, to review the strengths and weaknesses found during the playtest, make sure the team is clear on them and that there are no misinterpretations. The second step is to revisit the team's design values to make sure that the way we translate the feedback into actual design tasks helps us get closer to the values that we identified in the beginning. Returning to the design values at every step of the way is like tuning an instrument or balancing the tires on a car so that we can move forward with them in mind as we make decisions about the game's design.

Incubate

With the strengths, weaknesses, and design values in mind, we then mull the specific issue over. Sometimes the issues are interconnected, making a solution that much more complicated to determine. Often, we begin with some time for everyone to think through the problems on their own, writing all their ideas for a given issue. This is a great way to let everyone think about solutions. How long everyone thinks on their own can vary. Sometimes we give ourselves 10 to 15 minutes. Sometimes we give ourselves a couple of days. Some people incubate best while running, or napping, or washing dishes. It really depends on the particular issues, where the game is in the design process, and other variables. The general rule, though, is the bigger the issue, the more time it can take to solve.

Brainstorm

Once the incubation phase is over, we gather to brainstorm ideas for strengthening our game. Capturing the ideas in a way everyone can see is always helpful. If in person, use a whiteboard, chalkboard, or a computer screen everyone can see. If remote, use a shared document, virtual whiteboard, or other shared method. These discussions should be inclusive, letting everyone share their ideas. (Remember the brainstorm rules?) Once all the ideas for each issue under discussion have been heard, it is time to start thinking about which solutions are best for the next prototype. Often, ideas combine or even lead to new ideas. Make sure all these are captured, too.

Here are a couple pointers for brainstorming solutions to your design. You'll likely come up with new ideas at this point to prototype and explore. That's great, but be careful. This is when you run the risk of overloading your design. It's key to identify the things that you absolutely need to do for your next prototype and playtest and the ones that are lower in priority. Sometimes the ideas that emerge here are great, but they're not perfect for the current game. So write them down, and save them for a future project.

Decide

With all the options discussed and their merits weighed, the team should make decisions about which solutions to implement. How do you know which are the right choices? Sometimes it is obvious, and sometimes it is really hard to figure out. But always keep the design values in mind, and let them help decide what is best for the game. It is better to make a decision than to spend too much time debating among the team. Getting to the next implementable prototype is much better than the perfect idea, so put emphasis on actionable decisions that are in the spirit of the design values whenever possible.

Document

With decisions made, it is time to divide tasks among the team to realize the solutions. First, capture the revisions that need to be made to the game design document. Then translate this into a series of tasks. Make certain everyone knows what they are responsible for. Using a tracking spreadsheet similar to what we described in Chapter 7, "Game Design Documentation," is helpful for this.

Schedule

Once everyone knows what they should be doing, the team should agree on a schedule for getting to the next prototype. This may be a couple of hours, it may be a couple of days, or it may even be a couple of months, depending on how big the game is, where you are in the process, and other commitments team members have outside the project. Again, a tracking spreadsheet is really helpful in working through all the details.

Summary

Evaluation is one of the more challenging and complex steps in the iterative game design process, but it's also where your game gets better. It's important to take your time, review the playtest feedback, and discuss and diagnose with your team. Consider your basic game design tools and the mechanisms by which players engage with your game as you do, and brainstorm solutions before jumping to conclusions. Of course, everything is guided by a review of your design values and documented so that you can stay on the path to finishing and releasing your game.

Following are the steps to evaluating your design:

1. *Review:* Look at the strengths and weaknesses exposed in the playtest, and review the design values to make sure the design is on track.

2. *Incubate:* With the strengths, weaknesses, and design values in mind, we take some time to consider the feedback and possible solutions.

3. *Brainstorm:* Brainstorm ideas for strengthening the game, using techniques from Chapter 9.

4. *Decide:* With all the options discussed and their merits weighed, the team should make decisions about which solutions to implement.

5. *Document:* Capture the revisions that need to be made to the design document and schematics, and break them down into tasks for the task list.

6. *Schedule:* Once everyone knows what to do, the team should agree on a schedule for getting to the next prototype.

CHAPTER 13

MOVING FROM DESIGN TO PRODUCTION

The first time through the iterative game design cycle isn't the end of the game design process—it is just the beginning. How many times a game needs to move through the process differs from game to game and team to team. And knowing when the design phase is finished is not always easy to determine. In this chapter we look at some of the diverse ways game designers move through the iterative process and think about the ways to tell when the design is complete.

"Ever tried. Ever failed. No matter. Try Again. Fail again. Fail better."[1]

These words of wisdom from Samuel Beckett sum up the most important lesson iteration teaches us—creativity is more about failure than it is success. That's the power of iterative design—it is a set of processes that embrace failure, and in time, use failure as the raw materials for creating good games. When we use the iterative cycle, we are posing a question that we theorize during the conceptualizing phase, we give form to during the prototyping phase, we answer during the playtesting phase, and we interpret during the evaluation phase. This leads to the next question, and thus, the next iterative loop. Sometimes these loops are trying again and again to answer the same question. Sometimes an iterative loop satisfactorily answers the question, and so the next iterative loop can move on to a different aspect of the game.

While the phases of conceptualize, prototype, playtest, and evaluate are pretty universal, there are many different ways to approach how the cycles of iteration actually play out. To show this range—including a case where the iterative approach is barely used at all—we have four case studies demonstrating different approaches to the iterative game design process. Each of the four examples shows how different the iterative process can be depending on the design values, the kind of technological tools used, and most importantly, the kind of play experience the gamemakers wanted to provide. These include Local No. 12's *The Metagame*, Die Gute Fabrik's *Johann Sebastian Joust*, Tale of Tales' The Path, and anna anthropy's *Queers in Love at the End of the World*.

Case Study: The Metagame

The Metagame (see Figure 13.1), a party game we both worked on, took many trips around the iterative cycle, in the process becoming several very different final games—from a game show to a conference game to a party game to an art project and finally, back to a party game. Originating in a design for an MTV game show by Frank Lantz and Eric Zimmerman, The Metagame became a game platform of sorts, leading to a new life as it exists now, a party game by Local No. 12, our company with Eric Zimmerman. Our first redesign of the original idea was to create a collectible card game for the 2011 Game Developers Conference (GDC). We wanted to create a game that fit naturally into the kinds of activities already present at GDC. One thing all of us had noticed was that people spent a lot of time between conference sessions and late into the evenings debating the merits of different videogames. So we looked for a way to develop a game around this already-present behavior. We spent about six months iterating on the gameplay, the art direction, the wording on the rules, and even how we would distribute the cards to conference attendees. We ran playtests at our respective schools, at small conferences and with small groups of friends—any opportunity we could find, really. The efforts paid off, as the conference game version of The Metagame caught on at GDC, with more than 3,000 people playing by the end of the conference.

---

1   From Beckett's novel, *Worstward Ho*, 1983.

Figure 13.1   A sampling of The Metagame prototypes created over the years.

At the end of the week, we launched a Kickstarter campaign to produce a full deck that we released a year later. This required a lot more than just taking the existing cards and packaging them in a box. The conference play sessions proved to be a large-scale playtest for us, allowing us to learn all sorts of things about the information on the cards, the approach to images, the kinds of conversations that emerged from the cards, and so on. All this informed the revisions we made to the game. We also had to rethink the game and its content to fit different play contexts. Instead of playing in conference halls and bars, we now had to design for living rooms, classrooms, and other spaces. We revised the basic game structure and began adding new play modes that were more conducive to smaller groups and contexts. This led to a period of tight iterative loops around the play modes and how they were captured in the rules booklet. While this was going on, we worked on new card ideas and illustrations.

After launching the boxed version of The Metagame Videogame Edition, we were approached to do a project for the art magazine *Esopus*. We decided to create another version of The Metagame, this time expanding the content from videogames to all kinds of culture—from film to fashion, literature to fine art, and beyond. This led to a new phase of iteration around broadening the content, but also making sure the play modes made sense to the new audience as well as rethinking the size of the cards and how they might be bound into a magazine.

The response from *Esopus* readers was great, so again, we gained the courage to run another Kickstarter campaign to release a boxed version with the broader range of content. The current version has ten games you can play with the deck—like a traditional deck of cards where you can play anything from poker to go fish. As with the previous versions, we iterated content and the games you can play with the deck hundreds of times, first using index cards and then working with a small-run Internet printer for a more genuine card feel. We also playtested with various age groups and cultural backgrounds, trying to get a good mix of content in the game that could appeal to an intergenerational audience—your family, after a holiday meal. Much of the content was inspired by these playtests, as people naturally recommended this or that television show, fashion design, or art piece.[2]

The Metagame, then, was an iterative process that spanned five years and involved different content, audiences, and forms. While the play modes, audiences, and content changed, the primary goal of the game—provide a playful structure for talking about pop culture—never wavered. Staying focused on this goal allowed us to have a clear set of goals for each successive version of the game and helped us maintain the spirit of the play experience even when almost everything else changed.

Case Study: *Johann Sebastian Joust*

Another party game, *Johann Sebastian Joust* (see Figure 13.2), had a decidedly faster path to completed design. In fact, the core play experience evolved over just 48 hours during the

Figure 13.2 *Johann Sebastian Joust*. Photo by Elliot Trinidad. Used with permission of the IndieCade International Festival of Independent Games.

---

2   For a more detailed look at the iteration on the game's visual design, see John's essay, "How the Metagame Cards Went from a Sports Card-Like to Dictionary Chic." www.heyimjohn.com/metagame-card-design/. 2015.

2011 Nordic Game Jam. Despite this fast design process, Douglas Wilson, the game's designer, describes the process as one with roots in a much longer exploration of motion-sensitive controllers. Douglas and his colleagues learned some valuable lessons experimenting with motion controllers that, at the time, may have felt like failed projects, but in the end, were just the right experimentation to help Douglas create *J.S. Joust*. The technical experience and knowledge of how motion-sensitive controllers could be used found its way to the game jam, with the interest in creating a game that emphasized player interaction without the mediation of the screen—a videogame without video. The discovery of the core game came from experimentation with the technology during the jam, with a focus on making a game that was multiplayer and used music as a core element instead of visuals on a screen.

The original intent was to try to create a racing game, where players would need to race in slow-motion so they wouldn't jostle their controllers. As Douglas and his collaborators were testing the sensitivity of the controllers, a happy accident occurred. He describes it:

> "The breakthrough moment soon followed when Nils and I happened to find ourselves walking towards one another from opposite sides of the room. Staring at one another, face-to-face, each of us silently hatched the same mischievous plan; as soon as we were in range, we shoved one another in an attempt to make the other lose. In that one instant, it became clear to us that the game we actually wanted to make was one that involved an antagonistic duel. In a certain sense, it is debatable whether I even "designed" *J.S. Joust*. As I see it, Nils and I pulled the game out of the social ether, collaboratively."[3]

This is a great example of how design and playtesting are intertwined, and often, how one might simply start playing with a technology to find the fun in the game. Douglas calls this approach "toy-centric" design. By exploring the play potential of a new piece of technology, motion controllers, Douglas sought out a way to turn those controllers into a toy around which to build a game. By serendipitously homing in on players simultaneously balancing their own controller while trying to jostle that of their opponents, Douglas and his collaborator had found that perfect toy around which to design a game. In the ensuing 24 hours, Douglas coded up the core play experience.

For a couple years, the game remained more or less the same—a game that required setup and oversight by Douglas or someone else who could provide the basic instruction and technical support to run the game—in some cases, up to 16 players, each with their own controller. These events became playtests for the core game, as Douglas was more often than not there to set up and run the game. This allowed small refinements to the play and the game software.

Several years later, *J.S. Joust* was released on the PlayStation in the local multiplayer compilation *Sportsfriends*, with much the basic design developed during that initial 48 hours. Of course,

---

3   Excerpted from page 120 of Doug Wilson's PhD thesis, "Designing for the Pleasures of Disputation—or—How to Make Friends by Trying to Kick Them!", 2012.

it wasn't as easy as simply porting the code from the game jam to work on the PlayStation platform. Changes to the technology (from Wiimote to PS Move controller) and subtle refinements in player feedback were implemented, as was building an infrastructure for players to be able to run the game for themselves. The biggest challenges came in the development of a stand-alone system for people to run the game themselves. This required the development of an interface and menu system for teaching players how to play and to walk them through the setup of the game. Designing and implementing this took two years, an order of magnitude longer than the initial design.

With *J.S. Joust*, we see a game that seemed to come together almost by magic in a short period of time. The reality, though, is that the year or more of experimentation around motion controls before the game jam and the two-plus years of design and development of a stand-alone version of the game afterwards were equally important. So while the Hollywood version of the *J.S. Joust* story might focus on those first 48 hours, the reality is that it took four years to create, despite that moment of design clarity at the Nordic Game Jam.

Case Study: *The Path*

Tale of Tales' *The Path* took a very different approach to iteration than the previous two examples. Instead of starting with an idea around gameplay or an interest in finding the fun in a piece of technology, Auriea Harvey and Michaël Samyn began with a setting (a path in the forest), a story (*Little Red Riding Hood*), and a genre (horror). All of these design motivations came together in the process of writing a grant proposal to support the development of the game—funding being a constraint we hardly address in this book, but a real one, and part of any development process. The funding they received was modest, so they made a choice early on to use tools with which they were comfortable and an engine into which they had already put some work. A previous project, *The Endless Forest*, provided the environment rendering system, and a partially completed project, *Drama Princess*, was shifted to serve as the character behavior manager.

With a setting, story, genre, and tools sorted out, there was still a lot left to think through with the game. An important inspiration came from the music of Kris Force and Jarboe, the musicians they would work with to create the game's soundtrack. Their music helped solidify the mood and emotional atmosphere that Auriea and Michaël wanted to capture in the game.

This is where *The Path* diverges from the previous examples (see Figure 13.3). To playtest the emotional effect of the game, its environments, art, and sound needed to be well developed. This meant it would be difficult to playtest without fairly advanced work already in place in modeling and texturing the environments and coding in the event sounds and score. So they focused early design cycles on creating a navigable world without much in the way of gameplay. Testing for emotional response sometimes involves bringing much of the art and media together in the prototype. Auriea and Michaël don't always playtest with outside playtesters, but for *The Path*, one of the goals was to appeal to gamers and nongamers alike—and to do so, playtesting was the only way to determine whether that was working. In Figure 13.3, you will see how closely Auriea and Michaël observed their playtesters, with Auriea sketching players as they played through the game.

Figure 13.3   A sketch drawn by Auriea Harvey of a playtester for *The Path*.

The engine they used to create the game, Quest 3D, also provided an unusual twist in the iterative process, blurring the lines between prototyping and playtesting due to the "live coding" nature of the development environment. If the behavior of a character was modified, it happened in real time, as if they were living beings inside the world with shifting motivations. A tweak to the color of the sky, or the scale of the flora would immediately take place, shifting other elements in the environment along with it. So in essence, while they were prototyping the game, Auriea and Michaël were also playtesting it—playing in a world and making changes to it in real time, similar to the way one might play with dolls. This allowed for a very fluid movement between playable prototyping and internal playtesting. Indeed, the process allowed for a lot of design decisions emerging from Auriea and Michaël's playtesting.

Eventually, after much internal and external playtesting of the fully realized game world, gameplay emerged. They created a series of adventure-game style puzzles and object collection goals that they designed and implemented. The gameplay changed radically after they heard the completed soundtrack by Kris Force and Jarboe. Auriea and Michaël realized that the game actions and the music didn't quite go together. So they removed many of the small puzzle-solving tasks they had designed and made the game more about exploration and discovery.

This is a great example of sticking with your design values: having a sense of the kind of emotional tones you want your game to generate and being willing to "kill your babies" when it's just not working. The iterative process of *The Path* is one that we probably wouldn't recommend to our students for their first game. Taking so long to get to a playable prototype and playtest can involve spending many hours of art production work that ends up on the cutting room floor. But, by the time *The Path* project started, Auriea and Michaël had clocked thousands of hours in previous projects that fed into the development process and helped them gauge scope. So while we would say, "don't try this at home," we think that this is an exceptional example of designing for emotional effect and being true to design values.

Case Study: *Queers in Love at the End of the World*

The final case study is anna anthropy's Twine game *Queers in Love at the End of the World* (see Figure 13.4). Though an experienced game designer, able to work in a variety of development environments herself, anna was attracted to the low barrier-to-entry of Twine—the tool allows pretty much anyone with access to a computer and basic English language literacy to create games. It was important to anna to create her Twine games without having to resort to any programming or visual design work so that her games could serve as models for aspiring gamemakers. This established one important design value for the game—showcasing the accessibility of Twine as a game creation tool.

A little earlier, anna encountered S. Astrid Bin's Twine game *PANIC!*, which had an interesting feature—a timer on all player decisions. anna thought this was a clever way to add challenge to the game, as it pushed on the core action of all Twine games—reading comprehension. Since the feature required programming, anna tucked away the idea for later use.

At some point, someone released an open source code snippet for adding timers in Twine, so anna felt it was okay for her to make use of it in a game. With this in hand, anna saw that an upcoming Ludum Dare challenge was creating a 10-second game. (Ludum Dares are 48-hour game jams, each centered around a theme.) This inspired anna to find a use for the Twine timer. Though she didn't participate in the Ludum Dare, she decided she would create a game that lasted 10 seconds—a great example of designing around constraint! She also decided she wanted the game to use the time constraint to create a social pressure rather than a test of skill

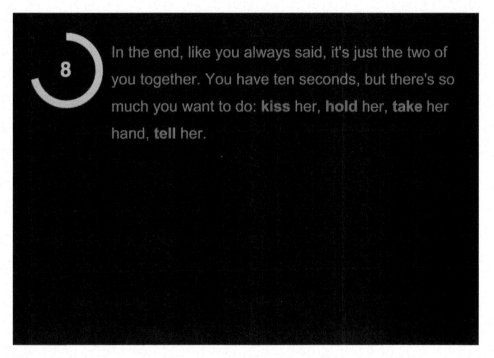

Figure 13.4 Screenshot from *Queers in Love at the End of the World*.

or puzzle-solving. anna was in a long-distance relationship at the time and felt she never had enough time with her partner. She began thinking about how she was always in a position of having to make the most of the time she had, which led her to have to make decisions about what she really needed when with her partner and what she was able to give her partner in return.

From there, she came up with the game's theme: a queer couple with only 10 seconds together before the world ends. She quickly came up with the first set of choices in the branching structure of Twine: "kiss her, hold her, take her hand, tell her." She then began working on the paths that emerged from the "kiss her" choice. Each choice begat more choices, until anna found herself writing hundreds of decision points. The game's poetic feel in part comes from the raw, impulsive nature of each decision point and the increasing franticness as the short time passes. To help maintain this feeling, anna kept her editing to a minimum, only revising decision points that didn't feel quite right or in the spirit of her own experiences as a queer woman.

Because the game was so much about a sense of urgency but also her own feelings about the pressures of time on love, playtesting differed from previous examples. anna focused the playtesting on making sure there were no technical problems such as the timer not always working or dead links in the branching narrative. anna was not looking for ideas for making the game better or input on adding content to the game. She simply wanted to make sure the game was playable as she designed it.

anna's concepting, design, and playtesting certainly unfolded over a period of months, but it lacks the cycle of loops the other case studies used as part of their design. *Queers in Love at the End of the World* only tangentially fits into the ideas of iterative game design as captured in this book. This is why we've used it as the final case study—to point out that not all games require a full iterative process to be created. In the same way it was important to anna to use Twine in a way that someone with game design or programming experience might, so too is it important to point out that a deep knowledge of iterative processes isn't a requirement for making games. In the same light, having the time and resources to devote to the iterative design process is not something that can be assumed. Sometimes all we have is a short period of time to work on a game.

How to Know When the Design Is Done

As the chapters in Part III, "Practice," make pretty clear, the iterative design process is one that takes a lot of time, patience, and energy. But it is also just the beginning: it is the design of the game. There is still another phase to go: production. Production is when the game's design, technical planning, and other related preparatory work is complete and what is left is building the final game. It's true, the team has likely already built the game a number of times during the design process through the repeated loops of the iterative cycle. But that was all in the service of conceptualizing, prototyping, playtesting, and evaluating the game's design. It wasn't about building a solid, stress-tested piece of software.

The rule of iterative design is fail faster. During iteration, the team is thinking about the final game but avoids getting hung up on doing things right. You know you will fail, so why waste time trying to make everything perfect? But in production, the opposite is true. Things have to be just right to keep them from failing—the team must create bullet-proof server code for handling the Internet traffic in some games or debugging collision detection code to withstand all the things players will try in others.

This brings up one of the more challenging aspects of game design—knowing when to phase out of iteration and design and into production. What are some signs that it's time to move into production? How does the team know when to stop building and testing prototypes and start building the final game that people will see and play?

- *Complete game prototype:* For one, the team has made at least one complete game prototype. This should include all of the game's features, including the core gameplay, interface elements like the menus, scores and buttons in the game, the art direction, and sound direction. In other words, all of the elements that make up the experience are decided on and locked.

  Once a fully tested complete game prototype has been tested, it should be pretty clear what issues remain open. There are no forks in the road ahead around big design decisions. There shouldn't be any difficult decisions about the sound or visuals, and there won't be questions about which platform the game will be published on. What's left is to simply complete the unfinished elements in your game.

- *Playtesting:* Knowing whether or not the complete game prototype is proving out the game's design takes plenty of playtesting and refinement. To really be certain, the team will have tested with people from your target audience. Their feedback is the litmus test for the game and how close it is to expressing the design values. New player and experienced player playtests are also really helpful. The new player playtests help you understand the learnability of your game. The experienced player playtests let you know the game holds up to repeated plays, that it doesn't lose its fun or become too easy to master over repeated plays.

- *Art direction:* Another important consideration is the visual and sound design of the game. The team has examples of the direction for the art and sound. This doesn't mean all the assets are created. For example, if the game has a lot of different types of dinosaurs, this might mean a few sample dinosaurs are already designed, like a stegosaurus, a velociraptor, a pterodactyl, but the team has only placeholder art for the tyrannosaurus rex, the brontosaurus, and the triceratops. Once the team tests all of the dinosaur code and their interactions in the game, there is still work remaining to the final models, textures, and so on. This is production.

- *Code:* The team has all of the code written and tested in the complete game prototype, but there might be some optimizing to do, some cleaning up and making sure it's well commented, and of course there will be work to integrate the final art and sound assets. There will be some final testing to do to squash any bugs in the code. It is often a wise decision to step back and create a plan for the final software that will guide the production. By creating diagrams of how the code works, how the various libraries interact, it is likely that the team will find ways to really optimize the code and make production time faster than it would otherwise be.

- *Text:* If there's any writing in the game, most of it will be written and tested in the complete game prototype, but you'll want to make final edits and check for accuracy and continuity.

- *Design values:* The team will have reviewed the complete game prototype against the design values. How close is the complete game prototype in realizing the design values? When players playtest the complete game prototype, is it hitting all the design values? Is there anything that could be added or taken away from the game to express those values more strongly and cleanly?

- *Documentation:* One of the clearest indications that a game is ready to move from design into production is when the game design document and accompanying schematics capture the full experience of the game. These should serve as the blueprints for production, including detailed information on the visual and sound production requirements of the game, and accurate schematics for interfaces and menus.

If you've hit all these points, then the team is probably ready to move out of iteration into production.

Getting Ready for Production

Once the team is ready to move out of the iterative cycle of concepting, prototyping, playtesting, and evaluation and into final production on the game, the team will want to create a production plan. The production process can be a real slog if not prepared for properly. The honeymoon phase of the design process is over. All the interesting decisions in the process have been made, and now it's just time to get it done.

Once the game design document, schematics, or any other materials are reviewed and up-to-date, the next step is planning out production. This is often handled by creating a new version of the task tracking spreadsheet discussed in Chapter 7, "Game Design Documentation."

Who is going to be part of the production team? It will likely be the same people who were part of the design process. But if you need any special skills, like someone to come in and help you do tasks that don't involve creative decisions, like resizing graphics or copyediting final text, you should bring them on.

Once you have the **who** of your production team figured out, it's time to identify and write down **what** they will be doing (see Figure 13.5). For *Ping!* we've been keeping a document to keep track of what we need to accomplish for our prototypes and who will do them. We also identify if there were any "dependencies," or tasks that can't be accomplished without another one being finished first.

PROTOTYPE	TASK	PERSON	TIME	DEPENDENCIES	NOTES
Core v3	**Basic elements - test with 5 designers**				
3 days	Interface to tweak paddle and ball physics	CM+AM	4 hours		
	Final Art Direction	JS	2 hours		
	Asset generation	JS+LB	8 hours	ALL: Review final art	
	Swappable paddle assets implemented	CM+AM	4 hours	JS+LB: Assets	
	Final sounds selected	JS	2 hours	ALL: Review final sound	
	Sounds implemented	CM	2 hours	JS: Sound selects	
	Scoring system - implement	CM	2 hours		Sets to matches
	Controller final prototype/test	BB	6 hours	ALL: Internal playtesting	
Complete v1	**Complete game playtest - test with 5 people**				
5 days	Final revisions to paddle and ball physics	CM+AM	4 hours	ALL: Internal playtesting	
	Controller v1	BB	8 hours		
	Visual asset revisions	JS+LB	4 hours	Designer test	
	Visual assets implemented	CM	3 hours	JS+LB: Visual asset revisions	
	Sound revisions	JS	2 hours		

Figure 13.5 A production spreadsheet.

Finally, as with any task, having clear deadlines is essential. Identify **who** is doing **what** by **when**. Without deadlines, nothing would get done. You will probably need to adjust deadlines as the team goes, especially for your first few games. It's human nature to underestimate the amount of time it takes to get something done. Try multiplying time estimates by 2 (that works for John), and then adjust this number as needed. Whatever formula, do try to set some deadlines in the process.

In addition to deadlines, you should set regular meetings with the team. While it seems like there's not much more to discuss because all of the open questions in the design process have been answered, there are still going to be things that come up and need the team's attention.

Regular meetings, whether they're weekly or more frequent, also keep you honest. How much did you accomplish in the past week? If there's nothing to report, that's a pretty clear indicator that you need to set aside more time to work on the game.

Considering the **who**, **what**, and **when** in your production process, and keeping track of these, will help you get to the finish line with your game. It's probably going to involve a lot of work and some late nights, but the reward of seeing your game out in the world getting played makes it all worth it.

Summary

All of the videogames we've talked about in this series were developed by small teams or individuals. Making videogames is challenging, and it takes a lot of practice. Start small, and don't be afraid of failure. It's just part of the process. Iteration is the way to take just a small kernel of an idea and grow it into a game. It just so happens that learning how to make games is its own iterative loop. Dive in, make a game, put it out there, and then make another one. We look forward to playing them.

Your game design is complete, you are ready to stop iterating, and you are ready to move into production when you have

- Created a complete game prototype
- Successfully playtested with target audience members
- Successfully playtested with new players
- Successfully playtested with experienced players
- Met your design values
- Solid art direction
- A strong code base for your target platform
- Most of the final text for the game
- An up-to-date game design document

WORKS CITED

Introduction

anthropy, anna, and Naomi Clark. *A Game Design Vocabulary: Exploring the Foundational Principles Behind Good Game Design*. Boston, MA: Addison-Wesley Professional, 2014.

Fullerton, Tracy. *Game Design Workshop: A Playcentric Guide to Creating Innovative Games*, 3rd edition. Bacon Raton, FL: CRC Press, 2015.

Salen, Katie, and Eric Zimmerman. *Rules of Play: Game Design Fundamentals*. Cambridge, MA: The MIT Press, 2003.

Chapter 1

anthropy, anna. *Queers in Love at the End of the World*. (browser game), 2014.

anthropy, anna, *Rise of the Videogame Zinesters: How Freaks, Normals, Amateurs, Artists, Dreamers, Drop-Outs, Queers, Housewives, and People Like You Are Taking Back an Art Form*. New York: Seven Stories Press, 2012.

Atari, Inc. *Pong*. Atari, Inc. (arcade), 1972.

The Chinese Room, *Dear Esther*. The Chinese Room (Macintosh), 2012.

Costikyan, Greg. "I Have No Words & I Must Design," *Interactive Fantasy*. No. 2, 1994.

Exquisite Corpse. Traditional parlor game.

Hickey, Dave. "The Heresy of Zone Defense," in *Air Guitar*: *Essays on Art & Democracy*. Los Angeles, CA: Art Issues Press, 1997.

Hopscotch. Traditional schoolyard game.

Meadows, Donella. *Thinking in Systems: A Primer*. White River Junction, VT: Chelsea Green Publishing, 2008.

Mojang, *Minecraft*. Mojang (Windows), 2009.

Salen, Katie, and Eric Zimmerman. *Rules of Play: Game Design Fundamentals*. Cambridge, MA: The MIT Press, 2003.

Soccer. Traditional sport.

Chapter 2

Atari, Inc. *Pong*. Atari, Inc. (Arcade game), 1972.

Burke, Liam. Dog Eat Dog. Liam Burke (tabletop roleplaying game), 2013.

Cardboard Computer, *Kentucky Route Zero*. Cardboard Computer (Steam), 2013–2014.

Chess. Traditional boardgame.

Coco & Co., *Way*. Coco & Co (Macintosh), 2012.

Costikyan, Greg. *Uncertainty in Games*. Cambridge, MA: The MIT Press, 2015.

Cziksentmihalyi, Mihaly, *Flow: The Psychology of Optimal Experience*. New York: Harper Perennial Modern Classics, 2008.

Darts. Traditional sport.

Foddy, Bennett. *Speed Chess*. Bennett Foddy (site-specific software), 2014.

Friedhoff, Jane, *Slam City Oracles*. Jane Friedhoff (Macintosh), 2015.

The Fullbright Company, *Gone Home*. Majesco Entertainment (Steam), 2013.

Go. Traditional boardgame.

Hide and Seek, *Tiny Games*. Hide and Seek (iOS), 2013.

Key, Ed, and David Kanaga, *Proteus*. Curve Digital (Steam), 2013.

Klamer, Reuben. The Game of Life. Milton Bradley (boardgame), 1960.

Leacock, Matt, Pandemic. Z-Man Games (boardgame), 2007.

Messhof, *Flywrench*. Messhof (Steam), 2015.

Naismith, James, Basketball. (sport), 1891.

Ninja. Traditional street game.

Nuchallenger, *Treachery in Beatdown City*. Nuchallenger (Macintosh), unreleased.

Number None, Inc. *Braid*. Number None Inc. (Xbox 360), 2008.

Nutt, Christian. "Road to the IGF: Lea Schüonfelder and Peter Lu's Perfect Woman" *Gamasutra*. February 24, 2014.

Pachinko. Traditional arcade game.

Pinball. Traditional arcade game.

Poker. Traditional cardgame.

Porpentine, *Howling Dogs*. Porpentine (browser game), 2012.

Roulette. Traditional casino game.

Salen, Katie, and Eric Zimmerman. *Rules of Play: Game Design Fundamentals*. Cambridge, MA: The MIT Press, 2003.

Schüoenfelder, Lea, and Peter Lu, *Perfect Woman*. Lea Schüoenfelder and Peter Lu (Macintosh), 2012.

Scott, Leslie. Jenga. Pokonobe Associates (puzzle game), 1983.

Secret Crush, *SUNBURN!* Secret Crush (iOS), 2014.

Squinkifer, Dietrich, *Conversations We Have in My Head*. Dietrich Squinkifer (Macintosh), 2015.

Suits, Bernhard. *The Grasshopper: Games, Life and Utopia*. Tonawanda, NY: Broadview Press, 2005.

Tale of Tales, *Sunset*. Tale of Tales (Steam), 2015.

Tennis. Traditional sport.

Young Horses, Inc., *Octodad*. Young Horses, Inc. (Windows), 2010.

Chapter 3

Abbott, Eleanor, Candy Land. Milton Bradley (boardgame), 1949.

Abe, Kaho, *Hit Me*. Kaho Abe (sport), 2011.

anthropy, anna. *Queers in Love at the End of the World*. (browser game), 2014.

Blackjack. Traditional cardgame.

Captain Games, *Desert Golfing*. Captain Games (iOS), 2014.

Charades. Traditional parlor game.

The Chinese Room, *Dear Esther*. The Chinese Room (Macintosh), 2012.

Chris Sawyer Productions, *Rollercoaster Tycoon*. MicroProse (Microsoft Windows), 1999.

Coco & Co., *Way*. Coco & Co (Macintosh), 2012.

Die Gute Fabrik, *Johann Sebastian Joust*. Die Gute Fabrik (PlayStation 3), 2013.

Foddy, Bennett, *QWOP*. Bennett Foddy (browser game), 2008.

Garfield, Richard, and Lukas Litzsinger, Android: Netrunner. Fantasy Flight Games (cardgame), 2012.

Gilliam, Leah. Lesberation: Trouble in Paradise. Leah Gilliam (tabletop game), 2015.

Hasbro. Twister. Hasbro (boardgame). 1964.

Hecker, Chris, *Spy Party*. Chris Hecker (PC), Early-Access Beta.

Juul, Jesper. "The Open and the Closed: Games of Emergence and Games of Progression." In *Computer Games and Digital Cultures Conference Proceedings*, edited by Frans Mäyrä, 323–329. Tampere: Tampere University Press, 2002.

Leacock, Matt, Pandemic. Z-Man Games (boardgame), 2007.

Love, Christine, *Analogue: A Hate Story*. Christine Love (Macintosh), 2012.

Magie, Elizabeth. The Landlord's Game. 1904.

Maxis, *SimCity*. Maxis (Macintosh), 1989.

Messhof, *Nidhogg*. Messhof (Steam), 2014.

Molleindustria, *The McDonald's Videogame*. Molleindustria (browser game), 2006.

Ninja. Traditional street game.

Nintendo. *Wii Sports*, Nintendo (Nintendo Wii). 2006.

Pope, Lucas, *Papers, Please*. 3909 LLC (iOS), 2013.

Poker. Traditional cardgame.

Porpentine, *Howling Dogs*. Porpentine (browser game), 2012.

Sampat, Elizabeth, Deadbolt. Elizabeth Sampat (tabletop game), 2013.

Semi-Secret Software, *Canabalt*. Semi-Secret Software (iOS), 2009.

Sirvo LLC, *Threes*. Sirvo LLC (iOS), 2014.

Soccer. Traditional sport.

Squinkifer, Dietrich, *Coffee: A Misunderstanding*. Dietrich Squinkifer (performance game), 2014.

Tale of Tales, *The Path*. Tale of Tales (Macintosh), 2009.

Team Meat, *Super Meat Boy*. Team Meat (Xbox 360), 2010.

Thekla, Inc., *The Witness*. Number None, Inc. (PlayStation 4), 2016.

Uvula, Wild Rumpus and Venus Patrol, *Tenya Wanya Teens*. (arcade), 2013.

Valve Corporation, *Portal*. Valve Corporation (PlayStation 3), 2007.

Valve Corporation, *Portal 2*. Valve Corporation (PlayStation 3), 2011.

Chapter 4

anthropy, anna. "level design lesson: to the right, hold on tight." *Auntie Pixelante*, 2009.

anthropy, anna. *Queers in Love at the End of the World*. (browser game), 2014.

Area/code, *Drop7*. Zynga (iOS), 2008.

Arkane Studios, *Dishonored*. Bethesda Softworks (PlayStation 3), 2012.

Bartle, Richard. "Hearts, Clubs, Diamonds, Spades: Players Who Suit MUDs." 1996.

Blendo Games, *Thirty Flights of Loving*. Blendo Games (Macintosh), 2012.

Burke, Liam. Dog Eat Dog. Liam Burke (tabletop game), 2013.

Cater, John, Rob Dubbin, Eric Eve, Elizabeth Heller, Jayzee, Kazuki Mishima, Sarah Morayati, Mark Musante, Emily Short, Adam Thornton, and Ziv Wities. *Alabaster*. (Windows), 2009.

Chess. Traditional boardgame.

Crampton Smith, Gillian. "What Is Interaction Design?" in Bill Moggridge, *Designing Interactions*. Cambridge, MA: The MIT Press, 2007.

Die Gute Fabrik, *Johann Sebastian Joust*. Die Gute Fabrik (PlayStation 3), 2013.

Fischer, Reece, "The Creation of Disneyland." *The Creation of Disneyland*. N.P., 2004. Web. 14 Jan. 2013.

Friedhoff, Jane, *Slam City Oracles*. Jane Friedhoff (Macintosh), 2015.

Garfield, Richard, and Lukas Litzsinger, Android: Netrunner. Fantasy Flight Games (cardgame), 2012.

Garrett, Jesse James, *The Elements of User Experience: User-Centered Design for the Web and Beyond (2nd Edition)*. San Francisco, CA: New Riders, 2010.

Gilliam, Leah. Lesberation. (tabletop game), 2008, 2015.

Gygax, Gary, and Dave Arneson, Dungeons & Dragons. TSR (tabletop game), 1974.

Juul, Jesper, *The Art of Failure: An Essay on the Pain of Playing Video Games*. Cambridge, MA: The MIT Press, 2013.

Key, Ed, and David Kanaga, *Proteus*. Curve Digital (Steam), 2013.

Kopas, Merritt, *Hugpunx*. Merritt Kopas (browser game), 2013.

Lemarchand, Richard. "Attention, Not Immersion: Making Your Games Better with Psychology and Playtesting, the Uncharted Way," Game Developers Conference 2011.

Messhof, *Flywrench*. Messhof (Steam), 2015.

Molleindustria, *The McDonald's Videogame*. Molleindustria (browser game), 2006.

Naismith, James, Basketball. (sport), 1891.

Nintendo R&D4, *Super Mario Bros.* Nintendo (SNES), 1985.

Norman, Donald, *The Design of Everyday Things*. New York: Basic Books, 2002.

Number None, Inc. *Braid*. Number None Inc. (Xbox 360), 2008.

Parsons, Talcott, *The Structure of Social Action*. New York: Free Press, 1967.

Porpentine, *Howling Dogs*. Porpentine (browser game), 2012.

Raskin, Jef. *The Humane Interface: New Directions for Designing Interactive Systems*. Boston, MA: Addison-Wesley Professional, 1994.

Romero, Brenda, *Train*. (installation game), 2009.

Schüoenfelder, Lea, and Peter Lu, *Perfect Woman*. Lea Schüoenfelder and Peter Lu (Macintosh), 2012.

Sharp, John. "Perspective," in *The Routledge Companion to Video Game Studies*. Ed. Bernard Perron and Mark J.P. Wolf. New York: Routledge, 2014.

Sirvo LLC, *Threes*. Sirvo LLC (iOS), 2014.

Tale of Tales, *The Path*. Tale of Tales (Macintosh), 2009.

Thatgamecompany. *Journey*. Sony Computer Entertainment America, Inc. (PlayStation 3), 2012.

Ubisoft Montreal, *Far Cry 2*. Ubisoft (PlayStation 3), 2008.

USC Game Innovation Lab, *Walden, a game*. (Macintosh).

Valve Corporation, *Portal 2*. Valve Corporation (PlayStation 3), 2011.

Yu, Derek, *Spelunky*. Mossmouth, LLC (Xbox 360), 2008.

Chapter 5

Dreyfuss, Henry, *Designing for People*. NY: Simon and Shuster, 1955.

IDEO, *Design Kit* (website).

Shewhart, Andrew Walter, *Statistical Method from the Viewpoint of Quality Control*. Washington, D.C.: The Graduate School, the Department of Agriculture, 1939.

Chapter 6

Atari, Inc., *Pong*. Atari, Inc. (arcade), 1972.

Bauza, Antoine, Hanabi. R & R Games Incorporated (cardgame), 2010.

Captain Games, *Desert Golfing*. Captain Games (iOS), 2014.

Chen, Jenova. "Designing *Journey*." Game Developers Conference 2013.

Chen, Jenova, and Robin Hunicke, "Discovering Multiplayer Dynamics in *Journey*." IndieCade 2010.

Clark, Naomi, Consentacle. Naomi Clark (cardgame), 2014.

Flanagan, Mary, and Helen Nissenbaum, *Values at Play in Digital Games*. Cambridge, MA: The MIT Press, 2014.

Garfield, Richard, and Lukas Litzsinger, Android: Netrunner. Fantasy Flight Games (cardgame), 2012.

Holm, Ivar, *Ideas and Beliefs in Architecture and Industrial Design: How Attitudes, Orientations, and Underlying Assumptions Shape the Built Environment*. Oslo, Norway: Oslo School of Architecture and Design, 2006.

Sharp, John, "Design Values." *Hey I'm John* website. November 12, 2015.

Thatgamecompany. *Journey*. Sony Computer Entertainment America, Inc. (videogame), 2012.

Zimmerman, Eric. "Play as Research: The Iterative Design Process" in *Design Research: Methods and Perspectives*. Ed. Brenda Laurel. Cambridge, MA: The MIT Press, 2003.

Chapter 7

Llopis, Noel. "Indie Project Management for One: Tools," *Games from Within* website. August 5, 2010.

Chapter 8

anthropy, anna. *Queers in Love at the End of the World*. (browser game), 2014.

Burnett, Rebecca, Brandy Blake, Andy Freeze, Kathleen Hanggi, and Amanda Madden, *WOVENText version 2.2*. New York: Bedford St. Martin's, 2012.

Captain Games, *Desert Golfing*. Captain Games (iOS), 2014.

Hartnett, Tim. *Consensus Decision-Making* website.

Hunt, Jamer. "Among Six Types of Failure Only a Few Help You Innovate." *Fast Company* website. June 27, 2011.

Kniberg, Henrik, "Spotify Engineering Culture (part 1)." *Spotify Labs* website. March 27, 2014.

Kniberg, Henrik, "Spotify Engineering Culture (part 2)." *Spotify Labs* website. September 20, 2014.

Chapter 9

anthropy, anna, *dys4ia*. Auntie Pixelante (browser game), 2012.

anthropy, anna, *Rise of the Videogame Zinesters: How Freaks, Normals, Amateurs, Artists, Dreamers, Drop-Outs, Queers, Housewives, and People Like You Are Taking Back an Art Form*. New York: Seven Stories Press, 2012.

Atari, Inc. *Breakout*. Atari, Inc. (arcade), 1976.

Bell, Chris. "Designing for Friendship: Shaping Player Relationships with Rules and Freedom." Game Developers Conference 2012.

Cavanagh, Terry, *vvvvvv*. Distractionware (iOS), 2010.

Coco & Co., *Way*. Coco & Co (Macintosh), 2012.

Cooper, Alan, *The Inmates Are Running the Asylum: Why High Tech Products Drive Us Crazy and How to Restore the Sanity*. Boston, MA: Sams - Pearson Education, 2004.

Die Gute Fabrik, *Johann Sebastian Joust*. Die Gute Fabrik (PlayStation 3), 2013.

The Fullbright Company, *Gone Home*. Majesco Entertainment (Steam), 2013.

Granell, Craig. "The Weekend Read: How Canabalt Jumped from Indie Game Jam to the Museum of Modern Art." *Stuff* website, June 12, 2015.

IDEO, *Design Kit*.

Meadows, Donella. *Thinking in Systems: A Primer*. White River Junction, VT: Chelsea Green Publishing, 2008.

Molleindustria, *McDonald's Videogame*. Molleindustria (browser game), 2006.

Osborn, Alex F., *Applied Imagination: Principles and Procedures of Creative Problem-Solving*. New York: Scribner, 1979.

Semi-Secret Software, *Canabalt*. Semi-Secret Software (iOS), 2009.

Thatgamecompany. *Journey*. Sony Computer Entertainment America, Inc. (PlayStation 3), 2012.

Wilson, Douglas, *Designing for the Pleasures of Disputation—or—How to Make Friends by Trying to Kick Them!* PhD dissertation, 2012.

Wilson, Douglas. "The Unlikely Story of *Johann Sebastian Joust*." GDC China 2012.

Chapter 10

Atari, Inc., *Pong*. Atari, Inc. (arcade), 1972.

Cancienne, Kevin, *Dog Park*. Kevin Cancienne (PC), 2014.

DeBonis, Josh, and Nikita Mikros, *Killer Queen*. Josh DeBonis and Nikita Mikros (arcade), 2013.

DeBonis, Josh, and Nikita Mikros, "Swords and Snails: The *Killer Queen* Story." IndieCade East 2014.

Friedhoff, Jane, *Slam City Oracles*. Jane Friedhoff (Macintosh), 2015.

Harvey, Auriea. "The Making of Ruby." *The Path* development blog, March 10, 2008.

Local No. 12, *Losswords*. Local No. 12 (iOS), 2016.

Schüoenfelder, Lea, and Peter Lu, *Perfect Woman*. Lea Schüoenfelder and Peter Lu (Macintosh), 2012.

Tale of Tales, *The Path*. Tale of Tales (Macintosh), 2009.

Thatgamecompany. *Journey*. Sony Computer Entertainment America, Inc. (PlayStation 3), 2012.

Chapter 11

Cancienne, Kevin, *Dog Park*. Kevin Cancienne (PC), 2014.

Foddy, Bennett, *FLOP*. Die Gute Fabrik (PlayStation 3), 2013.

Hecker, Chris, *Spy Party*. Chris Hecker (PC), Early-Access Beta.

Isbister, Katherine, *How Games Move Us: Emotion by Design*. Cambridge, MA: The MIT Press, 2016.

Local No. 12, The Metagame. Local No. 12 (cardgame), 2015.

Chapter 13

anthropy, anna. *Queers in Love at the End of the World*. (browser game), 2014.

Beckett, Thomas, *Worstward Ho*. In *Nohow On: Company, III Seen III Said, and Worstward Ho*. New York: Grove Press, 2014.

Bin, Astrid, *PANIC!*. Astrid Bin (browser game), 2012.

Cardboard Computer, *Kentucky Route Zero*. Cardboard Computer (Steam), 2013–2014.

Esopus magazine.

Die Gute Fabrik, *Johann Sebastian Joust*. Die Gute Fabrik (PlayStation 3), 2013.

Die Gute Fabrik, *Sportsfriends*. Die Gute Fabric (PlayStation 4), 2013.

Local No. 12, The Metagame. Local No. 12 (cardgame), 2015.

Number None, Inc. *Braid*. Number None Inc. (Xbox 360), 2008.

Sharp, John. "How The Metagame Cards Went from a Sports Card-Like to Dictionary Chic." *Hey I'm John* website, April 16, 2015.

Tale of Tales, *Drama Princess*. Tale of Tales (software), 2006.

Tale of Tales, *The Endless Forest*, Tale of Tales (PC), 2005.

Tale of Tales, *The Path*. Tale of Tales (Macintosh), 2009.

Wilson, Douglas, *Designing for the Pleasures of Disputation—or—How to Make Friends by Trying to Kick Them!* PhD dissertation, 2012.

GLOSSARY

AAA AAA, or "triple-A" games are games designed by large studios with large budgets.

Absorption A state of player engagement to the extent that a game captures a player's complete attention.

Abstraction There are three forms of abstraction in games. Abstraction applies when elements in the game don't refer to anything in the world (for example, Go). Abstraction can also refer to games that represent real-world activities, such as how the game *Pong* represents tennis. Finally, there is the abstraction in which a systems model is created to represent a real-world phenomenon, such as the board game Pandemic's abstraction of the spread of diseases. Abstraction always involves some form of reinterpretation, simplification, and modeling.

Achievers Based in Richard Bartle's classification of players in online MUDs (Multi-User Dungeons), achievers are interested in setting and obtaining goals in a game.

Action Theory Talcott Parsons' theory for what happens when people interact with things. People have beliefs that shape their understanding of a given situation, which lead to reactions, which lead to desires, around which people create intentions, which finally lead to actions.

Actions The primary things players are doing in a game. Actions include direct and indirect actions. **Direct actions** are those in which the player has immediate interaction with objects and the playspace (the ball and flippers in pinball), while **indirect actions** are those that occur without direct contact by the player or the primary objects they use while playing (the bumpers, ramps, and other features in a pinball machine).

Active Skill A form of skill-based play utilizing the player's motor skills in performing the actions in the game. Hitting the ball in tennis is an example. *See also* Mental Skill.

Adaptive Processes An iterative approach to designing in which the designer allows the design to develop based on the feedback on and observations of interactions with a prototype. Adaptive processes differ from predictive processes, in which design emerges from the designer without external feedback.

Affective Conflicts One of three forms of conflict identified by Rebecca Burnett's *WOVENtext*. Issues arising in collaborative teams relating to team members' feelings, which in turn relate to their goals, needs, and wishes for the project. Affective conflicts often emerge from differences in values, which often derive from factors like gender, creed, culture, class, age, and sexual orientation. *See also* Procedural Conflicts and Substantive Conflicts.

Affordances The theory explaining people's innate understanding of what we perceive an object is used for before using it. There are four kinds of affordance: perceptible affordance, hidden affordance, false affordance, and correct rejections.

Altgames A loose grouping of games and gamemakers that are connected by a move away from genre and market considerations. Altgames tend to be smaller and more experimental in their search for more expressive play experiences.

Art and Sound Prototype A model of the sound and imagery in the game, used to test and try out visual and audio approaches.

Asymmetrical Competition A multiplayer game where players are trying to win against each other using different actions or objects.

Asymmetrical Cooperation A multiplayer game where players are collaborating to win against the game and have different actions and abilities.

Asymmetrical Information A form of play where players have access to different information about the game's state.

Asymmetrical Play A form of multiplayer play that gives players different roles and abilities in the game.

Asynchronous Competition A game where players compete by comparing their performance in a game played separately, and possibly at different times. The long jump in track and field is an example where players take turns jumping, and the distances are compared to determine winners.

Attention A player's understanding of what is currently happening in a game. There are two types of attention: reflexive and executive. Reflexive attention is from the back and side regions of the brain and is activated when loud noises, quickly moving objects, or anything novel is presented to us. Executive attention (sometimes called voluntary attention) refers to those things that we decide to pay attention to. Examples include looking at a health meter, for instance, or reading a sign in the road.

Brainstorming A process developed by Alex Faickney Osborn meant to generate many ideas around a specific question or problem. Brainstorming has rules to guide the process: defer judgment, quantity over quality, no buts (just ands), go wild, get visual, and combine ideas.

Challenge The resistance a game puts in the way of a player in their attempt to achieve a goal, or through the difficulty of a game's content or subject matter.

Chance The introduction of randomness that impacts a player's ability to predict the outcome of direct and indirect actions.

Code/Tech Prototype Prototypes where the focus is on exploring questions relating to the technology or production of a game.

Collaboration Working together toward the same goal. Given the complex nature of game development, many games are designed and produced collaboratively.

Competitive Play Play that pits players against each other, leading to winners and losers.

Complete Game Prototype An almost final version of the game, with art assets and most of the play experience in place. Complete game prototypes allow a full review of a game's design.

Conceptualize The first step in the four-step iterative game design cycle, involving brainstorming and idea generation as well as identifying motivations and design values.

Consistency In Gillian Crampton Smith's five characteristics of well-done interaction design, consistency provides players patterns from which they can develop an understanding of how a game works and what their role is in it.

Constraint For players, a way to make a play experience more difficult and interesting, such as the no-hands rule in soccer. For designers, this is a form of restriction on the game's design—often leading to innovations within the restrictions.

Context The time, place, and other environmental factors that impact the quality of a play experience.

Cooperative Play A form of gameplay that emphasizes player collaboration to meet the game's goal. This can include symmetrical and asymmetrical cooperative play.

Core Game Prototype A form of prototype that allows players to experience the core actions, objects, and other central elements of a game.

Correct Rejections One of the four forms of affordances. Correct rejections occur when people can determine what an object is not used for. For example, a pillow won't work as a hammer. *See also* Affordances.

Decision-Making The process by which a player evaluates their options and the choices they make for their next action.

Design Document The primary written documentation for a game. Design documents are used to share the specifics of how a game works.

Design Values The experiential goals set for a game. Design values are guideposts used to ensure a game's design stays focused throughout the iterative process. They include experience, theme, point of view, challenge, decision-making, skill, strategy, chance and uncertainty, context, and emotions.

Direct Actions Actions that the player initiates and controls. Direct actions differ from indirect actions, where objects in the game interact without player control.

Dynamics The shifting relationships between elements in a system. The outcomes of players and objects interacting in a game.

Emergent Play A term coined by Jesper Juul to understand player experiences that take shape from within a designed set of rules. This is in contrast to progressive play in which the player experience moves through predetermined paths.

Evaluation The fourth step in the iterative game design process, wherein the results of play-tests of a prototype are used to identify strengths and weaknesses in a game's design.

Experience-Based Play A kind of play that emphasizes an exploratory, sensory-based play experience.

Explorers Based in Richard Bartle's classification of players in online MUDs (Multi-User Dungeons), explorers like to understand the full breadth of a game's space of possibility.

Expressive Play A kind of play that de-emphasizes player choice and instead emphasizes either authorial or player experience.

Failure A primary experience in games and game design. Failure reveals the working relationships between things and is often how we learn. Jamer Hunt identifies six types of failure: abject failure, structural failure, glorious failure, common failure, version failure, and predicted failure.[1]

False Affordances One of the four types of affordances. False affordances are misinterpretations of what an object can do. We see a wax apple and think we might be able to eat it; we see a door in a 3D game but cannot open it. *See also* Affordances.

Feedback The response a game provides to a player's actions. One of Gillian Crampton Smith's five characteristics of well-done interaction design.

Frame Layer In our play adaptation of Jesse James Garrett's planes of user experience, the player's understanding of the game's space of possibility informed by their experiences as a player and more broadly as a person. *See also* Sensory Layer, Information Layer, Interaction Layer, and Purpose Layer.

Game Design The process of conceiving of and creating the way a game works, including the actions, goals, rules, objects, playspace, and number of players.

Game Development The overall process of making a game, including its design and production.

Game Production The process of making a game as indicated by the game's design.

---

1   Jamer Hunt, "Among Six Types Of Failure, Only A Few Help You Innovate," Fast Company Design, 2011 (http://www.fastcodesign.com/1664360/among-six-types-of-failure-only-a-few-help-you-innovate).

Game State The current moment in a game, including current time, score, location of objects in the playspace, and other elements in flux due to player actions and game reactions.

Goals The outcome players try to achieve through their play, whether they are measurable or purely experiential. Sometimes goals are measurable and determined by the game, but in other cases, goals are looser and open ended.

Head-to-Head Competition Direct competition between players. Both ping pong and basketball are examples of head-to-head competition.

Hidden Affordance One of four types of affordances. A hidden affordance is an interaction that is present in an object but is not obvious from its appearance. You wouldn't realize you can drink from a hat, but you can; you wouldn't know a brick up in the air could be hit to release a coin, but it will, sometimes. *See also* Affordances.

Imperfect Information Not all of the game state is visible or accessible to the player. Poker is a game of imperfect information, as players are exposed to different information based on the cards in their hand.

Independent Games Games developed and published by individuals or small teams.

Indirect Actions A tool of game design. Indirect actions are those that occur without direct contact by the player or the primary objects they use to perform actions.

Information Layer In our play adaptation of Jesse James Garrett's planes of user experience, the information the player discerns about the game via the appearance. *See also* Sensory Layer, Frame Layer, Interaction Layer, and Purpose Layer.

Information Space Games have information spaces that players explore. *Perfect information spaces* are those in which everything to be known about a game is visible to the player. *Imperfect information spaces* are those in which some information is hidden from players either by the game itself or by other players.

Interaction Layer In our play adaptation of Jesse James Garrett's planes of user experience, what the player understands he can do while playing the game. *See also* Sensory Layer, Frame Layer, Information Layer, and Purpose Layer.

Interactive Fiction The term used to describe text-based videogames where player actions are carried out through either entering text commands or selecting from text-based options.

Interface Prototype Interface prototypes explore the place where the player comes in direct contact with the game.

Intuitiveness The ease with which a player can understand and perform actions within a game. Intuitiveness is one of Gillian Crampton Smith's five characteristics of well-designed interactivity.

Iterative Design A process of creating games through the development and testing of prototypes before the final design is developed. The steps in the iterative design process are conceptualize, prototype, playtest, and evaluate.

Jump Cut A filmmaking term used to describe an edit without transition from one shot to another. Jump cuts usually indicate a passage of time.

Killers In Richard Bartle's classification of players in online MUDs (Multi-User Dungeons), killers are interested in disrupting or destroying other players or thwarting their attempt at achieving the goal.

Local Multiplayer Game A two or more player game where players compete or collaborate with each other while sitting in the same space together.

Lusory Attitude A term coined by Bernard Suits in the book *The Grasshopper: Games, Life and Utopia,* describing the willingness of players to submit themselves to arbitrary rules of a game to experience play.

Mental Model The way a player perceives a game to work, in terms of both what they should do to play, but also what their actions mean within the game's space of possibility. From Gillian Crampton Smith's five characteristics of well-done interaction design.

Mental Skill A type of skill-based play utilizing the player's ability to solve problems and form strategies. *See also* Active Skill.

Motivations The designer or team's point of emphasis for a game's design. Motivations include designing around the main thing the player gets to do, designing around constraints, designing around a story, designing around personal experiences, abstracting the real world, and designing around the player.

Navigability The ability of a player to understand how to navigate through the spatial, information, interaction, and goals of a game and its space of possibility. Navigability is one of Gillian Crampton Smith's five characteristics of well-designed interactivity.

Non-Player Character Characters in a videogame controlled by the computer.

Objects The things players use while playing a game. The ball or nets in basketball are an example.

Paper Prototype A nondigital prototype, made of paper or index cards, that tests ideas for a game.

Perceptible Affordances One of the four types of affordances. A perceptible affordance is what a player assumes something does based on what they can see, hear, or feel. *See also* Affordances.

Perfect Information Full access to the current state of the game, with nothing hidden from the player.

Performative Play A play experience in which player actions are the primary form. Performative play is often ideal for spectating.

Personas A tool for designing interactive software developed initially by Alan Cooper in his book *The Inmates Are Running the Asylum*. Personas are functional players that are based on the attributes we think our players will have.

Physical Prototype A nondigital prototype that models the rules and actions in a game. Physical prototypes are distinct from paper prototypes in the sense that they usually model physical action over the information space of the game.

Play As a noun, play is the act of experiencing a game. As a verb, play is any activity that goes beyond the requirements of the moment.

Playable Prototype A digital prototype (if it's a prototype for a videogame) that allows players to experience the core actions of the game.

Play-Centric A form of game design that prioritizes the experiences players have.

Player A person who interacts with a game.

Player Character The onscreen representation of the player.

Playspace The designed space within which a game is played.

Playtest The third step in the iterative game design cycle: observing how a prototype operates when played. Playtests can be internal tests, game developer tests, friend tests, target audience tests, new player tests, and experienced player tests.

Predictive Processes A design process by which the final product is well understood and can be produced without having to make changes to its design from testing. Predictive processes assume the designer is going to be right the first time around in contrast with adaptive processes, which are iterative processes that leave room for error, but also new ideas that can improve upon the original.

Procedural Conflicts One of three forms of conflict identified by Rebecca Burnett in her book *WOVENtext*. Procedural conflicts relate to misunderstandings or disagreements on the processes through which a team collaborates. *See also* Affective Conflicts and Substantive Conflicts.

Progression Jesper Juul's concept of games of progression are those in which the player makes decisions, but all possible outcomes are already defined by the game's creators. While this approach provides less open-ended play, it provides richer, authored storyworlds to investigate.

Prototyping The second stage in the iterative cycle, involving making a tangible version of the game or some aspect of it. Types of prototypes include paper, physical, playable, art, sound, interface, code/tech, core game, and complete game.

Pseudocode Code written in no specific syntax that models the logic of a program.

Purpose Layer In our play adaptation of Jesse James Garrett's planes of user experience, the purpose layer is the player's goals for the game. *See also* Sensory Layer, Frame Layer, Information Layer, and Interaction Layer.

Role-Playing A form of play that enables players to inhabit and perform as a character.

Rules The instructions for how a game works.

Schematics Blueprints for the game showing the basics of how a game looks to help explain what it will be like to play and what needs to be built.

Second-Order Design Designing games is a second-order design activity because we create the play experience indirectly through a combination of rules, actions, and goals. The game only takes form when activated by the player.

Sensory Layer In our adaptation of Jesse James Garrett's planes of user experience, the sensory layer is the surface of a game, or what the player sees, hears, and feels when playing the game. *See also* Frame Layer, Information Layer, Interaction Layer, and Purpose Layer.

Simulation-Based Play A form of play that models a real-world system.

Skill The measurement of a player's mastery of a game's actions.

Socializers In Richard Bartle's classification of players in online MUDs (Multi-User Dungeons), socializers are interested in interacting with other players over anything else in the game.

Space of Possibility Because games are interactive, they provide players with a variety of possible actions and interpretations. While a designer can't predetermine all of the possible actions and experiences players will have, they can limit or open up the space of possibility through the game's combination of actions, rules, goals, playspace, and objects.

Story Beat Important moments in a story. Jack and Jill running up the hill is one of a number of story beats that together compose the folk tale of Jack and Jill.

Storytelling A series of tools for shaping player experience that borrow from traditional narrative structures.

Storyworlds Spaces within which players inhabit characters and carry out actions via their avatars, designed to embody the place, setting, and time of the game.

Strategy A player's theory for how to best play a game and achieve goals (either those of the game or of the player's).

Substantive Conflicts One of three forms of conflict identified by Rebecca Burnett's book *WOVENText*. This may include team conflicts relating to the game itself—things like what kind of game it is and what kind of experience the team wants to provide players. These conflicts can help teams arrive at an understanding of the game together. *See also* Affective Conflicts and Procedural Conflicts.

Symbiotic Cooperation Play situations in which players are reliant on one another to play a game and achieve goals established either by the game or by the players themselves.

Symmetrical Competition A form of *Competitive Play* that provides the same abilities, roles, and challenges to each player.

Symmetrical Cooperation A form of *Cooperative Play* that provides the same abilities, roles, and challenges to each player.

Symmetrical Information All players have access to the same information about the state of the game.

Systems Dynamics An approach to understanding how things work by seeing them as objects that interact toward a particular purpose.

Team Agreement Team agreements spell out how the team is going to interact, how decisions are made, how ownership of the game is handled, and many other important elements of collaborations between individuals.

Theme The logical framework for how a game is represented.

Tracking Spreadsheet A document that captures the big-picture and moment-to-moment tasks necessary to design, prototype, and playtest a game.

Turn-Based Play Play that involves waiting for each player to decide on and execute their actions.

Uncertainty The unpredictable nature of what will happen when a game is played.

Whimsical Play Whimsical play emphasizes silly actions, unexpected results, and creating a sense of euphoria by generating dizziness and a play experience that you need to feel to understand.

Yomi The Japanese concept for knowing the mind of your opponent. It's usually applied to one-on-one competition but can also be found in sports, where one team analyzes the other team's past plays to predict future actions, all in service of gaining strategic advantage.

Index